IMAGES
of America

GLOCESTER
RHODE ISLAND

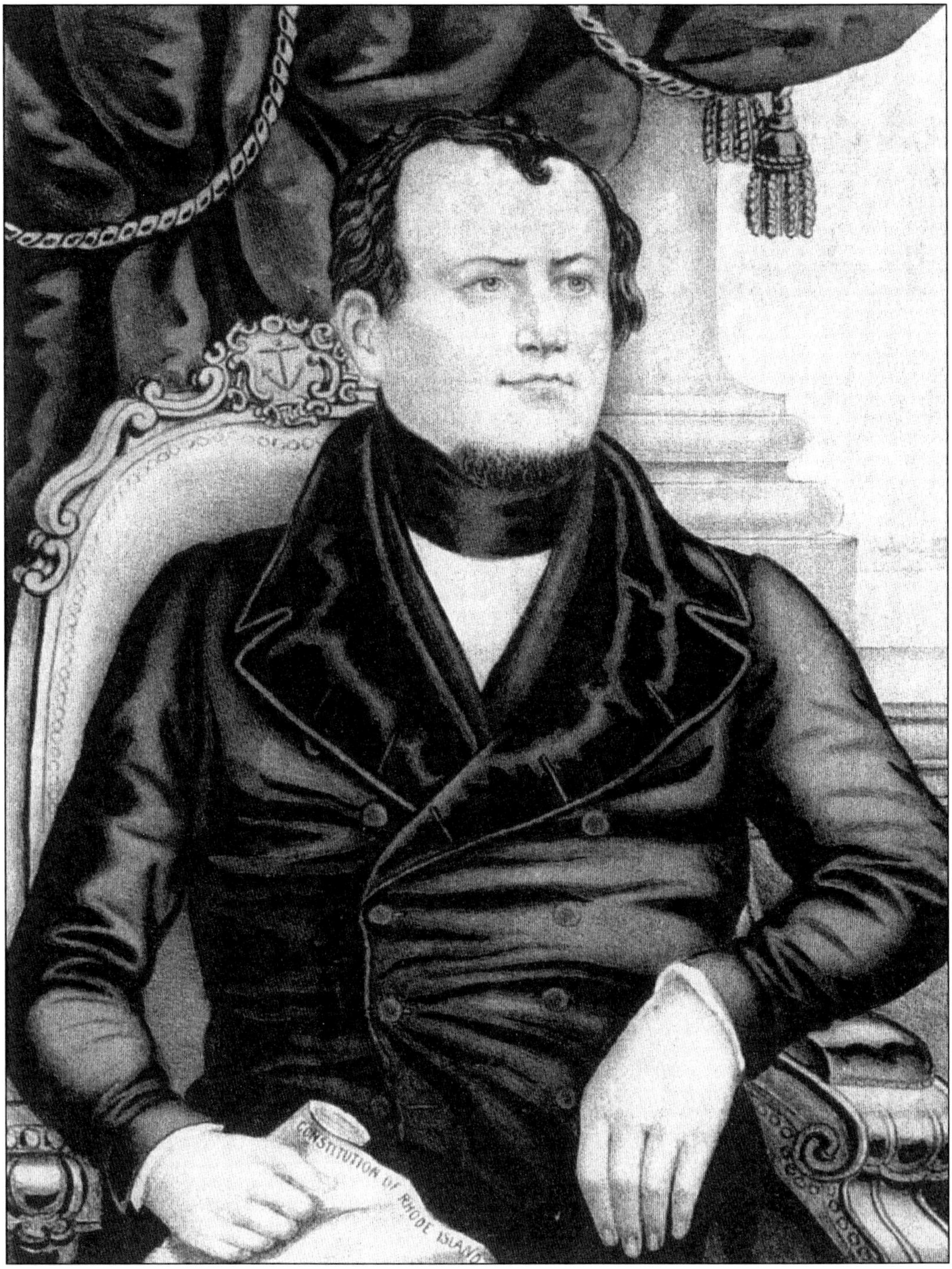

Thomas Wilson Dorr, lawyer, statesman, and advocate of popular sovereignty, was elected governor of Rhode Island by the People's Party on April 18, 1842. A power struggle ended in the Dorr Rebellion on June 28, 1842, at Acote's Hill. His words remain a part of our voting rights to this day. A memorial monument was erected by the State in his honor at Acote's Hill, Chepachet, in 1912.

IMAGES
of America

GLOCESTER
RHODE ISLAND

Edna Whitaker Kent

ARCADIA
PUBLISHING

ISBN 978-0-7385-9010-3

Published by Arcadia Publishing
Charleston, South Carolina

Printed in the United States of America

For all general information contact Arcadia Publishing at:
Telephone 843-853-2070
Fax 843-853-0044
E-mail sales@arcadiapublishing.com
For customer service and orders:
Toll-Free 1-888-313-2665

Visit us on the Internet at www.arcadiapublishing.com

Contents

Acknowledgments

This photographic essay of Glocester is but a sampling of photographs and memorabilia from the private collections of Glocester residents, those with "family ties" with the town, and the C.G. and E.M. Kent Collection. Most of the views have never been seen by the general public. Information was obtained for each caption from the historian's private research files and collected over the past 30 years from authoritative texts, town records, and personal interviews.

This book could not have been completed without the dedication and expertise of Patricia Zifchock Mehrtens, who typed and transferred to disk all written information, and Louis Doucett, who put it all on film. Also, I want to especially thank my husband, Richmond, whose patience helped me to achieve my goal.

I wish to thank the following people for their kind generosity and willingness to share their treasured photos and memorabilia with future readers: Clifford W. Brown Jr., Betsy Baker, Diane Bartlett, Jacqueline Blanchard, Anna Capron, James Chase, Elizabeth Clarke, Jennifer Cooke, "Ellie" Cutler, Andrew Demaine, Louis Doucett, Fred Everett, Martha Fogarty, Carole Fry, Shirley Greenhalgh, Molly Harrington, Henry Hawkins, Lois Hawksley, David Inman, Marjorie Lawton, Priscilla Lowell, Madelaine MacLean, Patricia Mehrtens, Lori Morin, Averill Maher, Herbert Newman, Wilton Newman, Irene Salisbury, Mrs. Charles Sherman, Ann Chapman Soule, Edd Spidell, Frances Steere, Harvey Steere, Robert Steere, Mildred Thoman, Howard Tucker, Miriam Wilcock, and those who wish to remain anonymous.

Introduction

As early as the 1680s, settlers, some herding cattle and sheep, made use of Native American trails through the wilderness of Rhode Island's northwest corner. One such trail became our Putnam Pike of today, which slices diagonally across Glocester. Another trail, possibly much older, is Snake Hill Road, which meanders from east to west in the southern region.

For the first 75 years after Glocester's incorporation in 1730–31, the inhabitants established their homes and wrestled with the rocky soil, dense forests, and problems with roads, while the town government struggled to govern the extraordinary size of Old Glocester. In 1806, the northern half was set apart and named Burrillville.

Our largest village is Chepachet, seat of government since Glocester's incorporation, and a trading center during the 18th and 19th centuries which attracted travelers from Woonsocket, Providence, Uxbridge, and Danielson. In 1842, Thomas Dorr, finding support and legal counsel at Chepachet, made his headquarters at Sprague's Tavern. His final stand was Dorr's Rebellion at Acote's Hill, near today's busy intersection of Putnam Pike (Rt. 44) and Chopmist Hill Road (Rt. 102).

Several settlements have lost their identities. However, Harmony, situated on Putnam Pike, continues to flourish. Williams' Mills, Skeeterville, Hawkins' Village, Clarkville, Cherry Valley, Spring Grove, Waldron's Corner, and Evans' District are no longer found on current maps. They played their special roles in history, too, as proud residents there might be quick to point out.

The following images have been picked from over 800 privately owned photos. The choices were often difficult and required additional interviews and readjustments to the outline. I hope you find this collection enjoyable and informative. May it bring back many happy memories.

Edna Whitaker Kent
Glocester Historian

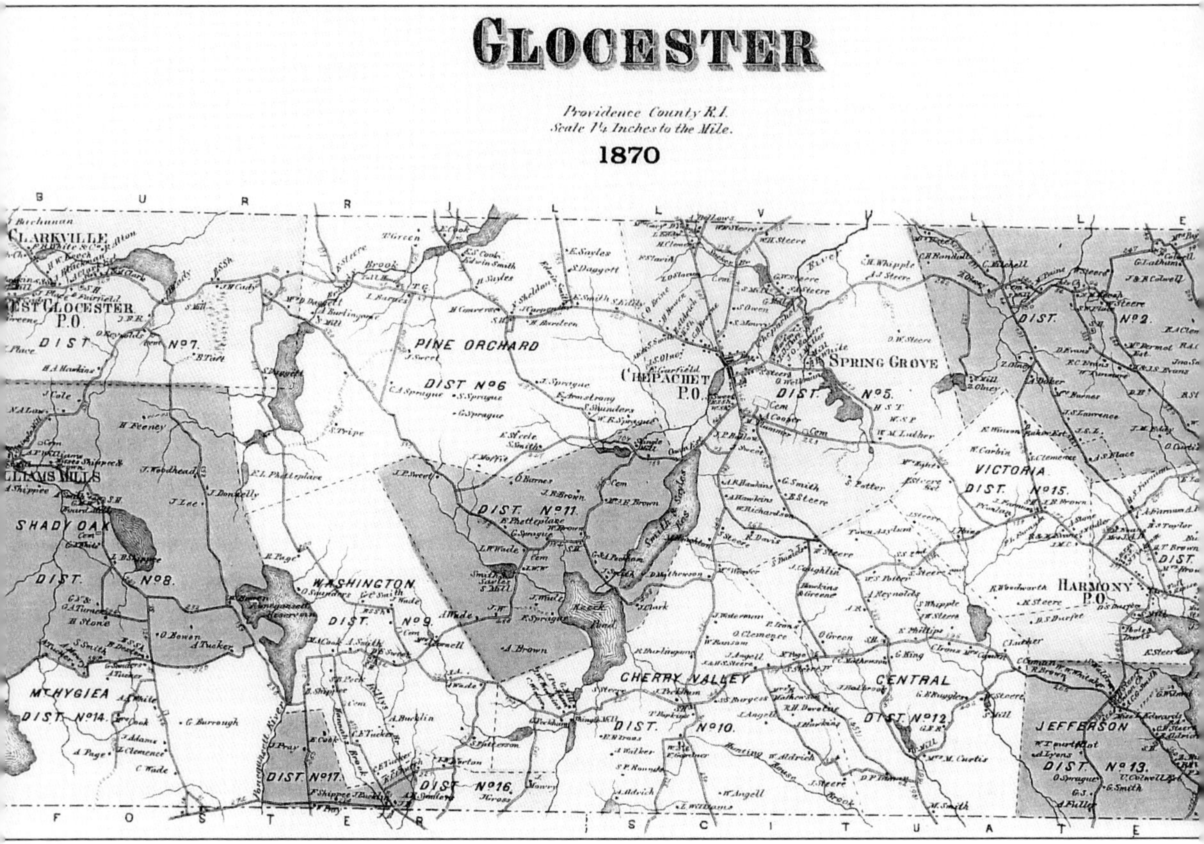

The Town of Glocester in the County of Providence was incorporated in 1730–31. The northern half of Glocester was set apart as the Town of Burrillville in 1806.

One

Turnpike and Country Roads

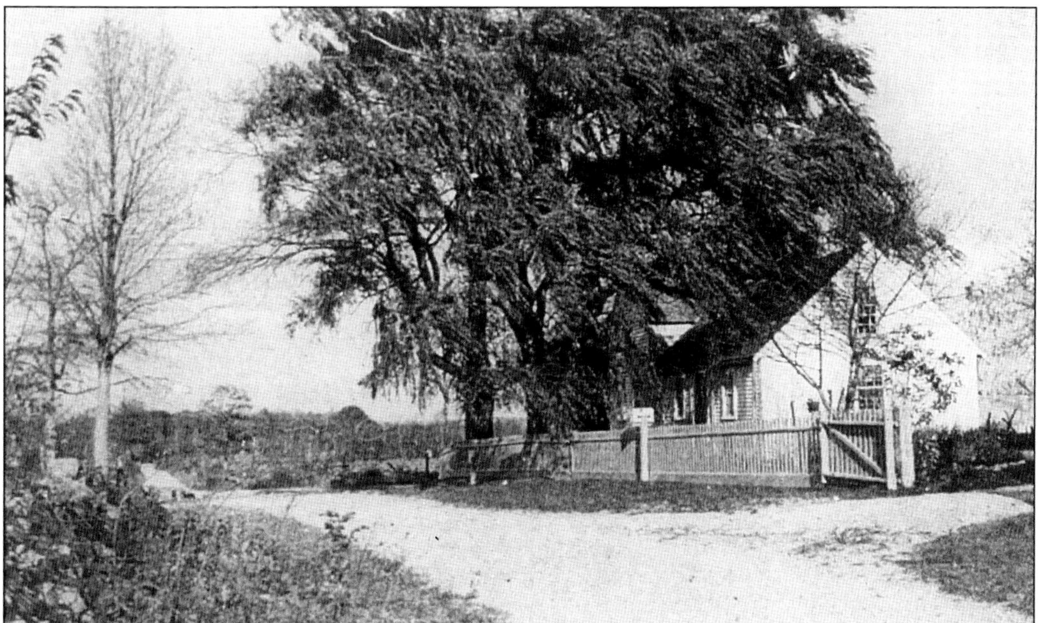

This typical country crossroad was probably known as Waldron's Corner as early as 1800 since the house was originally owned by Dr. Edward Waldron. It became Seth A. Steere's home in the late 1800s. This turn-of-the-century photo pre-dates the building of Laurel Grange, which now stands at the northeast corner of the Sawmill Road and Snake Hill Road intersection.

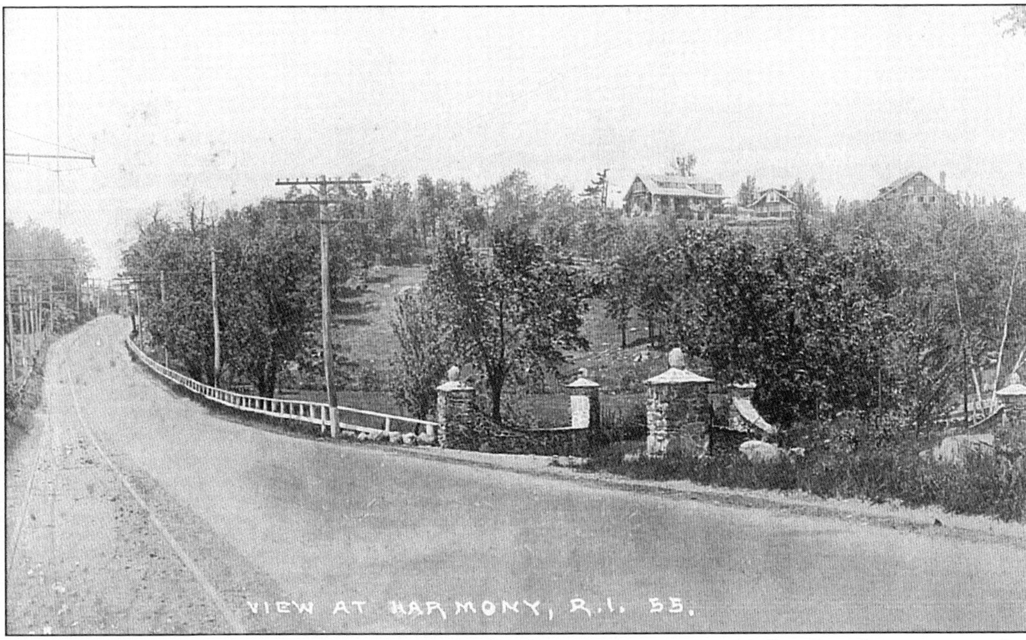

Although Putnam Pike has been widened, the fine stone posts at Valley Road remain to this day. Notice the trolley tracks on the left and the trolley wires overhead, which would date the photo between 1914 and 1924. Harmony Hotel can be seen in the distance down the road. The area to the left of the road is now the Glocester Country Club's golf course.

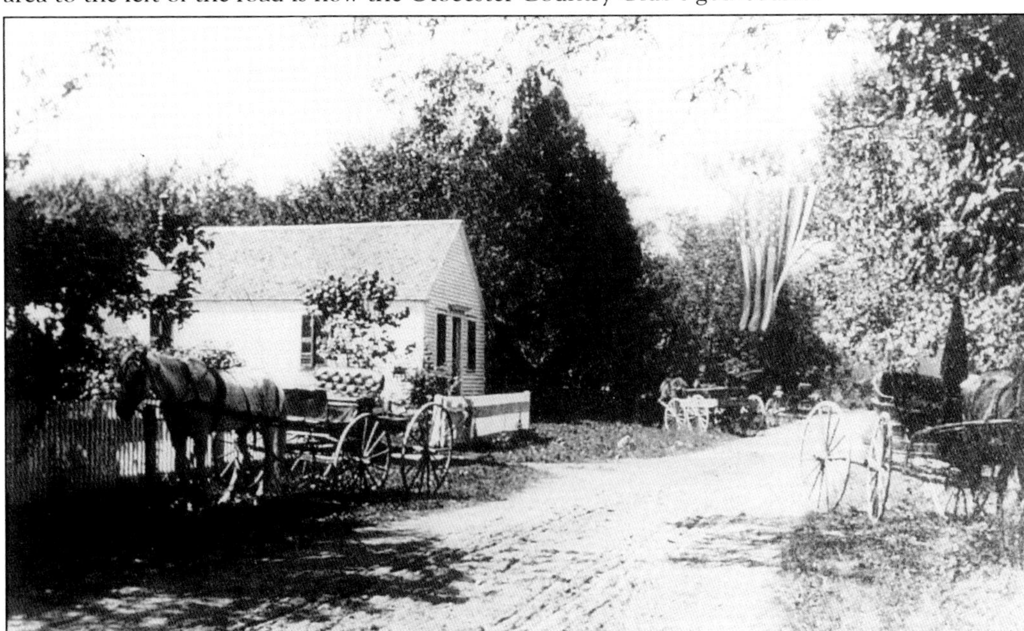

In September 1908, Laurel Grange members held their first Field Day to raise money to build a hall. Horses and wagons lined Snake Hill Road near Waldron's Corner. The white building is Union Chapel. Originally built as a school for the Jefferson District, it was purchased in 1860 for religious meetings. It has since been converted into a residence.

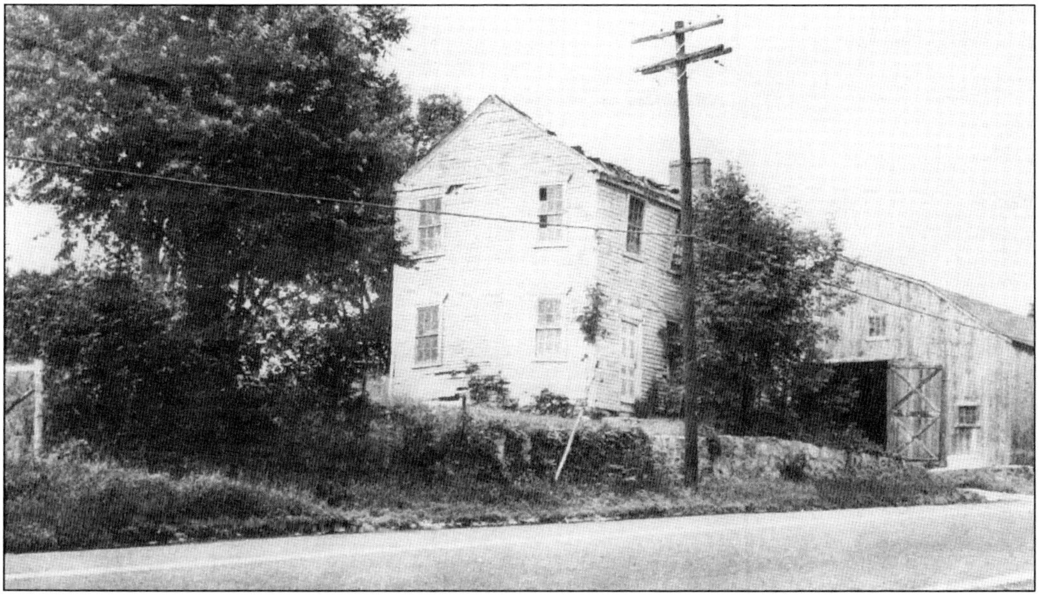

Beginning in 1824, Cutler's Stand (at right) next to Farnum's Hotel operated a tollgate on Putnam Pike in Harmony. To use the pike, travelers paid their toll, drove through the long barn, and out the opposite end. Some of the tolls were as follows: horse and rider, 5¢; horse and wagon, 6¢; and coach, 40¢. Sometime during the next 30 years, the tollgate was moved to the corner at Cooper Hill Road, and by 1856 Putnam Pike was free to all. The old hotel land is now part of Glocester's Land Conservancy Program.

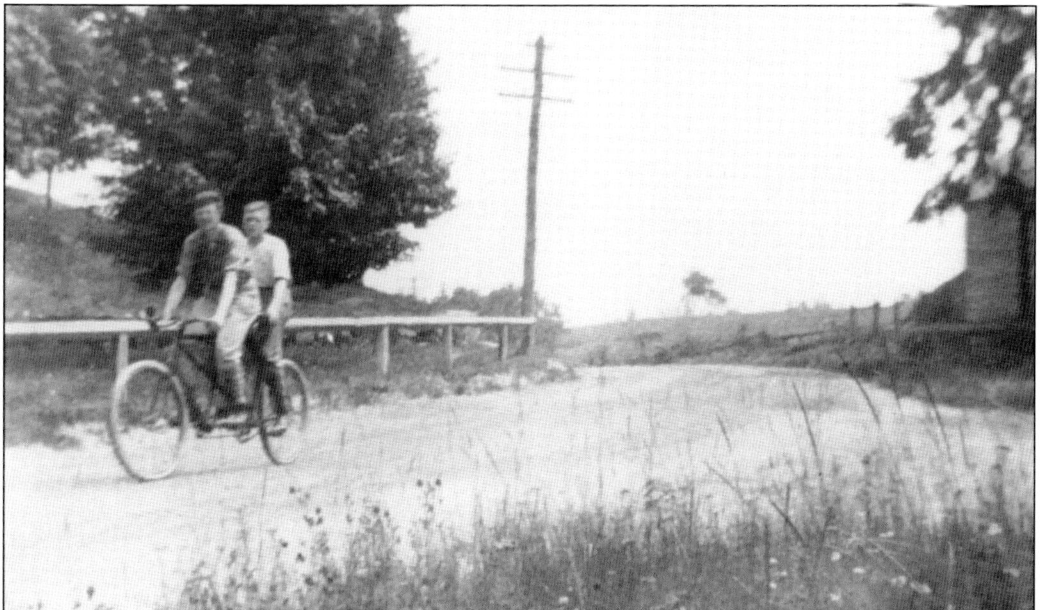

In this turn-of-the-century photo, cyclists enjoy a sunny summer's day on their tandem bicycle at the curve around Acote's Hill in Chepachet. Notice the poles are for telegraph and telephone wires only. The photographer took this shot near the bandstand which stood in the center of the intersection at Putnam Pike and Chopmist Hill Road (Rt. 102).

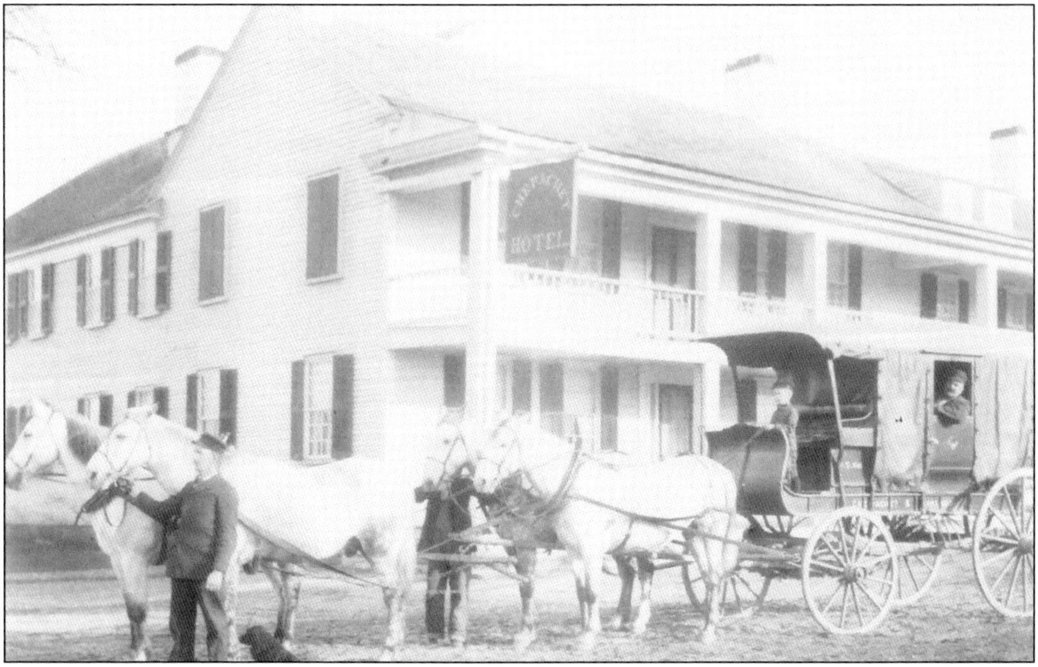

A trip to Providence entailed boarding the Chepachet & Oakland Stagecoach, which regularly took passengers to the train at the Oakland Station. In this picture, posed for the photographer about 1900, Jim Angell holds the front horse, while Dana Capron adjusts harnessing on the other side, young Walter Capron holds the reins, and David Webster leans out of the passenger compartment. Behind them is the nearly century-old Chepachet Hotel at the corner of Douglas Hook Road and Putnam Pike.

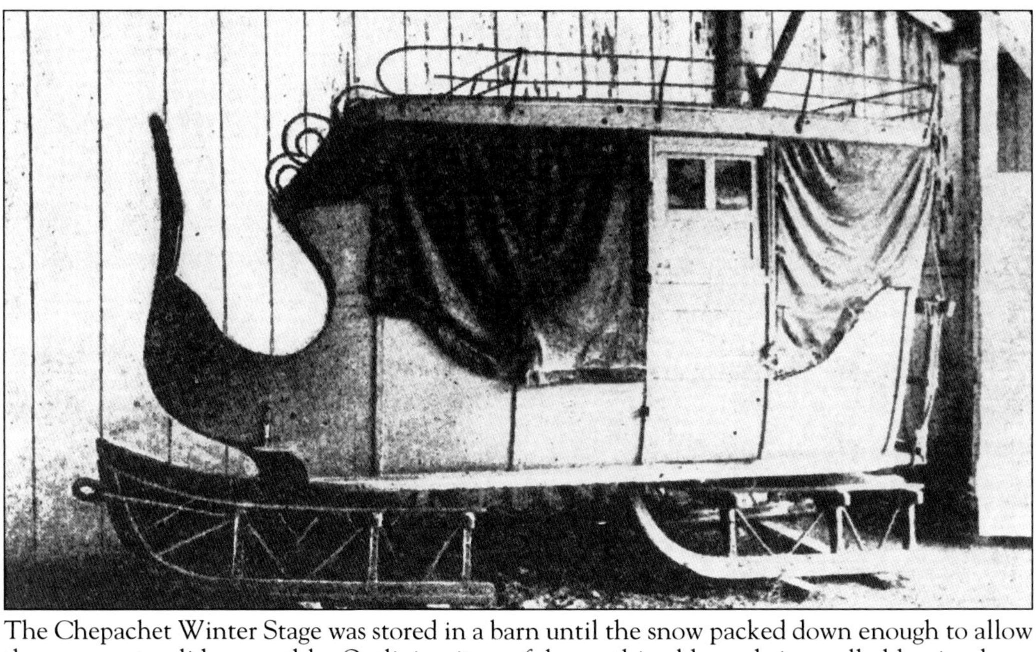

The Chepachet Winter Stage was stored in a barn until the snow packed down enough to allow the runners to glide smoothly. Outliving its usefulness, this old coach is recalled having been left behind the barn next to the old town clerk's office for many years until it fell apart.

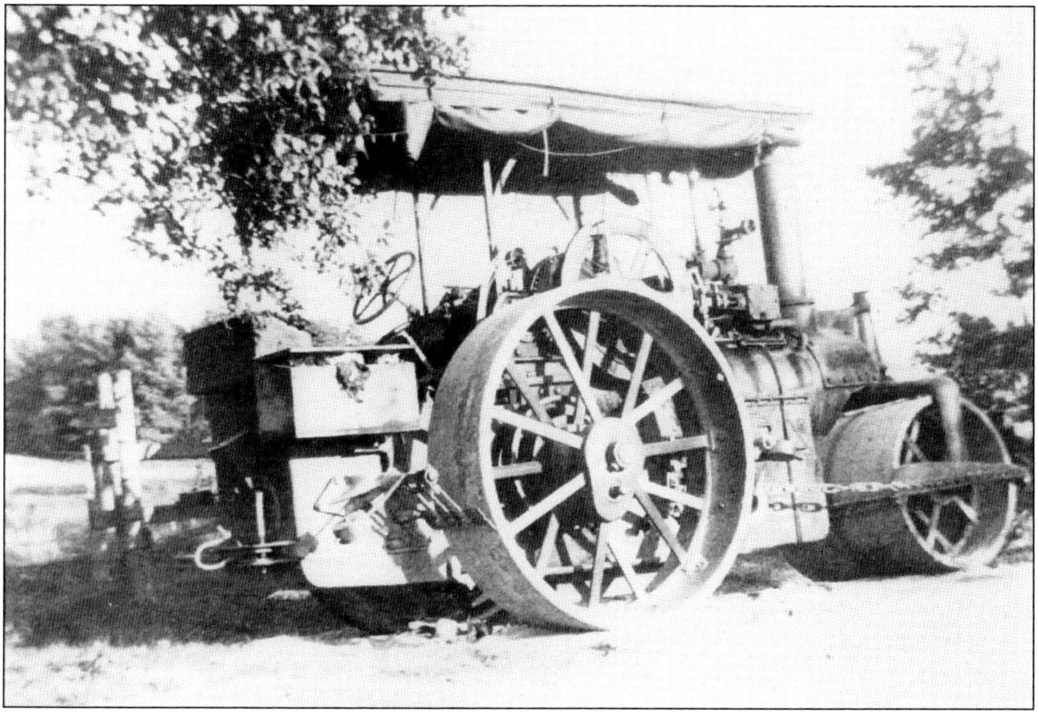

The steamroller compacted and smoothed the new road surface on Putnam Pike in the early 1900s. It is said that the particularly handsome young steamroller operator set the young ladies of the town "a flutter" in spite of their rather Victorian upbringing about 1909.

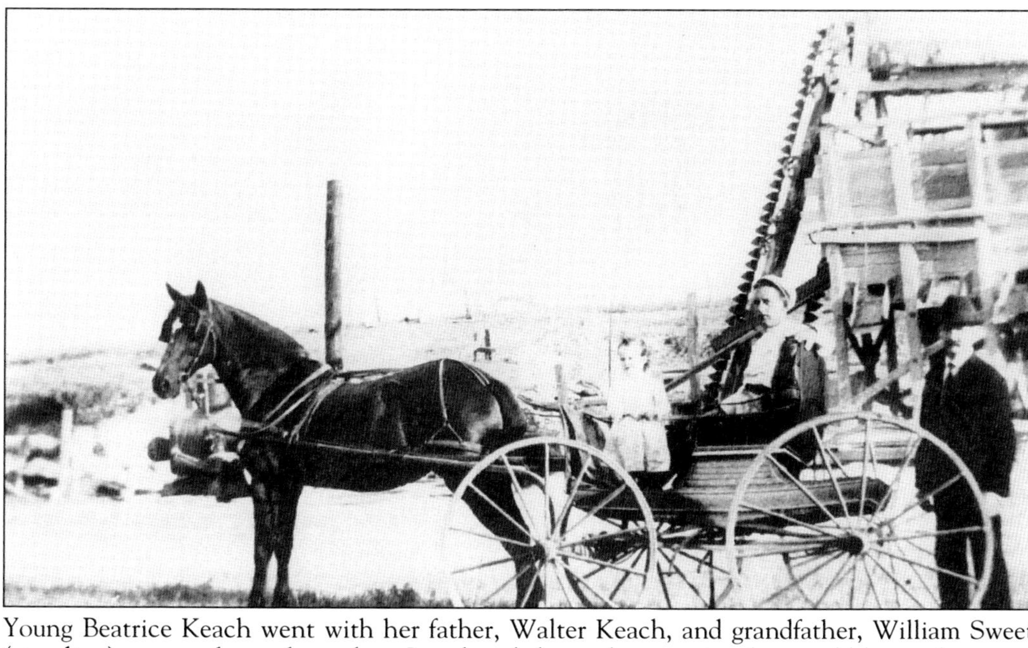

Young Beatrice Keach went with her father, Walter Keach, and grandfather, William Sweet (standing), to see the rock crusher. It reduced the rocks to a size that could be used to pave Putnam Pike. The exact location is unknown.

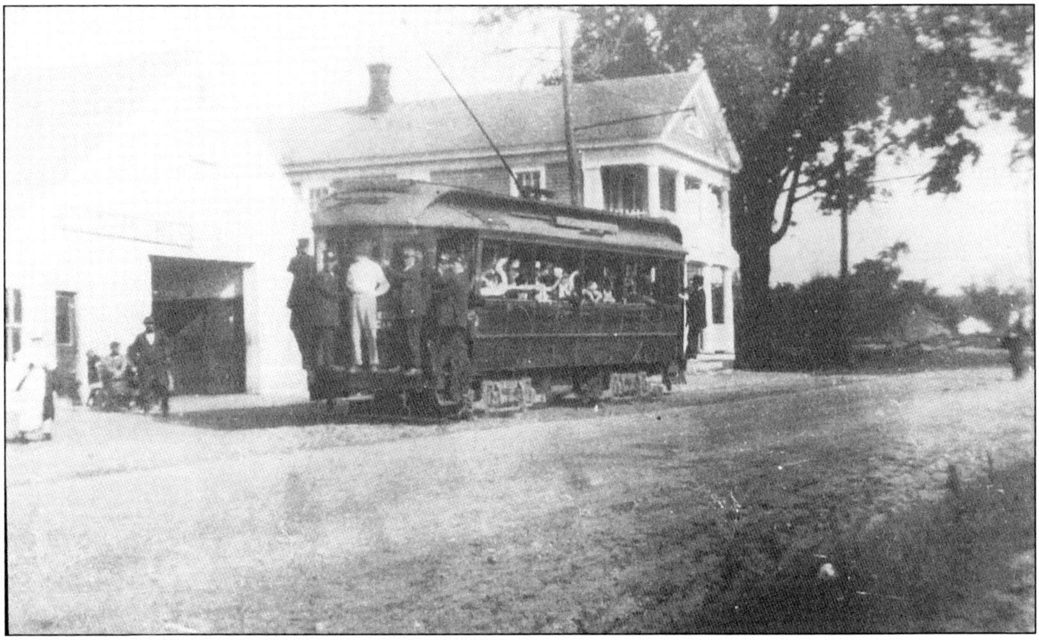

The photographer was fortunate to catch this shot of the hourly trolley passenger service from Providence stopped at Jim Steere's Stable. Martha Fitch, a *Providence Journal* reporter (at left), is on hand to scoop a new story for the newspaper. That is Deforest Richmond seated in front of the office door.

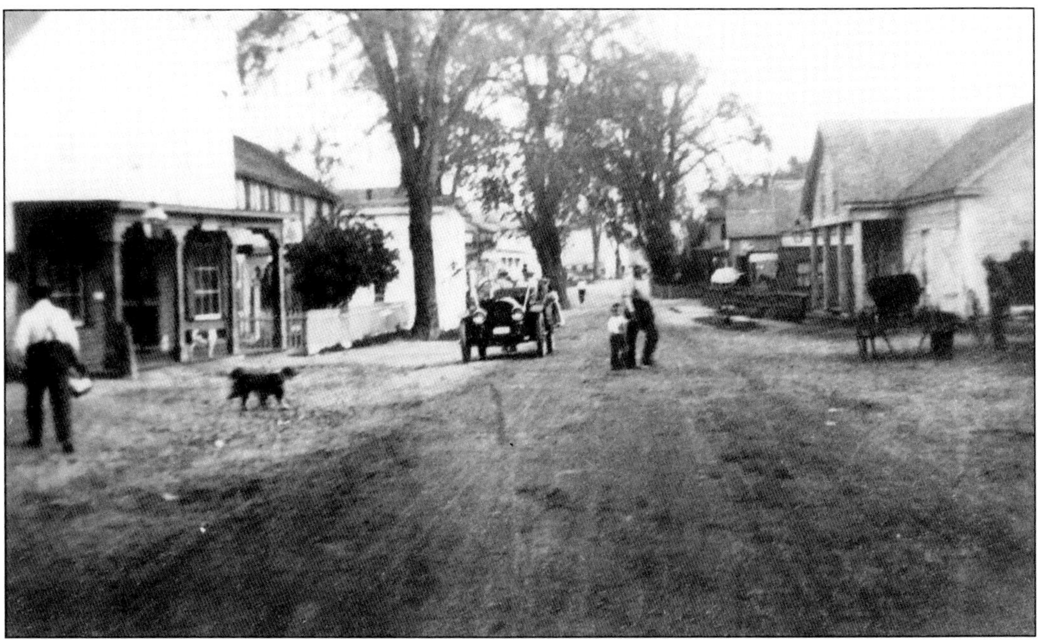

A tranquil afternoon about 1905 on Chepachet's Main Street is interrupted by a "horseless carriage." Potter and Brown would have been operating the store on the left. The bell sign proclaimed that a telephone was available within the store. The man and little boy are headed toward Abe Hawkins's blacksmith shop. At this time, an auto driver exceeding 6 miles per hour in thickly settled Harmony or Chepachet would be fined $10–$20.

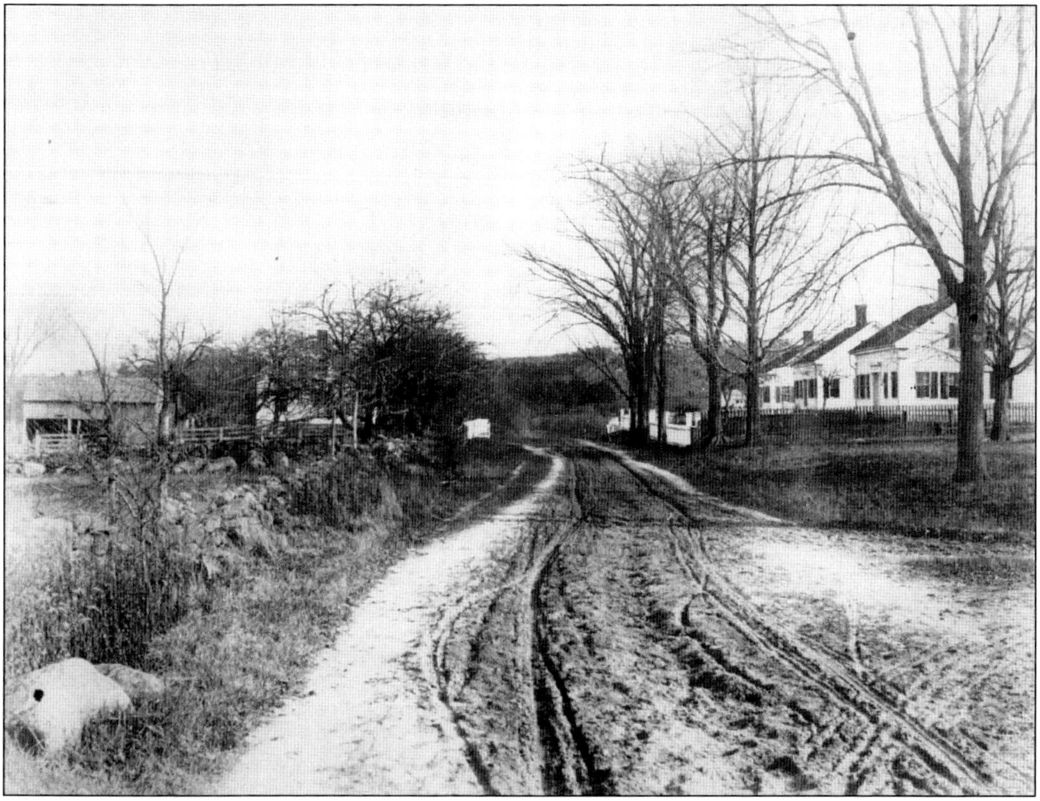

This early-1900s view of Douglas Hook Road with its row of neat white Greek Revival houses has changed very little except for the width and condition of the road and loss of the picket fences. The old Harrington farm is on the left and Seifert's house is on the extreme right.

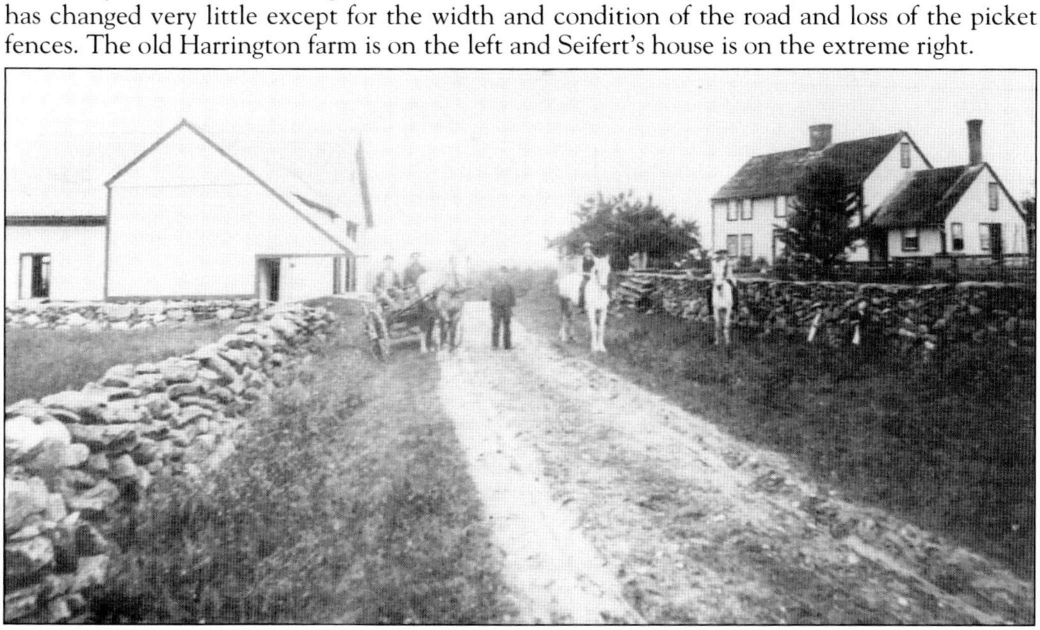

The photographer faced west on Douglas Hook Road to take this view of the old Enoch Steere homestead at Whipple Road. The farm maintained a very large apple orchard for many years. A windmill/water tower was a familiar landmark on the hill, but it has recently been dismantled.

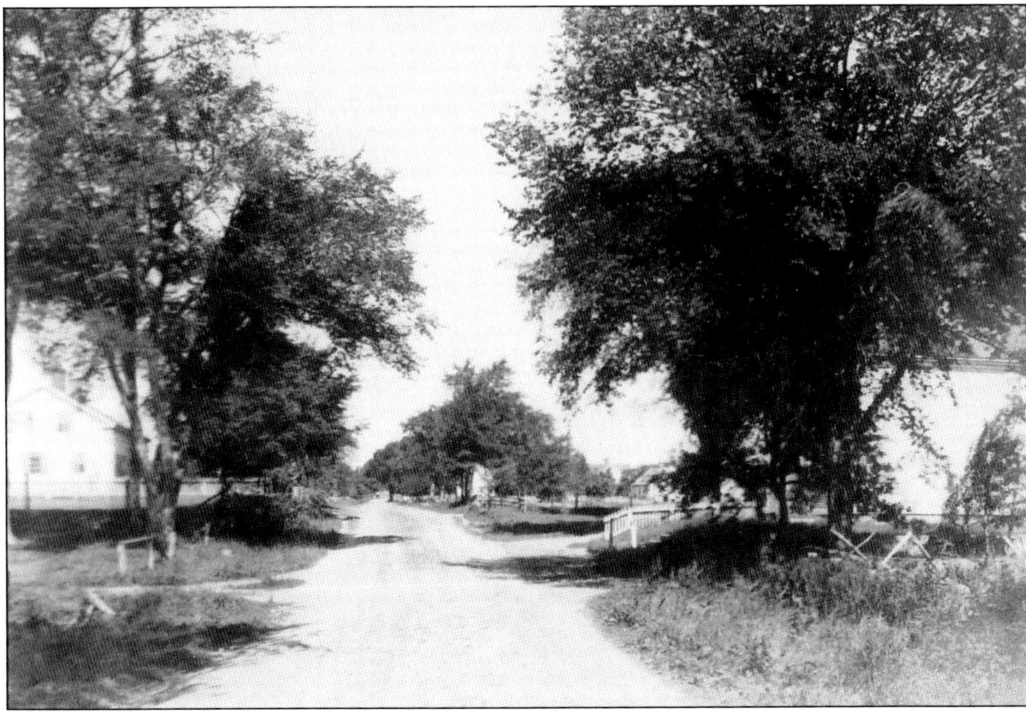

Nineteenth-century travelers may have had to urge their horses forward with the occasional snap of a whip in order to make it up this mile-long hill going west out of Chepachet on Putnam Pike. Between 1824 and 1856, the next toll would have to be paid at Cady's Stand, approximately 4 miles away. In the distance is a very large tree in the road—a popular meeting place for lovers.

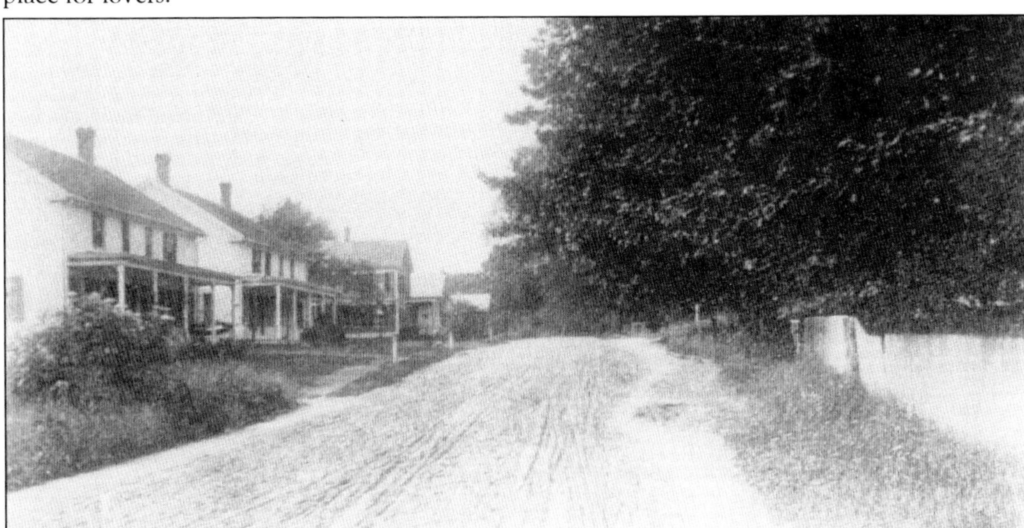

From this angle the heavy foliage obscures Will Hopkins's house at the middle of the fork in the road ahead. At one time this brief stretch was referred to as North Road, but over the years it has been called Pascoag Road or Money Hill Road (left road) and Oakland Road or Victory Highway (road that bends to the right). The picket fence at right belonged to the photographer, Edgar Potter.

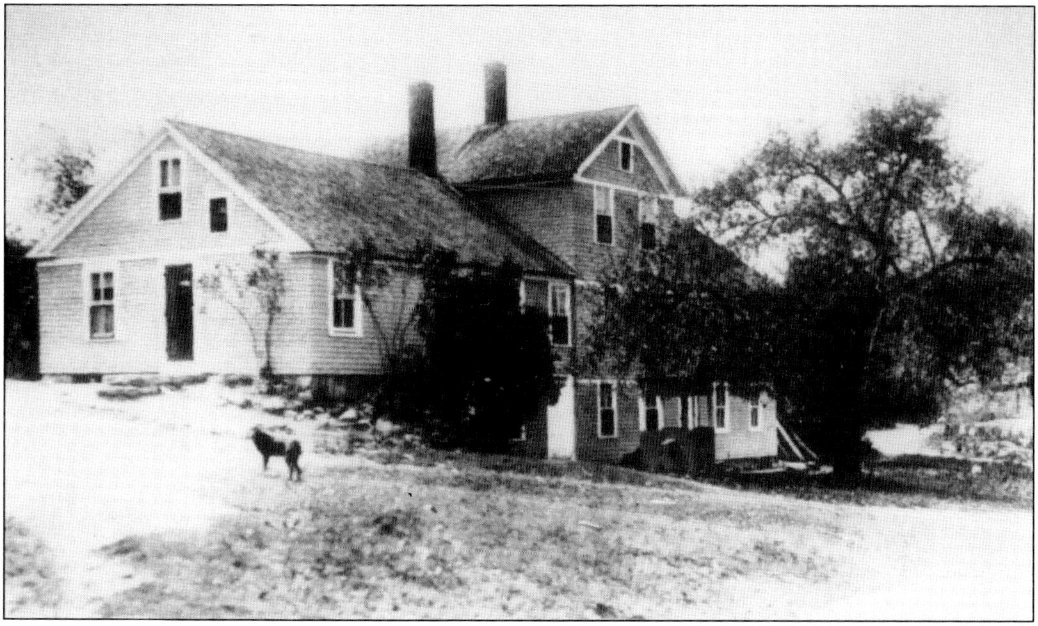

The old Captain Inman Shop has stood at the corner of Sprague Hill Road and Putnam Pike since sometime before 1790. It was expanded to accommodate the Barnes family, who still own it today. In 1923, H.P. Lovecraft stopped here in search of material for a book he planned to write.

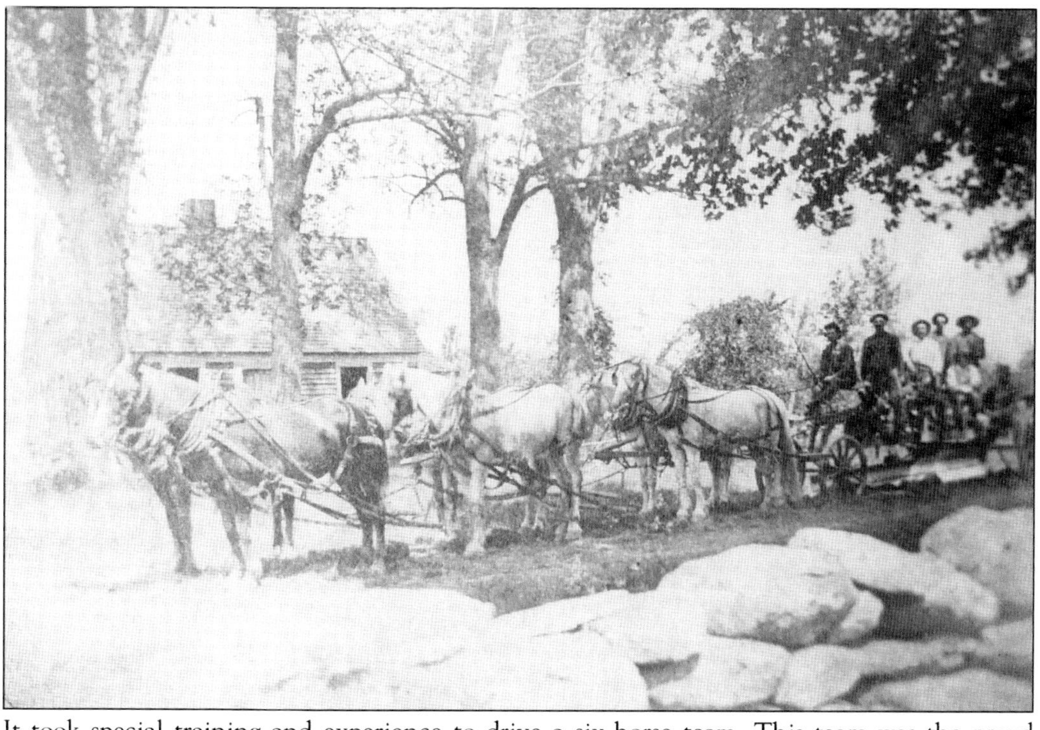

It took special training and experience to drive a six-horse team. This team was the proud possession of Walter A. and Helen E. Hawkins. The photo was taken in 1910 in front of the old Soule house on East Putnam Road near the Connecticut line.

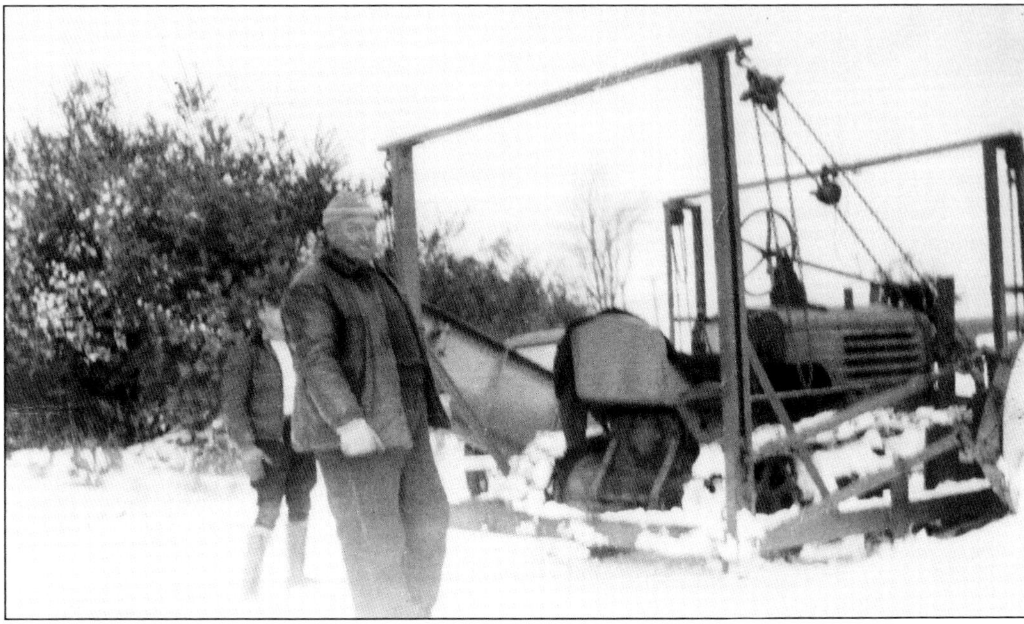

Snow shovels and strong backs moved snow back in the 1920s, but Walter Hawkins in West Glocester built his own snow plow. His nephew Henry (pictured here) referred to it as "the gas guzzler." Perhaps the unidentified man behind Henry has brought more gas to keep the vehicle going.

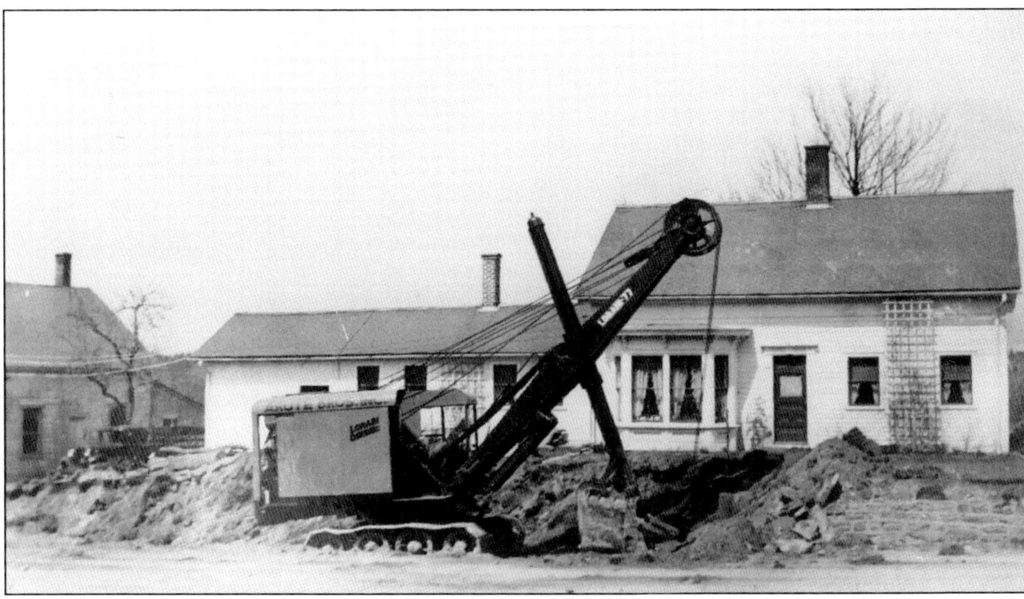

A steam shovel was used in 1938 to remove the stone walls and tree stumps and roots from Hawkins's front yard on Putnam Pike when the two-lane road was widened to four-lane macadam. Hawkins' Store is at the extreme left.

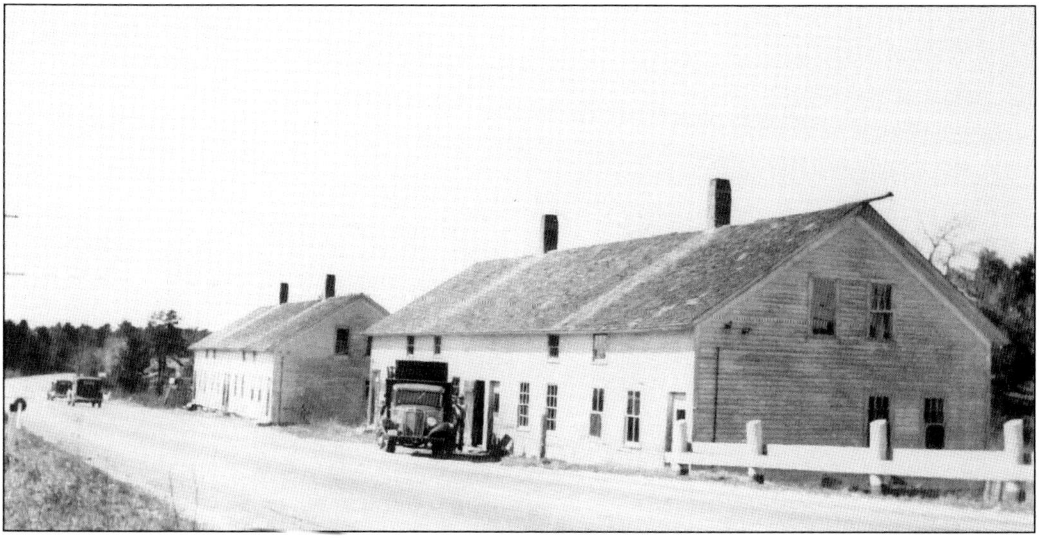

It was moving day for one of the tenants in the Hawkins' Mills tenements on Putnam Pike. A Hawkins' Lumber truck is at the door. Four families occupied each building. These tenements were torn down when the road was widened in 1938. The Connecticut state line is just ahead of the most distant car.

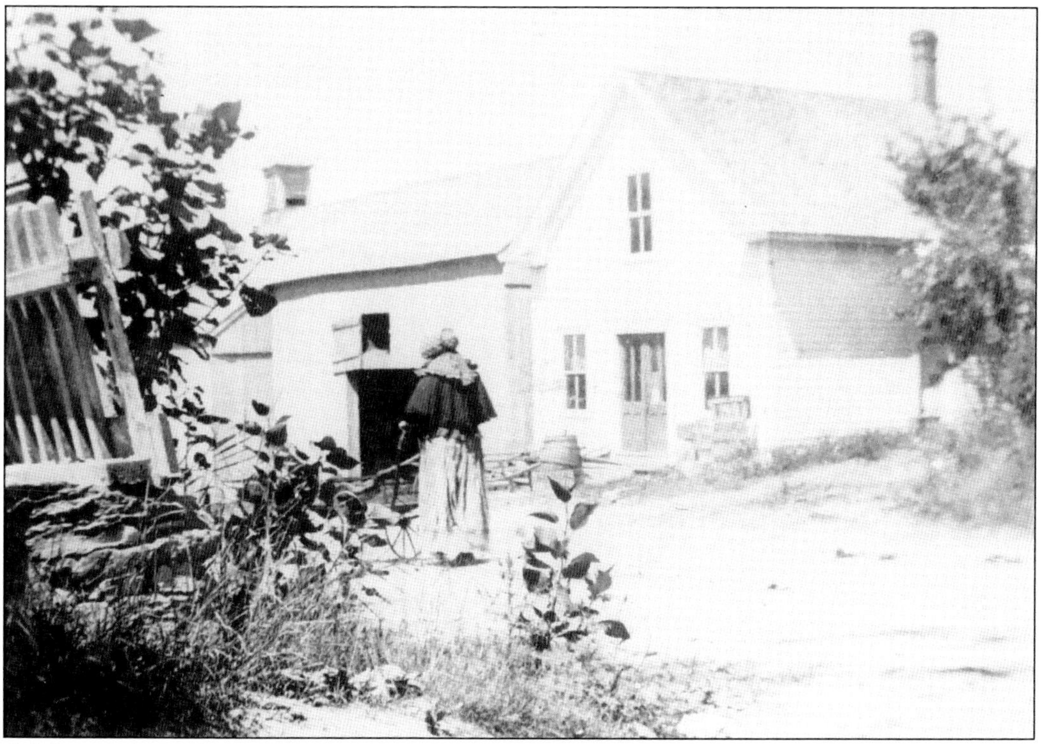

Adeline Baker, who lived in one of the big Hawkins' Mill tenements at the base of the hill, pushes a carriage down the narrow lane. Hawkins' Store and horse and cattle barns are in the background. This 1910 view of Putnam Pike clearly illustrates the size of the road at that time. Interstate traffic traveled east Putnam Road and the old Thompson Road (Pulaski Road).

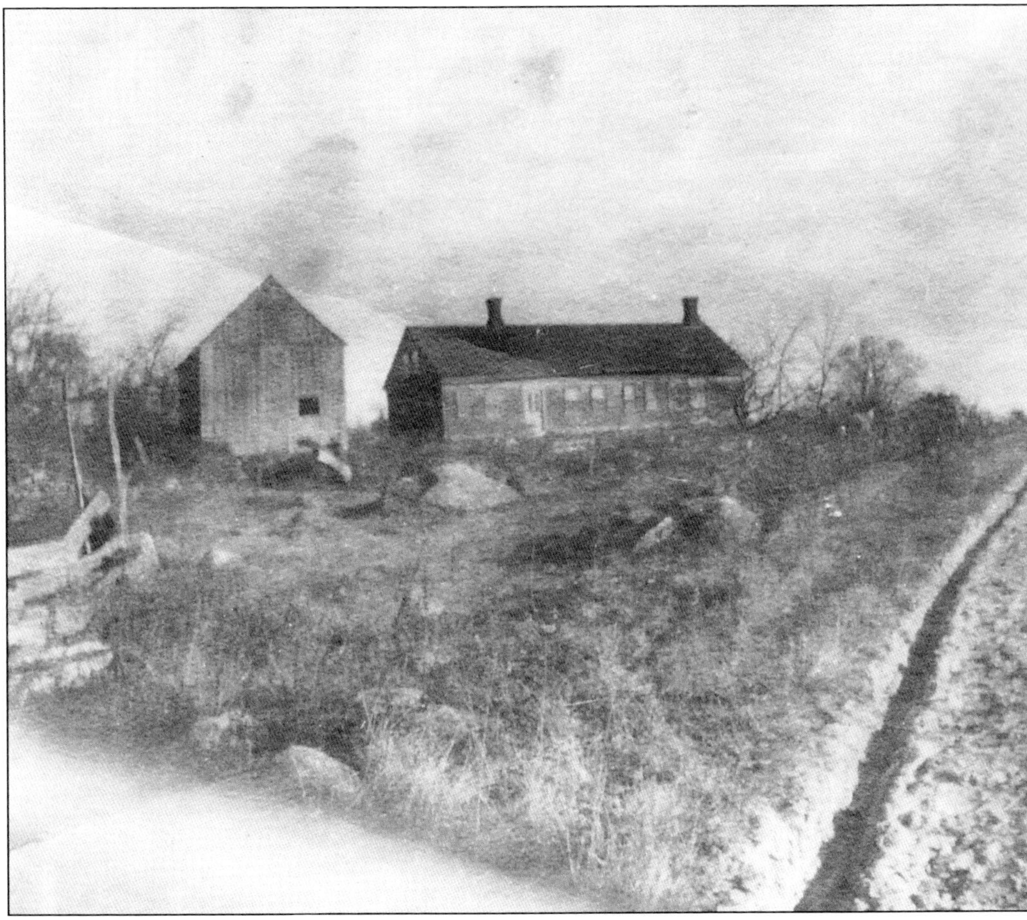

Travel would not be easy in this area as this 1920s view of the deep ruts proves at Anan Evans Farm in southwest Glocester. Today, Snake Hill Road curves south onto Anan Evans Road, upon which one may find the Ponaganset High School and Middle Schools. This photo faces north.

Two

Mills and Businesses

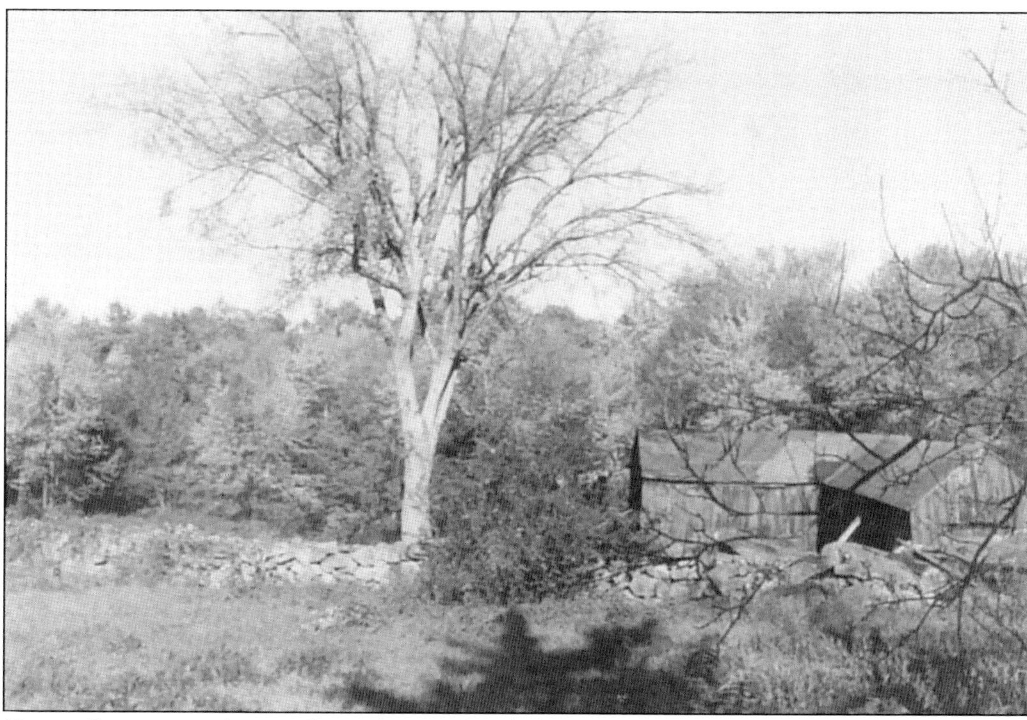

Gristmills were vital to early settlers. A hand-drawn map in 1808 identifies 12 gristmills in old Glocester; at least six are in the present Glocester area. Joseph Winsor's gristmill is drawn on the map where to this day Peckham's Saw and Grist Mills (pictured here) stand on the headwaters of the Chepachet River near Snake Hill Road.

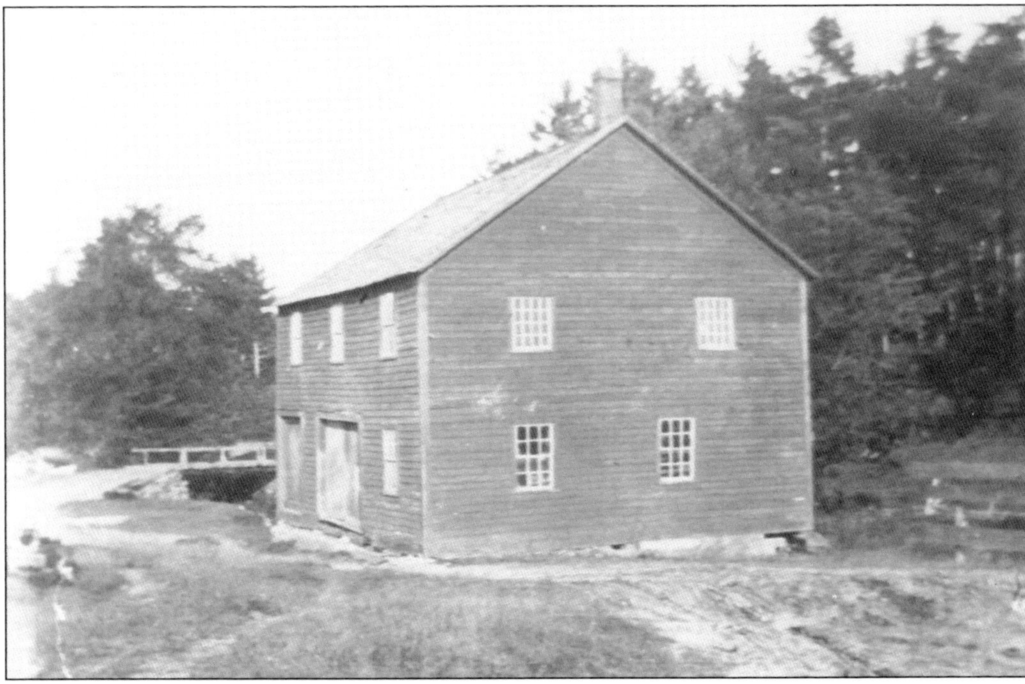

Steere's gristmill on the Chepachet River was located on John Steere's farm east of Chepachet. The mill was built in 1854 and survived for more than a century. The dam there is the only one that did not give way to the enormous flow of water from the freshet of 1867.

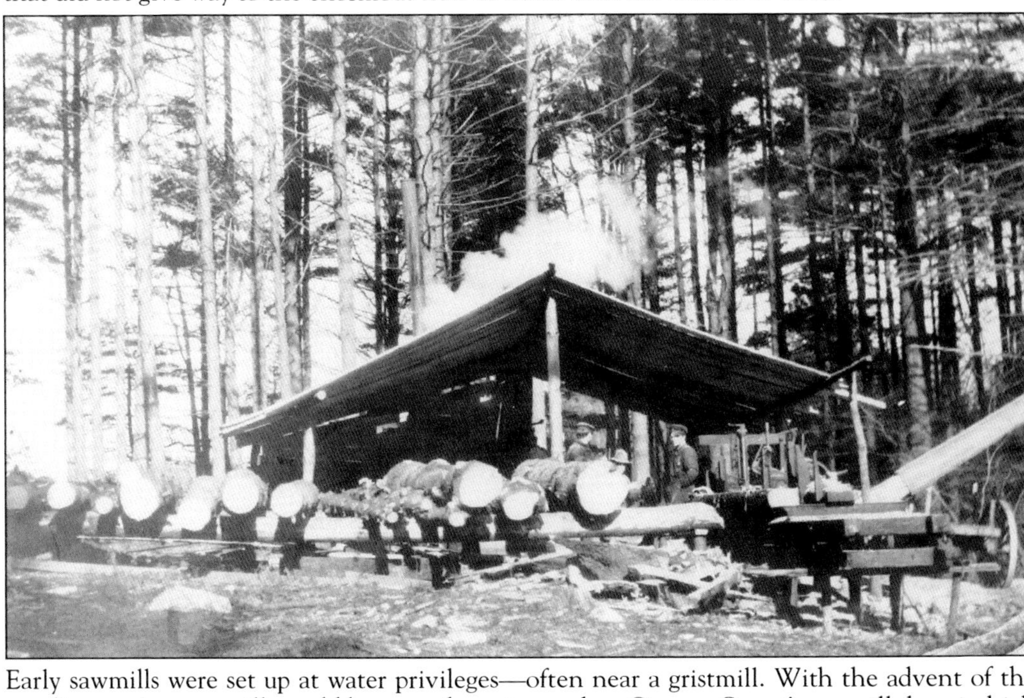

Early sawmills were set up at water privileges—often near a gristmill. With the advent of the gasoline engine, sawmills could be moved on site, such as Simeon Sweet's sawmill deep in high timber in this early-1900s photo. By the early 20th century, much of Glocester's prime timber had been taken for building and manufacture.

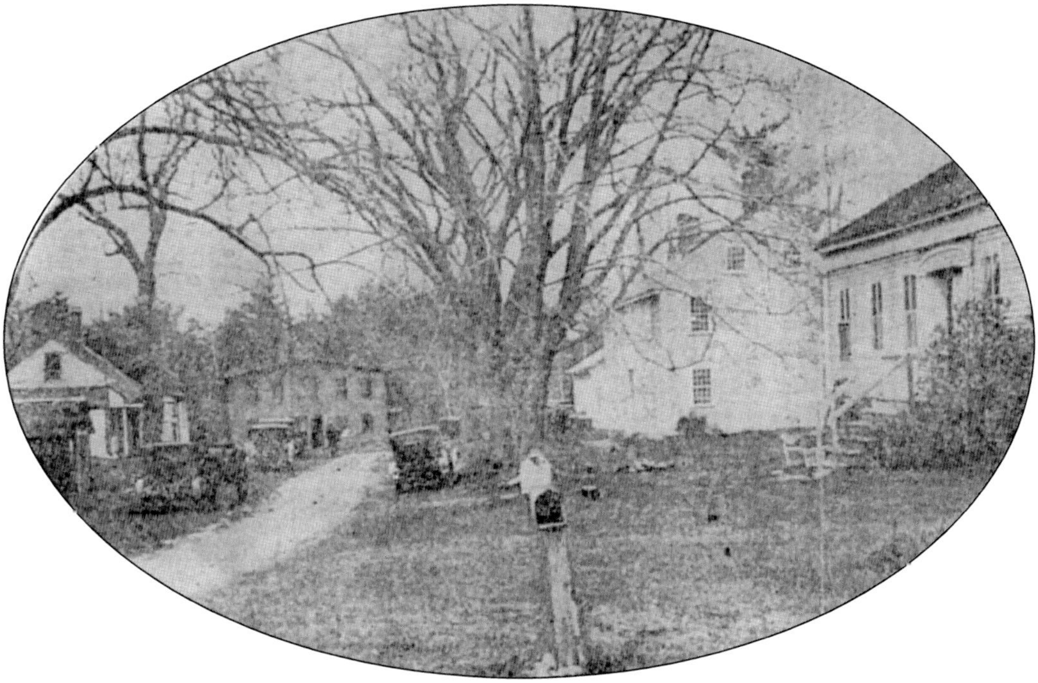

At the time this photo was taken in the early 1900s, Smith Mowry's old mill (center) operated as Spring Grove Worsted, running 24 broad looms and 12 narrow looms. The mill was built in 1838 and first produced cloth and then shoddy during the Civil War. Located on Spring Grove Road east of Chepachet, the little settlement remains to this day.

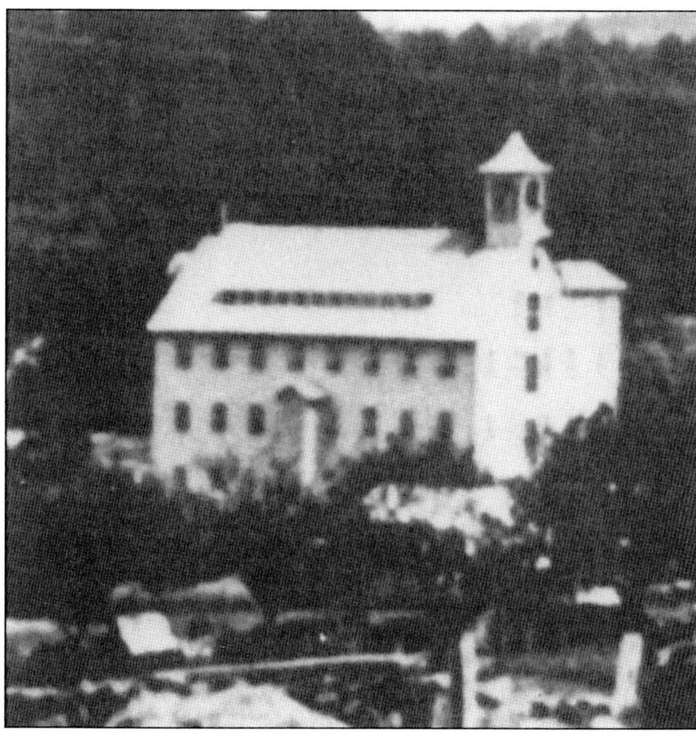

This 18th-century fulling mill was first called the Benefit Mill. It supported a store, a school, and several houses and was operated by Amey Gadcomb, who was widowed in the 1790s when her husband drowned in the river. Later it became known as Point Mill and manufactured cloth. Seriously damaged in the freshet of 1867, it never recovered and burned in 1889.

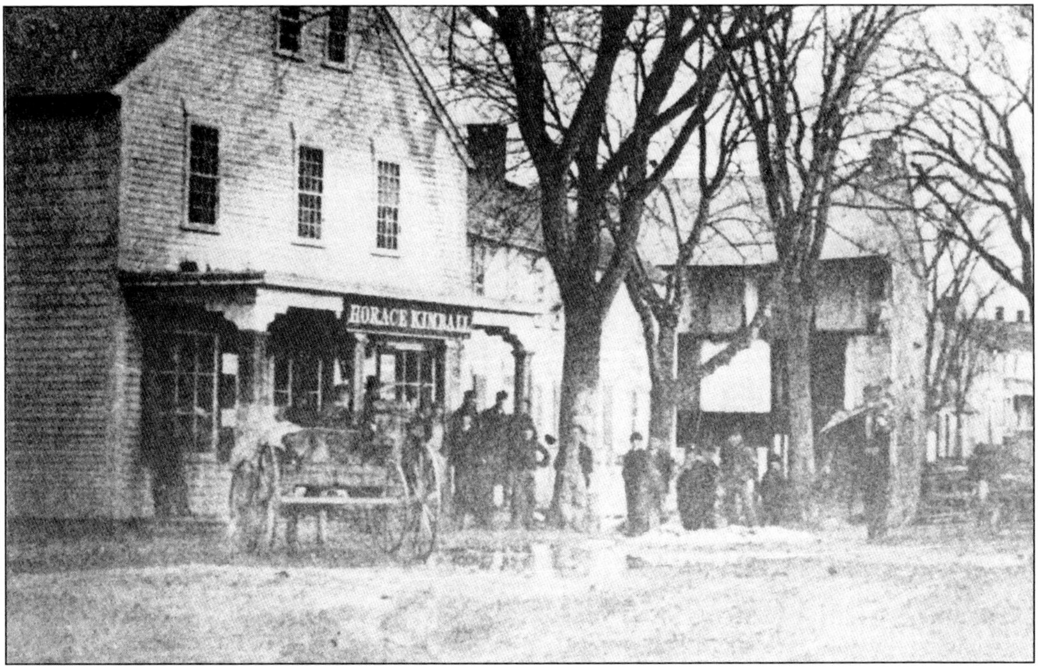

Townspeople are viewing damage done by the freshet on February 10, 1867. A torrential rain with a rapid temperature rise overnight caused the quick melt of 12–15 inches of snow. Thawing ice, 20 inches thick the night before, crashed through two dams. Seething yellow floodwaters tore away river banks and buildings. Mills on the river were devastated, and the bridge was gone. The north wall of the 1814 Stone Mill was torn away.

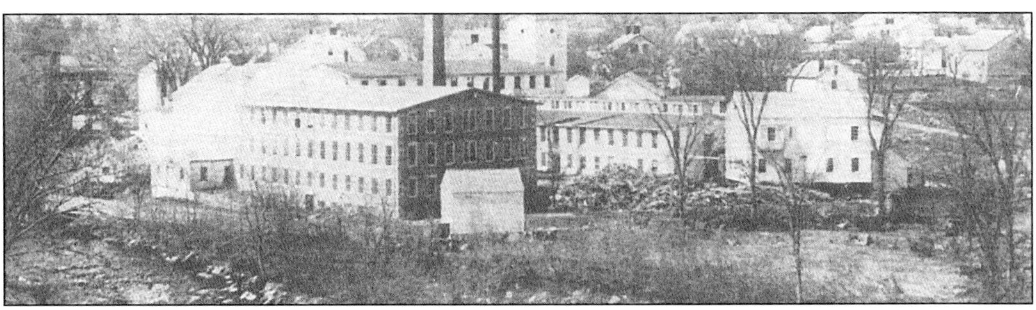

This picture of White's Mill was taken between 1887 and 1889 from the Point Mill's belltower facing west into the village. The Chepachet River, the Stone Mill, and Chepachet Bridge can be seen on the left. A 100-foot addition for carding and spinning was completed in 1886. Eight broad Crompton looms produced fancy worsteds and suitings. The entire mill complex burned in 1897.

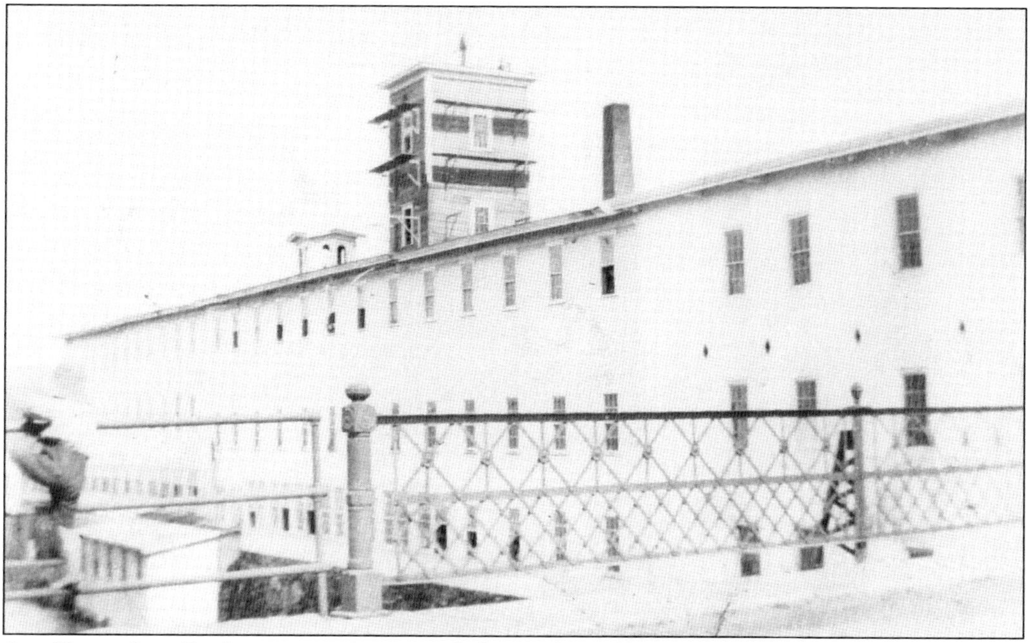

At Chepachet Bridge, a much expanded textile mill, complete with two towers, was photographed before the turn of the century. Built in three stages, the center connected the two separate mills. The original stone structure was built in 1814 by Lawton Owen. All that remains today is the 1814 Stone Mill and the old powerhouse on Point Lane.

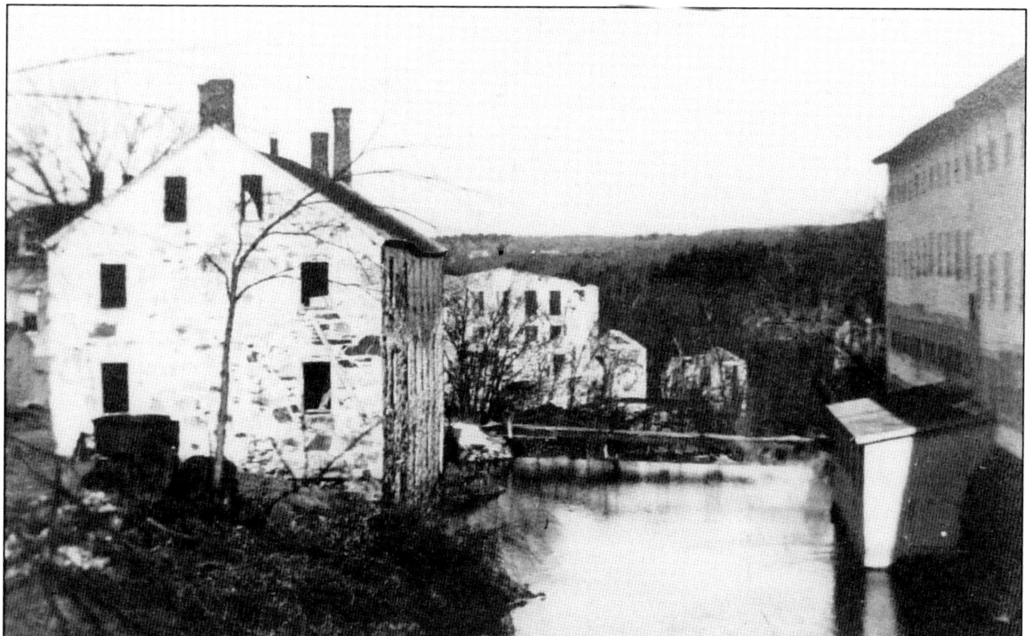

A turn-of-the-century view from Chepachet Bridge reveals the crumbling stone house that was undermined by the freshet and also the charred ruins of White's Mill downstream. Notice the footbridge across the dam. It connected the mill with the mill office on the river's north bank on Tanyard Lane.

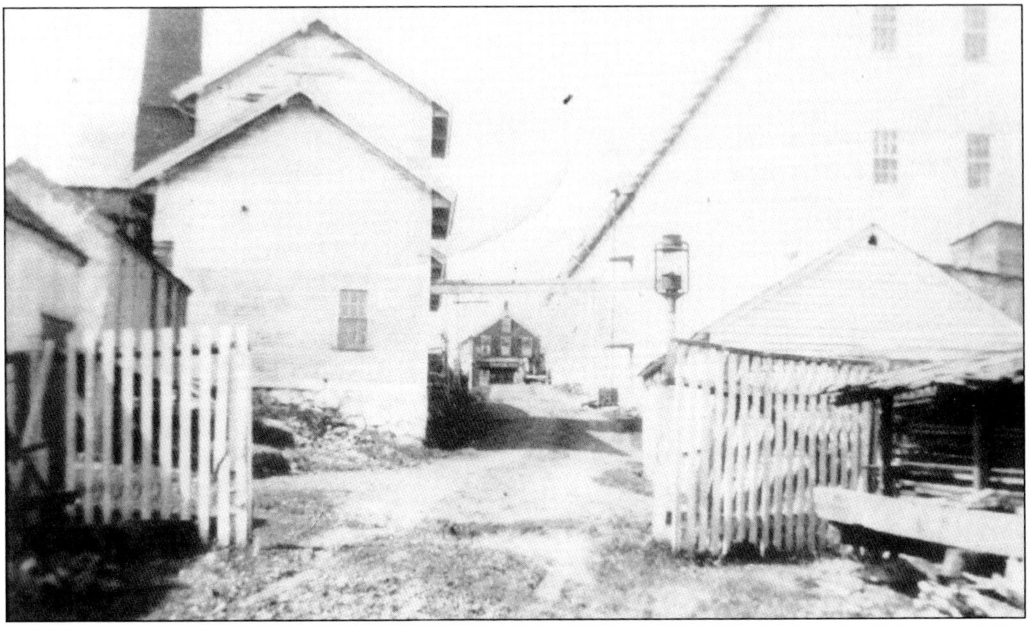

Point Lane was a narrow drive beside the Stone Mill that led to the Point Mill houses. The mill yard was enclosed by a high fence with a gate at the street, which was closed every night. Between the powerhouse at left and the mill was a shaft that transferred power to the machinery in the mill. The old tin shop converted into the fire station is in the distance.

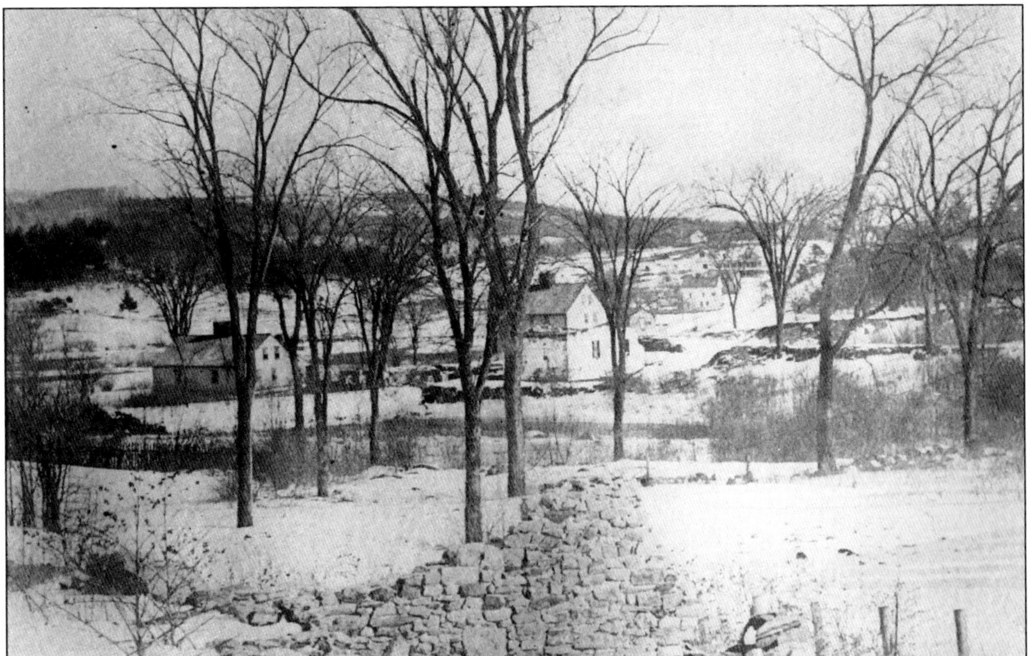

Over the ruins of White's Mill can be seen the old foundation of Point Mill and the mill houses beyond. In the distance is the little Spring Brook School and Spring Grove Road leading up Page Hill. This early-1900s view was taken near the site of the old tannery on Elbow Street which connects Tanyard Lane with Oil Mill Lane.

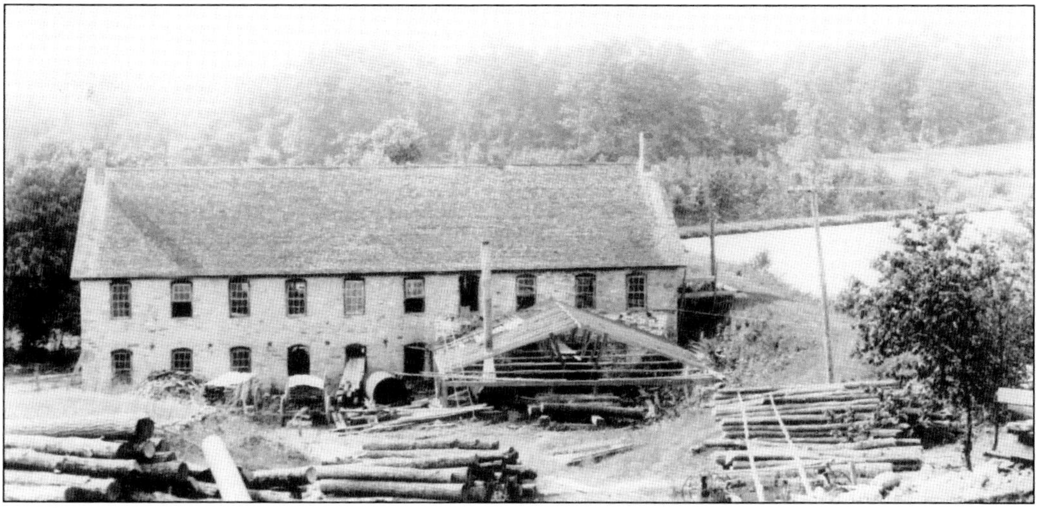

Hawkins' Mill was north of Putnam Pike near the Connecticut line. This mill sawed and planed lumber, made clothboards, wainscoting, and twine, manufactured picnic tables and rowboats, and sold baled shavings. The shaving shed is the addition on the front of the mill. One of the two ponds of Hawkins' Mill ponds is visible at right. This mill had burned many years before and had been rebuilt, but a fire on July 4, 1946, totally destroyed it.

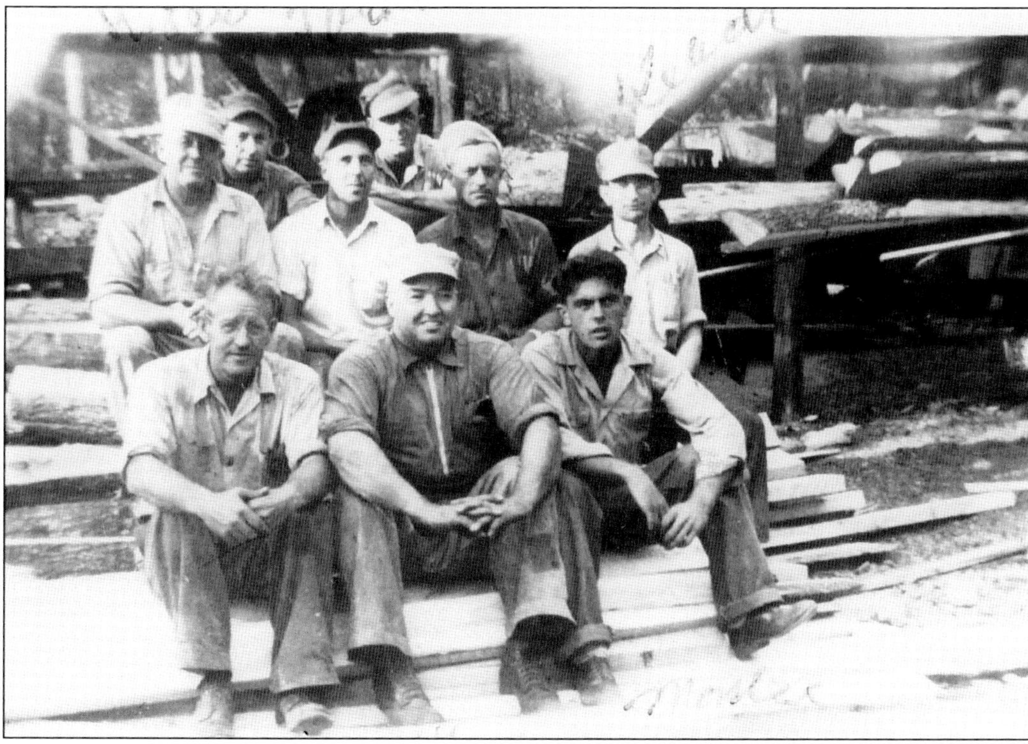

Here are Hawkins' Mill workers in 1940 resting after a hard day's work—hauling logs out of the pond where they were preserved until ready to cut. The workers, from left to right, are as follows: (front row) Ernest Cutler, Henry Hawkins, and Normand Montie; (middle row) Randall Law, Tom Adams, Conrad Montie, and Francis Keach, planer; (back row) Ernest Child and ? Glenner.

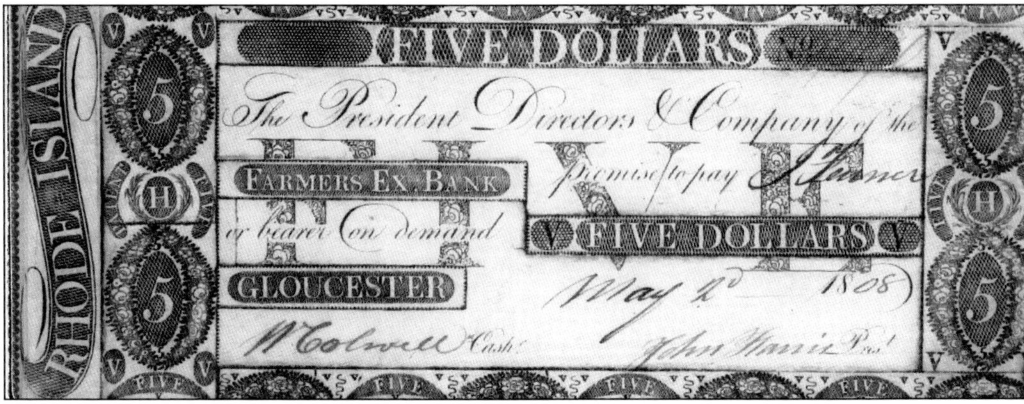

The Farmers' Exchange Bank $5-note pictured here may not have been good for long— if at all. The bank failed in 1809 due to mishandling of funds. Nine years later, Franklin Bank opened in Chepachet to serve the financial needs of Glocester and continued successfully until the National banking system was established in 1865.

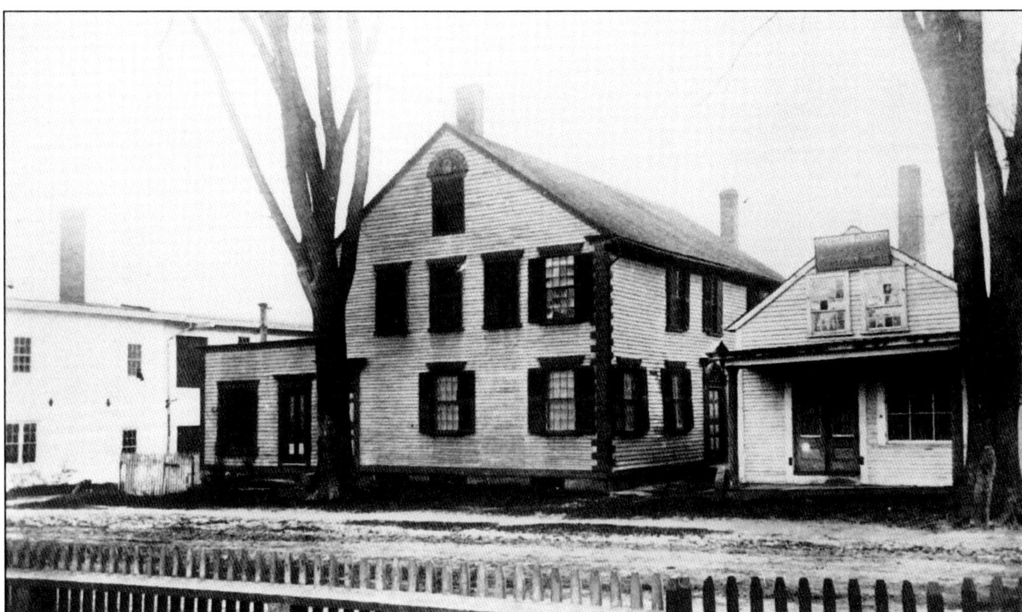

The Farmers' Exchange Bank in Chepachet operated from 1804 to 1809 on the first floor of the two-story Masonic building in the center of the photo. The second floor belonged to Friendship Lodge #7 F & AM Masons. The bank's unique overnight safe may have left some question as to reliability. The day's money was lowered by rope through a trap door in the floor into a dry well.

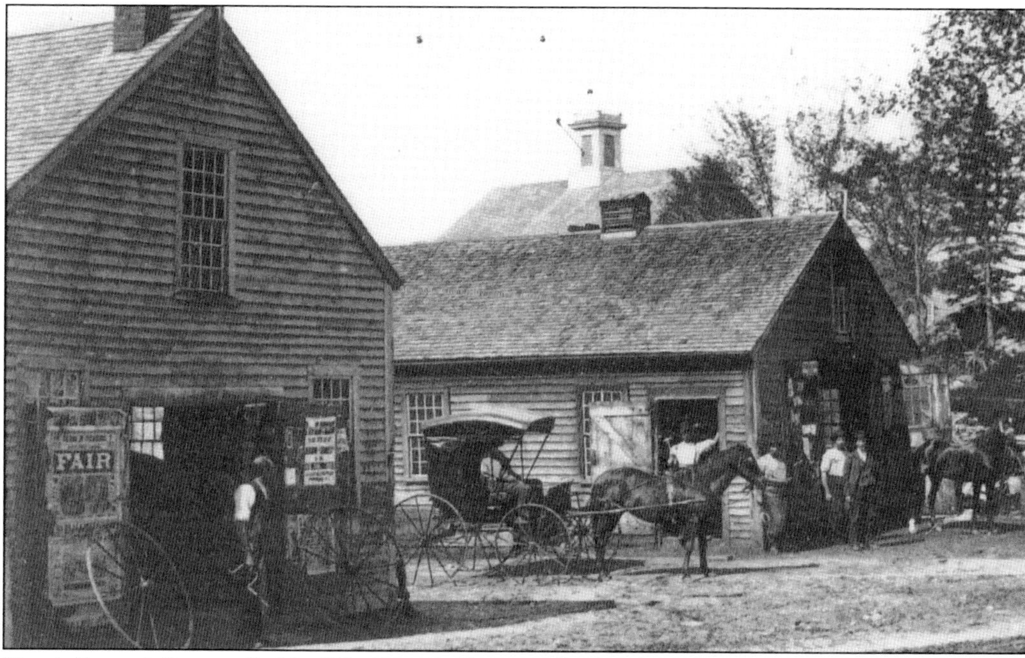

Harris Steere's Livery Stable, Blacksmith Shop, and Wheelwright Shop stood on the southwest side of Putnam Pike at the intersection with the Oakland Road (Rt. 102). The photographer took great care to pose everyone with their tools of trade in this 1880s scene. This site is now the approximate location of the Kesteloot Building. The barn was made into an apartment house and has recently been torn down.

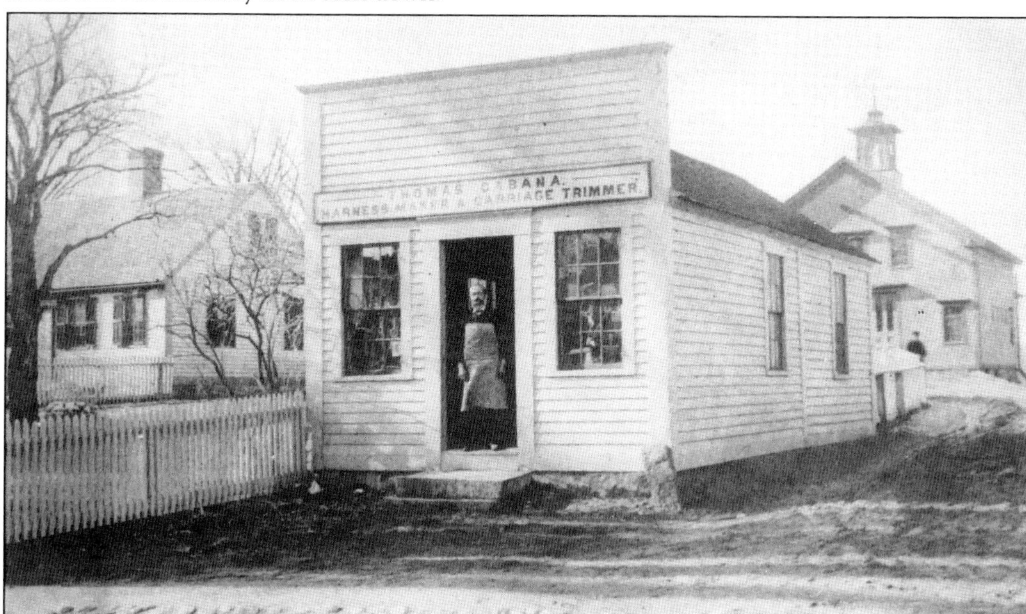

Thomas Cabana stands at his shop's door in this 1890s photo. His shop stood where the new addition to the Chepachet Fire Station has been built. This two-room shop began as Dr. Mowry's office. It was also the first home of Glocester's Manton Free Public Library. The little building was sold at auction for $85 in 1939 and moved to Money Hill Road.

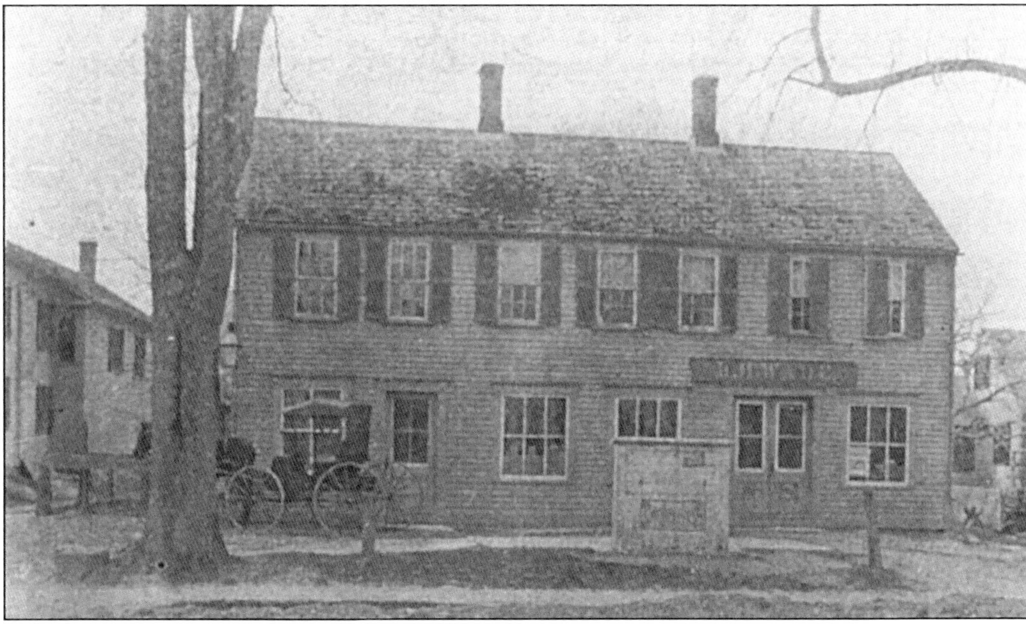

This rare 1880s photo is of Bob Wade's Store, which stood where Lawyer Bradley Steere's office is today. It was a general store with at least two apartments upstairs. The store, three houses, and three barns burned in 1907 in one of the most disastrous fires ever to strike the village of Chepachet.

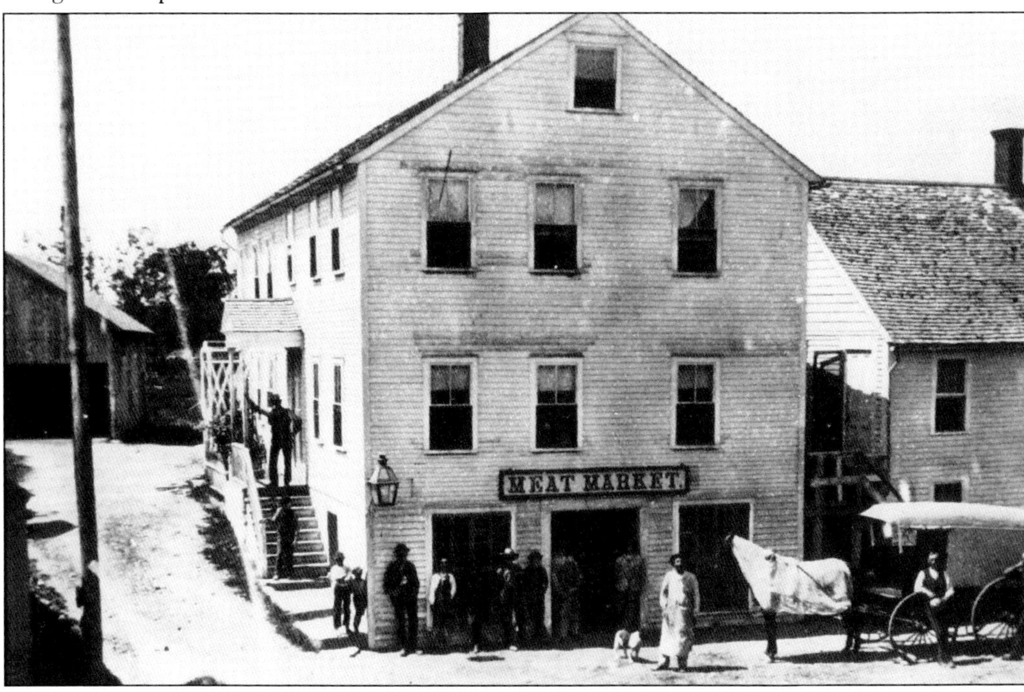

Job Armstrong's old house and barn look very much the same today as they did in this 1890s photo. Two meat markets and a variety of other shops have occupied the space below the house—Mr. Armstrong being the first, before his big store across Main Street was built. The Places had several meat markets and slaughterhouses in Chepachet and made home deliveries.

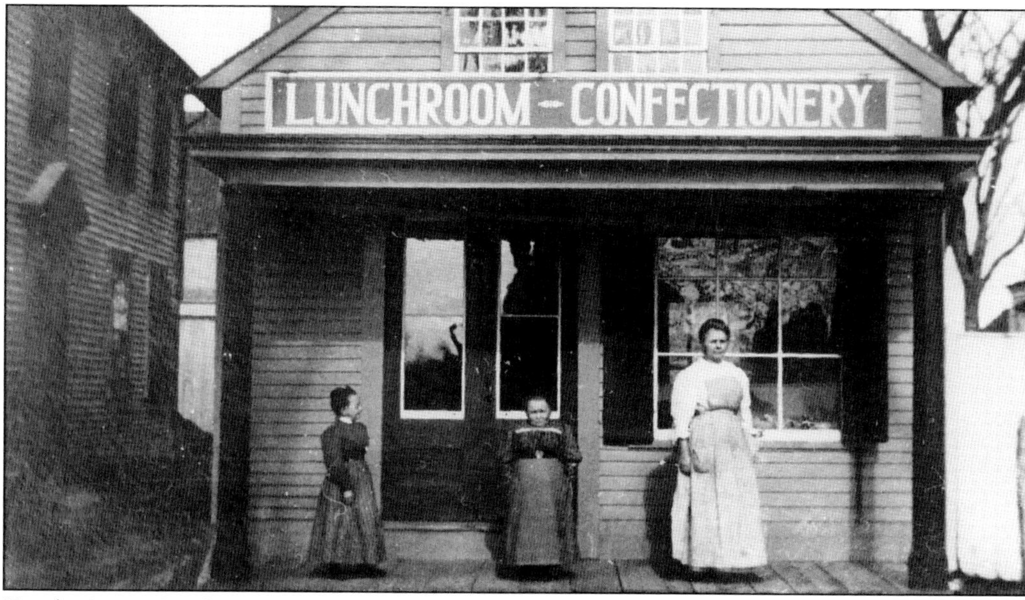

"Little Annie Reuben"—as she was affectionately called—ran this shop next to the Masonic Hall. In 1910, her friend, Sadie Belton (on the left), of the nationally renowned Lilliputian Opera Company, traveled from her home in Watkins, New York, to tend the store so that "Annie" could take care of her husband, Reuben Steere, who had pneumonia.

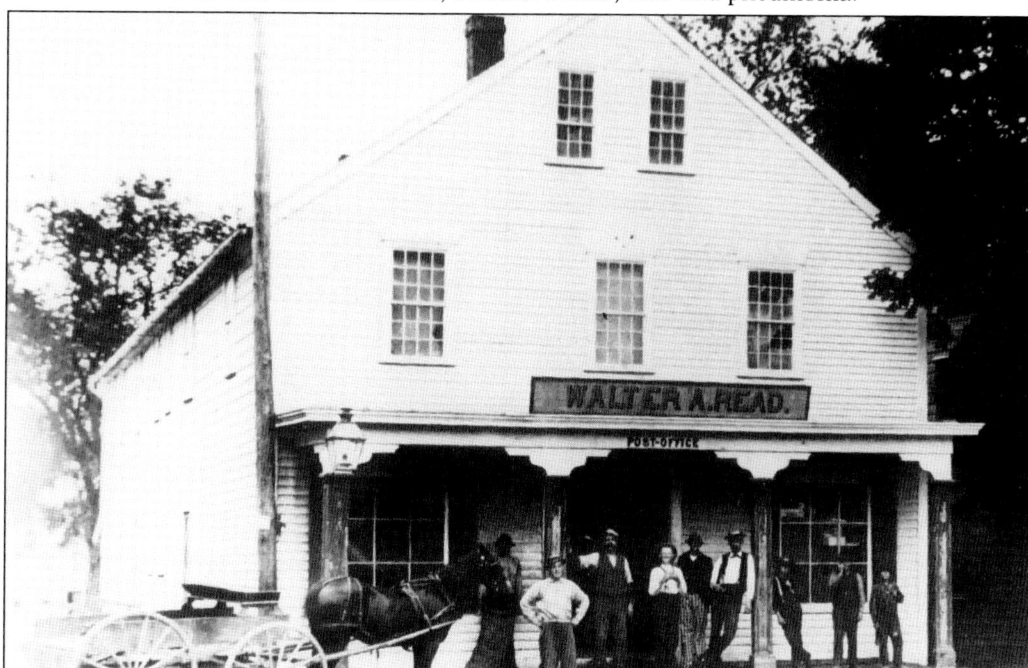

After Captain Walter Read returned from three years in the Civil War, he tended store with Augustus Wade and then as sole owner 19 of the 26 years as storekeeper; he also served as the postmaster. Many recalled that wagonloads of merchandise bearing the initials W.A.R. came to the store. It may be Captain Read, with vest buttoned, who stands proudly with his hand on the porch post in this 1880s photo.

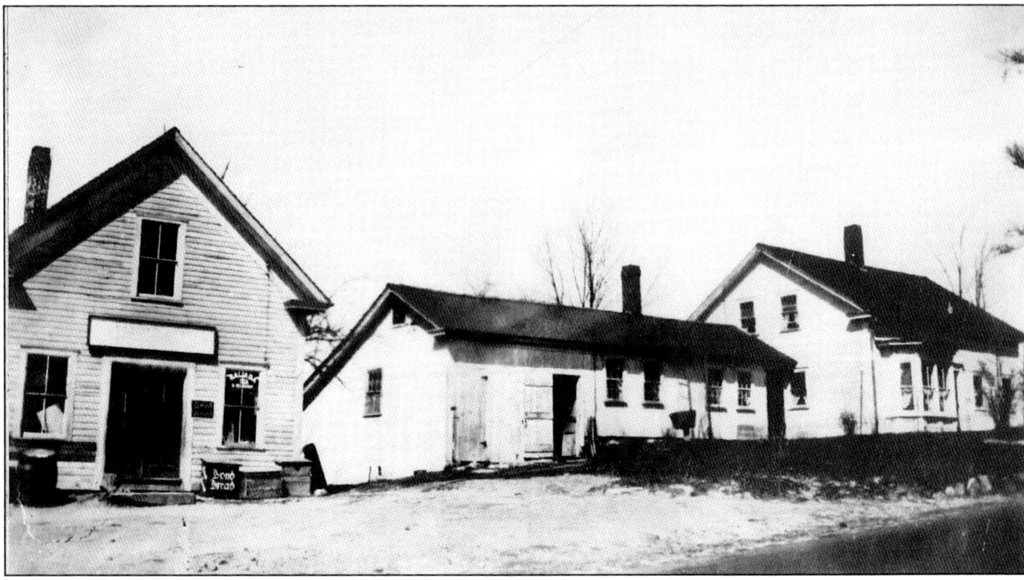

Hawkins' Store built in 1886 on Putnam Pike also held the West Glocester Post Office in the early 1900s. Mrs. Dexter (Elizabeth) Hawkins tended both store and post office. Fred Barnes, and sometimes his wife, Clara, delivered the mail. The "Star Route," a horse-drawn, covered black mail wagon driven by Charles Slocum, traveled from Putnam, stopping at Hawkins' Store three times a week.

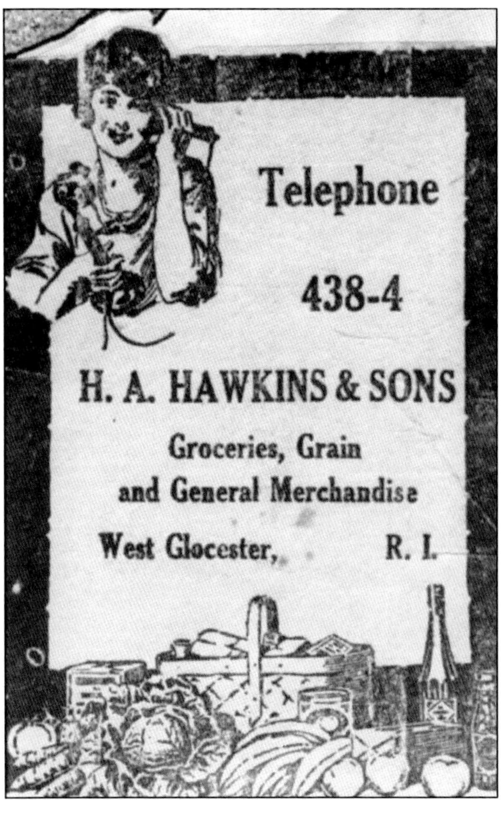

Some of the store's customers were Connecticut residents because the store was so close to the state line. When he was old enough to drive, Henry Hawkins delivered groceries to neighbors and shut-ins in the store truck. This 1890s ad was part of Hawkins's photo collection.

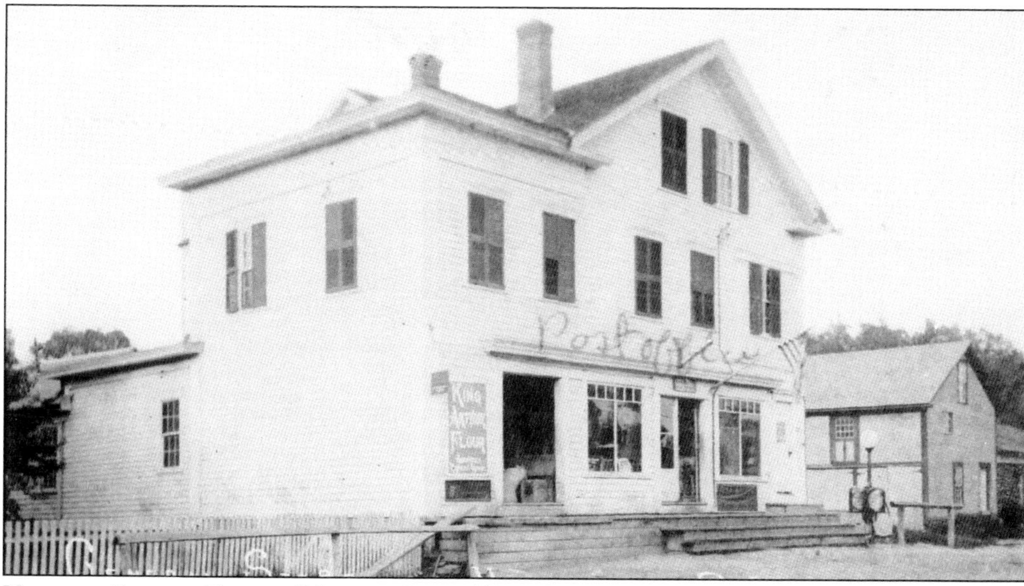

Harmony Store on Putnam Pike near Sawmill Road was built in 1838. C.P. Burlingame succeeded E.M. Aldrich and was dealing in general merchandise in 1870. The post office was installed in the store in 1883 by C. Whipple, followed by W. Hancock, Henry Randall, and Harry Staples. It was called Brown & Staples when this 1920s photocard was developed. Although closed for several years, it is still known as Dunn's Store to this day.

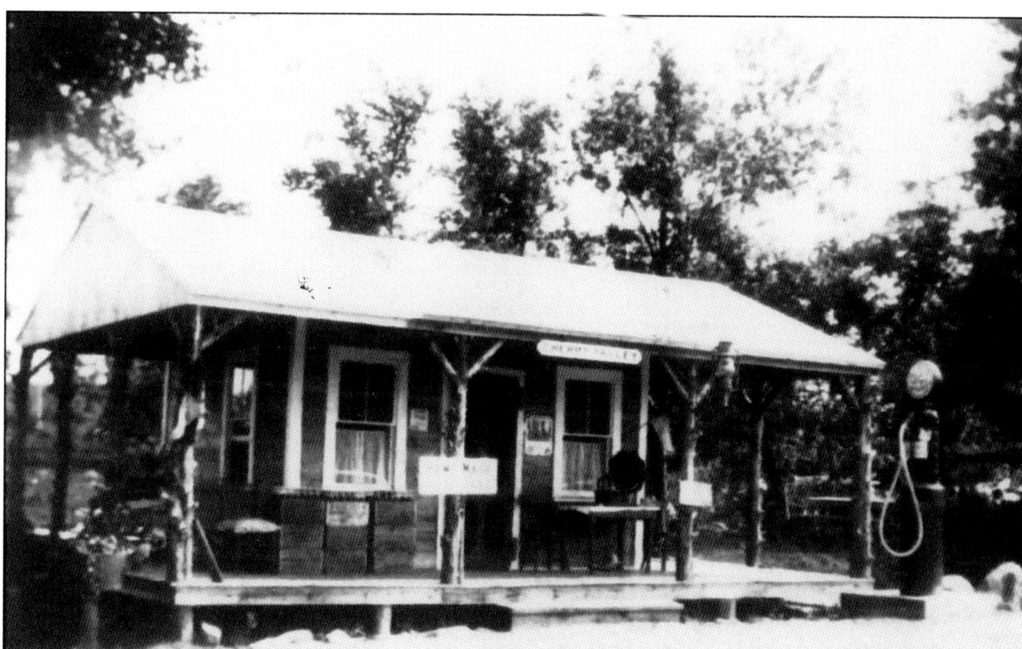

Ella Steere's Cherry Valley Store, a familiar landmark in South Glocester at the intersection of Chopmist Hill Road and Snake Hill Road, provided basic groceries, the local news, home-baked pies and cakes, and Socony gas from the pump next to the porch in the mid-1900s. The local children respectfully called her "Gramma."

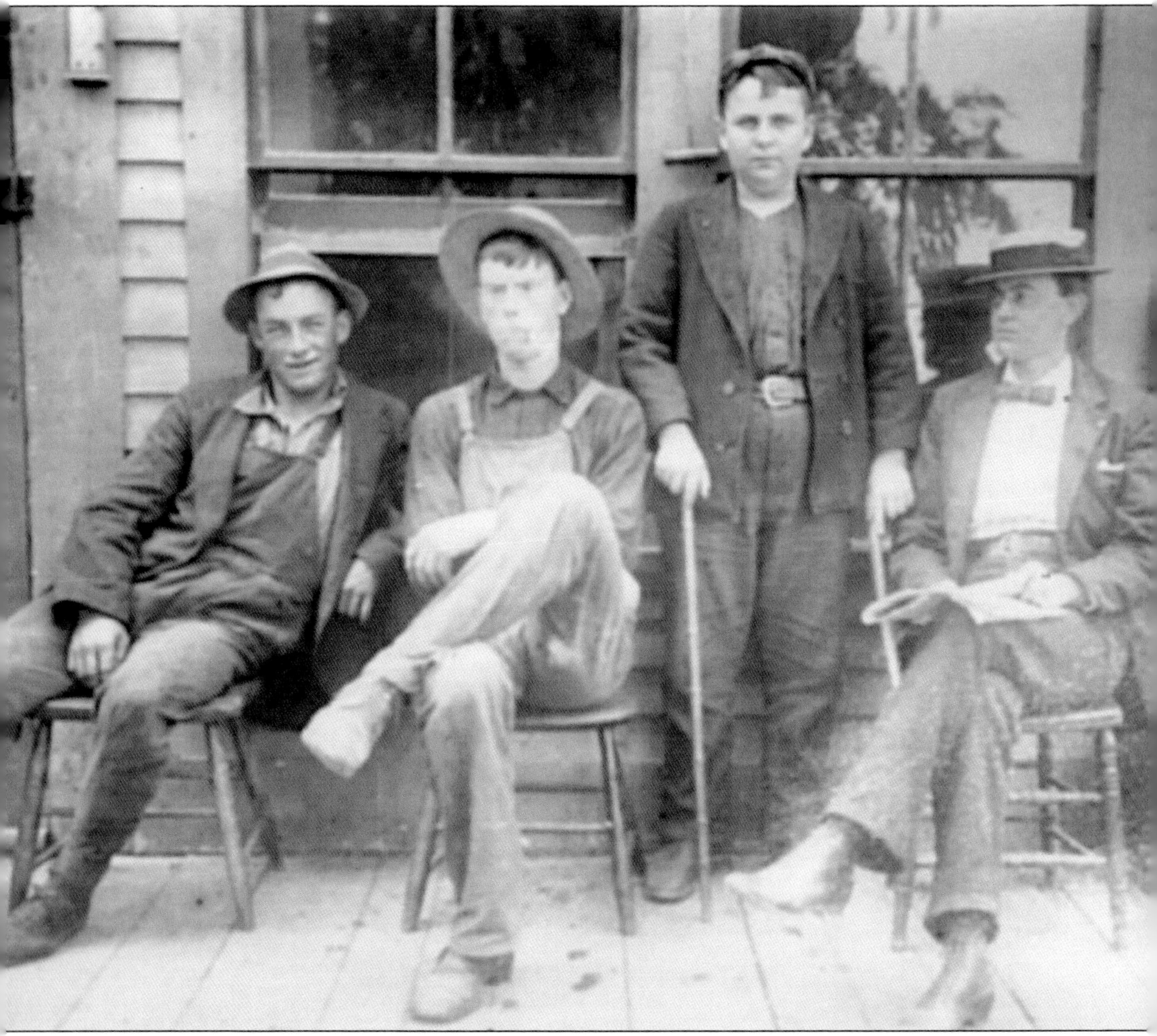

There were certain "regulars" who passed time at the local store chatting and watching passersby. The thin man smoking a pipe is believed to be Gus Irons. Although the other gentlemen are unknown, another familiar face at Trinque Brothers Store just south of Chepachet Bridge would have been "Fod" Richmond. Blind for many years, he turned the handle on the peanut roasting machine and listened to all the news from customers.

Three

Earth Industry

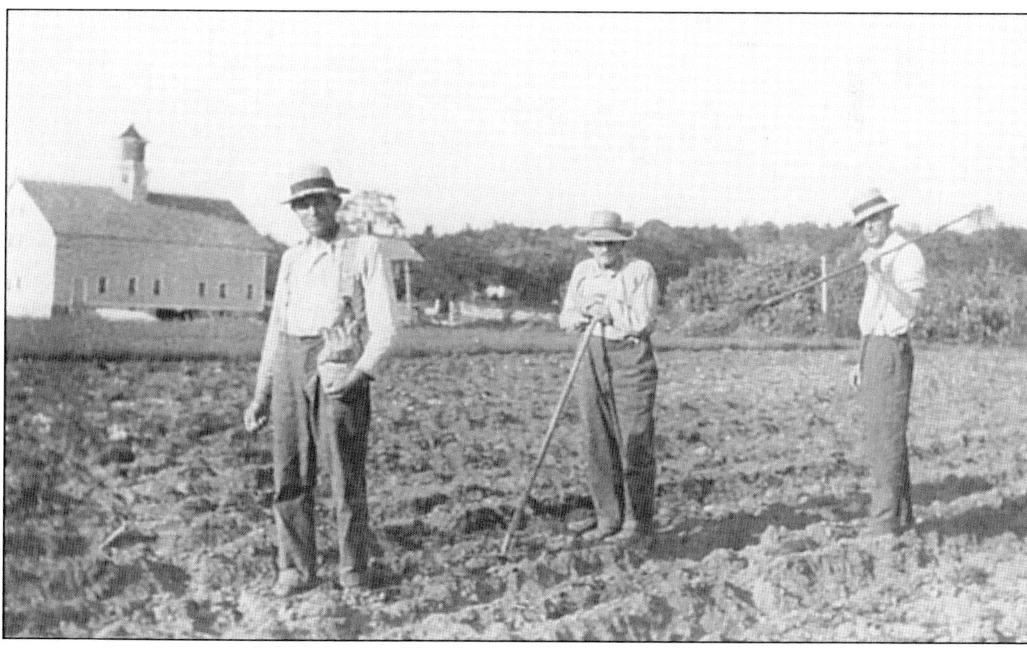

An extra hand or two during spring planting was always welcome. Henry Salisbury (center) and his son Charles (left) were glad for Frank Sturtevant's help the day they planted this cornfield. In this early-1900s view, Thomas Steere's barn on Chopmist Hill Road is in the distance. It was moved to the Roger Williams College campus and restored during the 1980s.

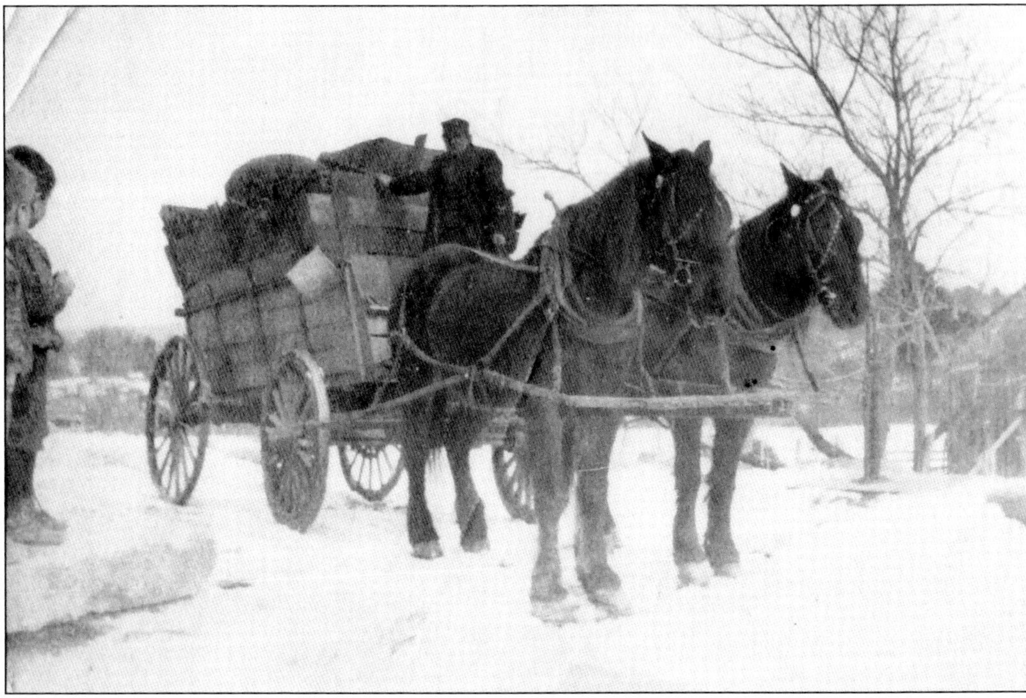

Jim and Elias Peckham stand on the stone step of the old Joseph Winsor house on Snake Hill Road looking at "Monk" Evans on the colliers' wagon. It is estimated that this photograph was taken between 1900 and 1910.

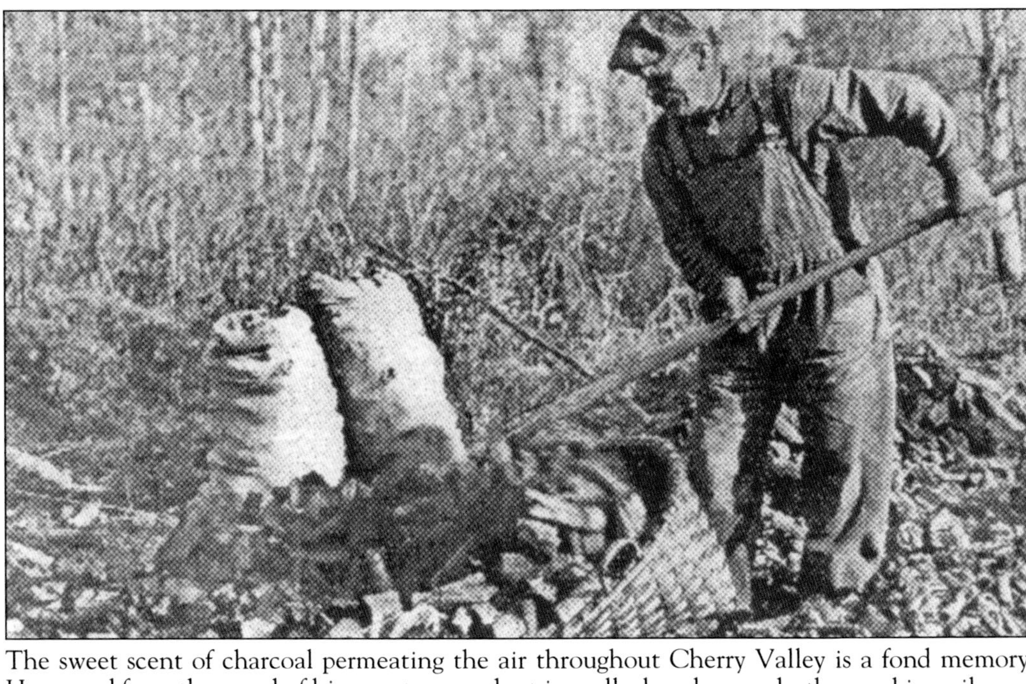

The sweet scent of charcoal permeating the air throughout Cherry Valley is a fond memory. Harvested from the wood of his own trees and set in well-placed mounds, the smoking piles are carefully tended around the clock for many days. Now blackened and brittle, the charcoal has cooled, and Mr. Peckham rakes the pieces into his basket.

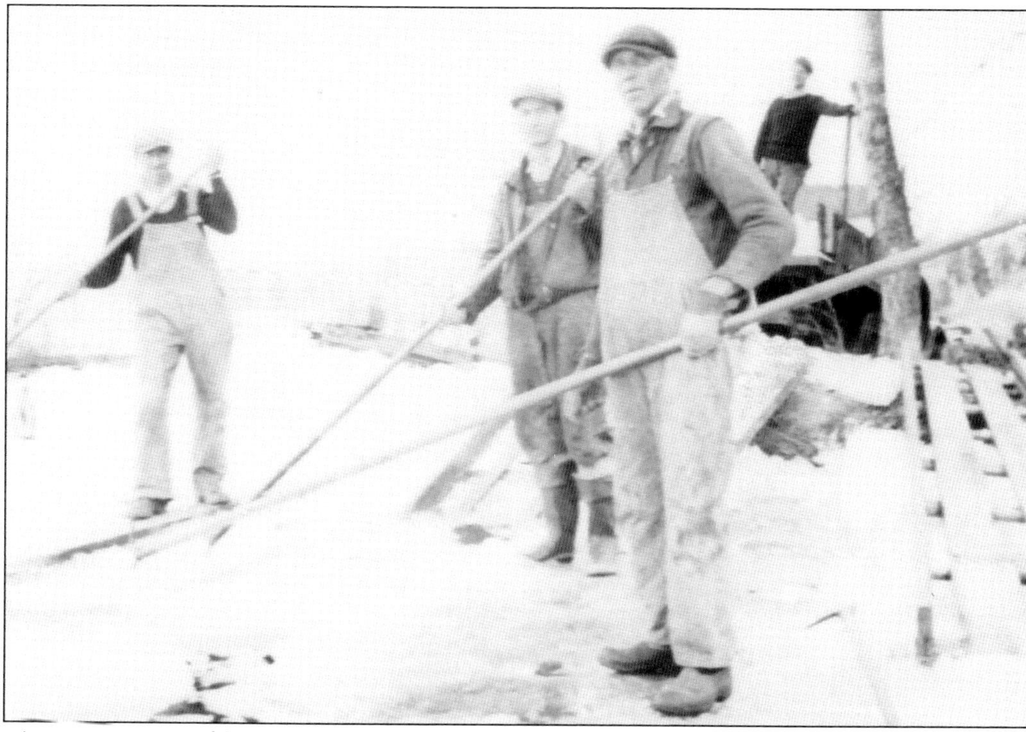

These men are holding long pikes used to guide the ice blocks on John Steere's pond east of Chepachet. Ice was sawn into blocks and slid to a huge icehouse on the property. There, insulated with thick layers of sawdust, the ice stayed solid well into the summer.

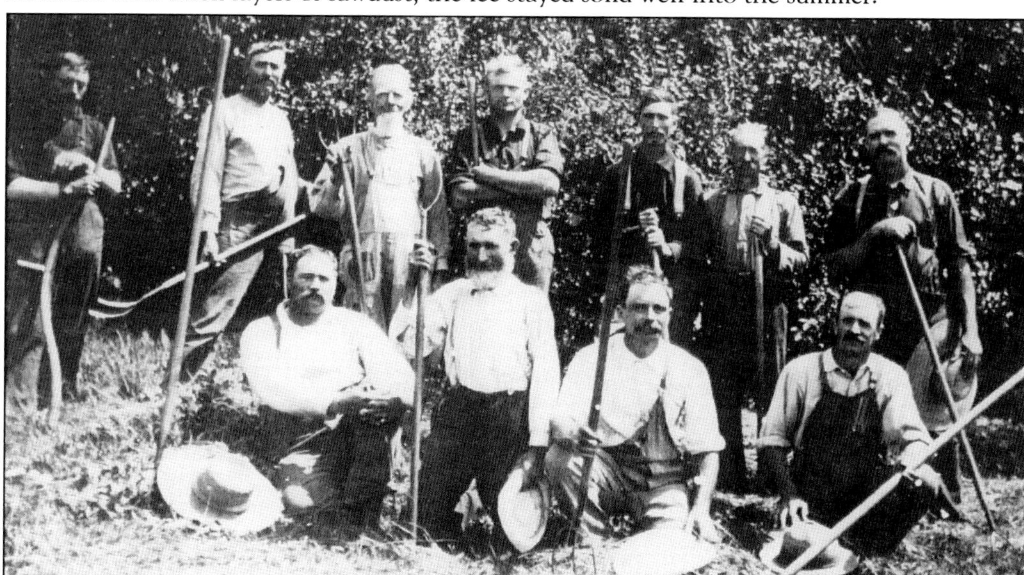

Cooperative weather and good teamwork got the haying done. This South Glocester haying team posed for the photographer in the 1890s. These hard workers are, from left to right, as follows: (sitting or kneeling) Arthur Place, Joseph Sarle, Eddie Cook, and Frank Peckham; (standing) Daniel Gleason, Welcome Place, Jonathan Eldredge, George Angell, Charles Shippee, Stillman Gross, and Fred Place.

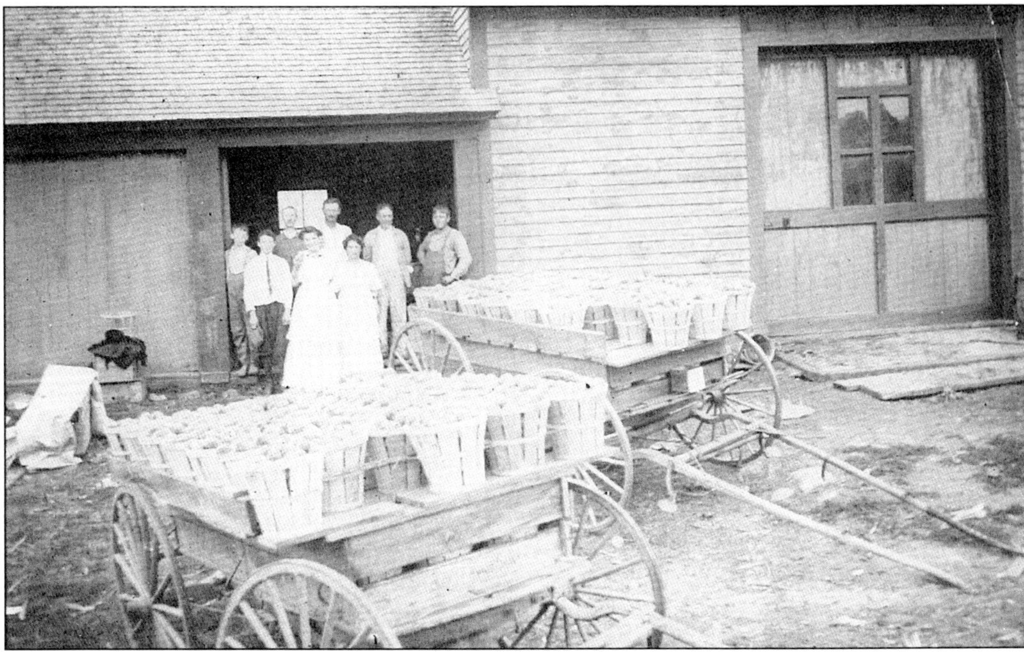

J. Curtis Hopkins's farm on Chestnut Hill Road called Prospect Hill Gardens produced apples, peaches, and vegetable plants. In this turn-of-the-century photo, the Hopkins family proudly displays their peach harvest. The tall man is J. Curtis Hopkins and the shorter woman is Jeanette Hopkins.

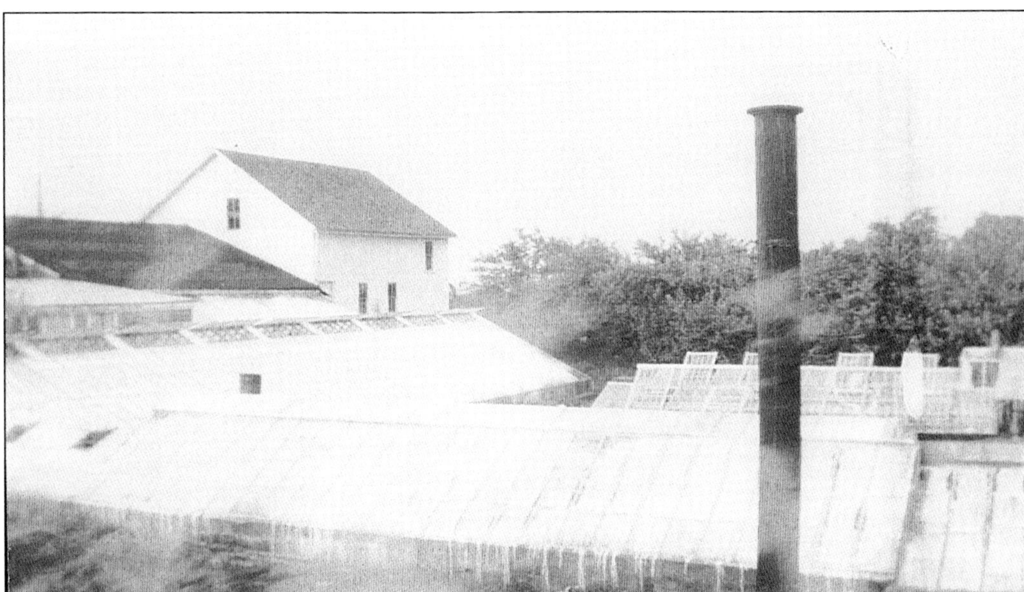

Vegetable plants were raised by J. Curtis Hopkins & Son in these enormous greenhouses atop Prospect Hill on Chestnut Hill Road. The barn and shed burned in 1938.

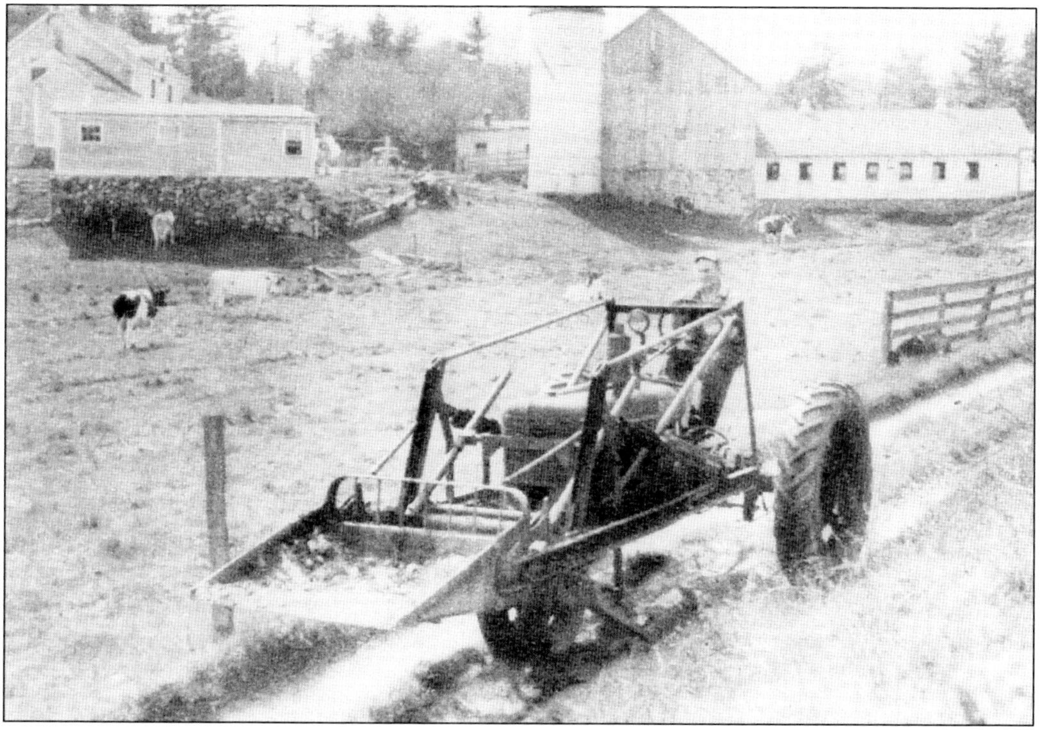

There were several dairy farms in Glocester. This picturesque farm was on the Oakland Road (Victory Highway) just north of Chepachet. Stanley Fitts, owner of the 70-acre farm, is driving the tractor. The road is in back of the house and barn in this 1947 picture.

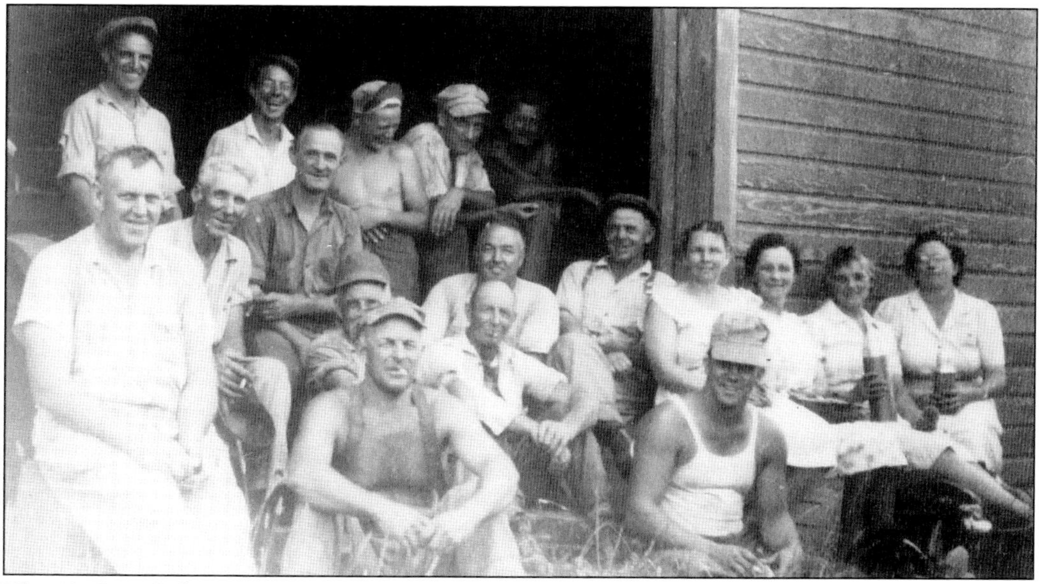

The 1945 apple harvest was a good one at Steere's Orchards on Douglas Hook Road. Gathered at Enoch Steere's barn are, from left to right, as follows: (front row) Leon Chase, ?, and Bonhomme Paul; (second row) ?, Raymond Steere, and ?; (third row, beginning with the man in the dark shirt) Henry Hawkins, Benny Steere, ?, Ruth Steere, Alcy Steere, Hortense Steere, and ?; (back row) Earl Salisbury, George Paquin, ?, ?, and ?.

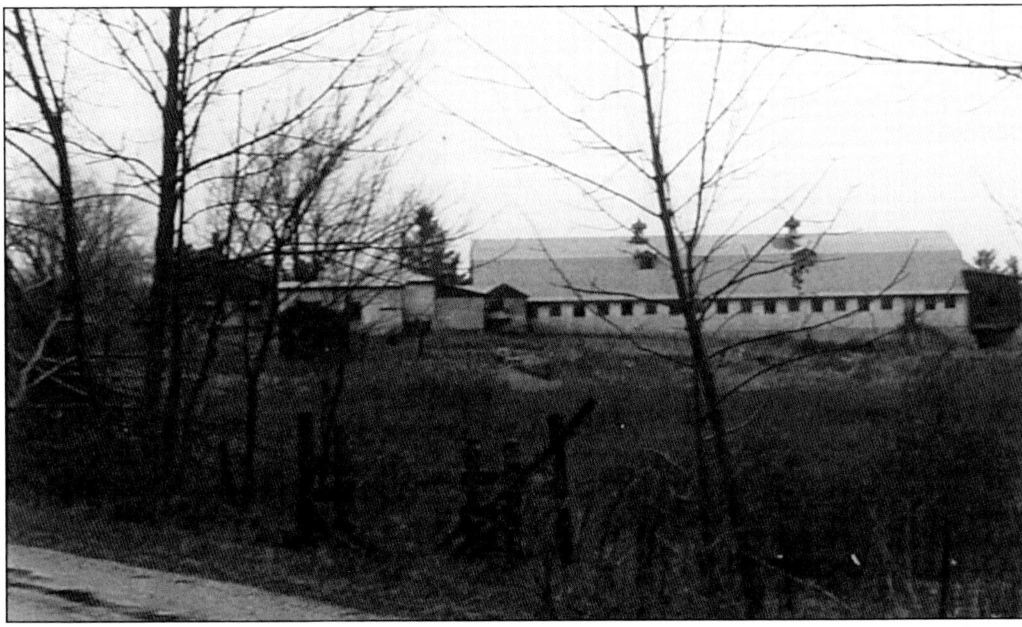

Johnny Mann's dairy farm was on the old Sweet farm just west of the intersection of Snake Hill Road, Chestnut Hill Road, and Durfee Hill Road. His Sunny Acres Farm milk truck, driven by Fred Everett, delivered to Glocester homes daily for many years. "Johnny" also drove the school bus from South Glocester to Chepachet. This is a 1980s photo.

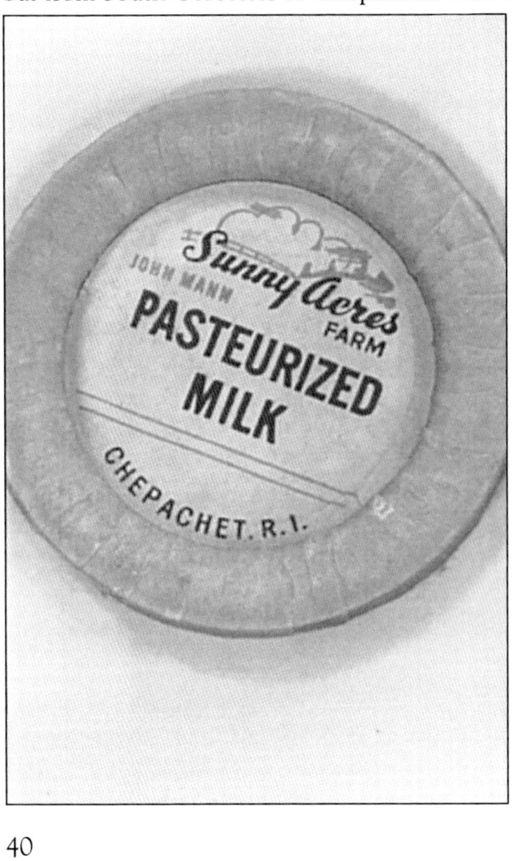

This is probably the only paper milk bottle cap with this imprint in existence, thanks to Fred Everett, who kept it as a memento of his many years working for Johnny Mann. When John was too busy to drive the school bus, Fred would fill in for him as school bus driver, too.

Four

Chepachet

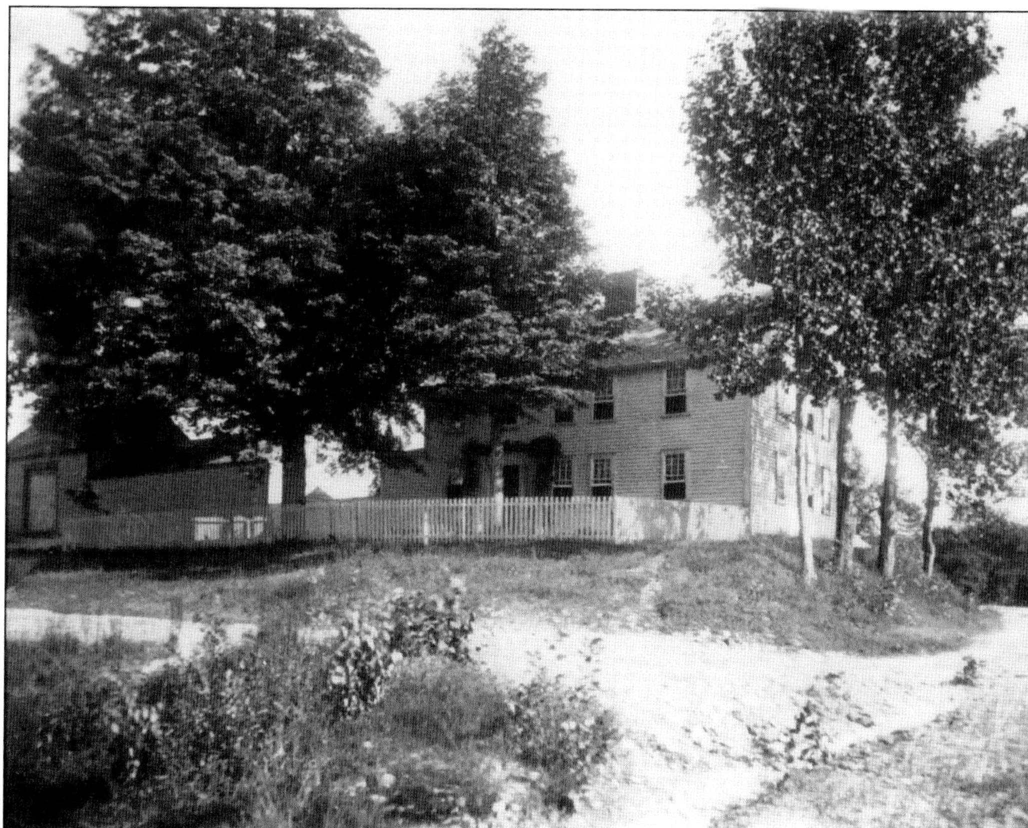

Marvin Plummers's house, photographed in the 1890s, stood at the Putnam Pike and Chopmist Hill Road intersection. Abraham Tourtellot II, son of Glocester's first settler, operated the first tavern here from 1743 to 1751. The Tourtellots owned land on both sides of Tourtellot Hill Road south to Sandy Brook Road. There, the pre-district Clay School, built in the late 1700s, is still owned by a Tourtellot descendant.

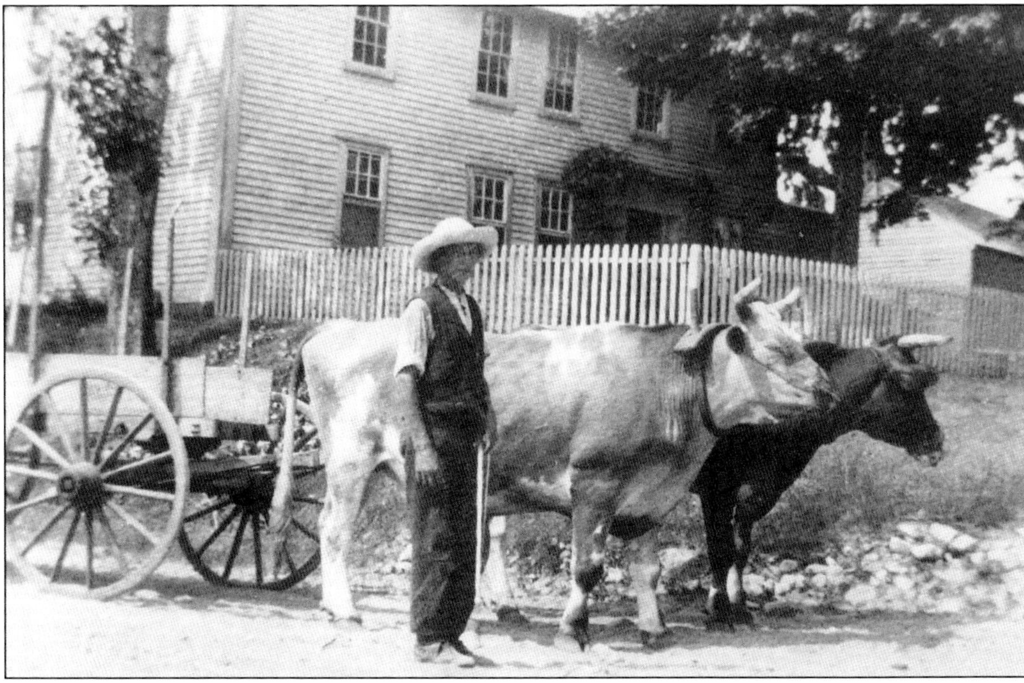

"Tot" Mars and his ox team were frequently seen in Chepachet. He halted his mighty oxen for the cameraman about 1910 beside the old Tourtellot house. Wherever there was a heavy load, an ox team was used. Most of our fine country stone walls were built with the aid of oxen.

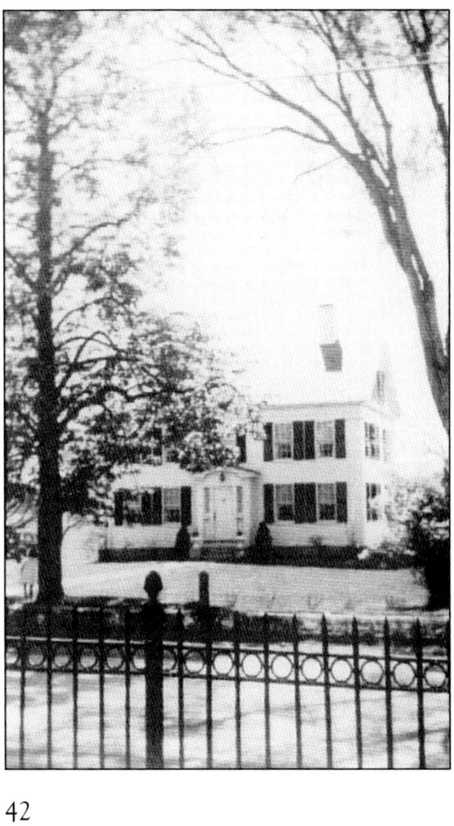

Lumberman Simeon Sweet's house was transformed into a bed and breakfast called Milmor Manor, operated by antique dealer Helen Miller. Its finely appointed rooms and delicious meals were enjoyed by traveling dignitaries, including the governor of Rhode Island. This 1937 photo was taken across Putnam Pike looking through H.C. White's Memorial fence from the foot of Acote's Hill.

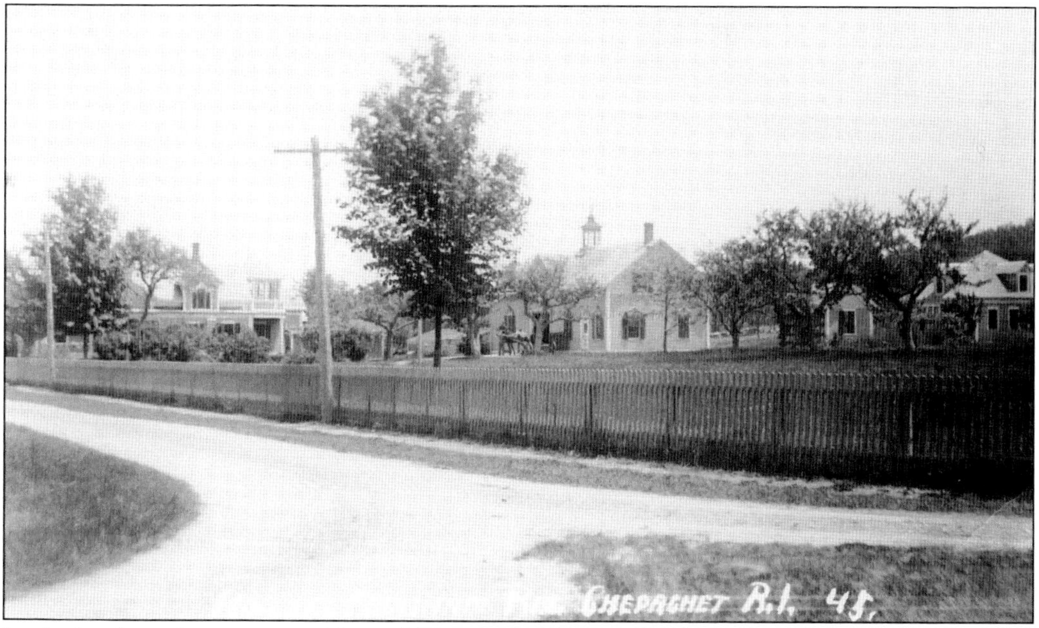

Look closely and you can see Howard Farnum hitching up his horse in front of the barn in this 1912 photo. The Farnum residence was on the corner of Main Street (Putnam Pike) and School Street (Dorr Drive) in Chepachet. His wife, Maude Read Farnum, became Rhode Island's first lady banker.

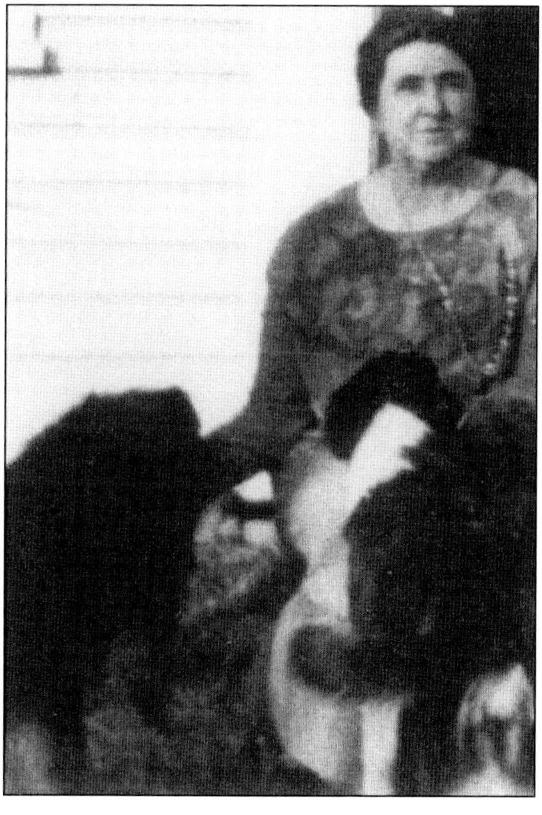

Maude Farnum is pictured here with friends sitting on Keach's steps at a Needlebook Club Meeting about 1920. Her local philanthropy was without equal. Among her many accomplishments, she opened the first free public library and operated it; she gave the land for the present Glocester Manton Free Public Library and set its cornerstone in 1930; and she donated the land that the Chepachet Cemetery Association now occupies at Acote's Hill.

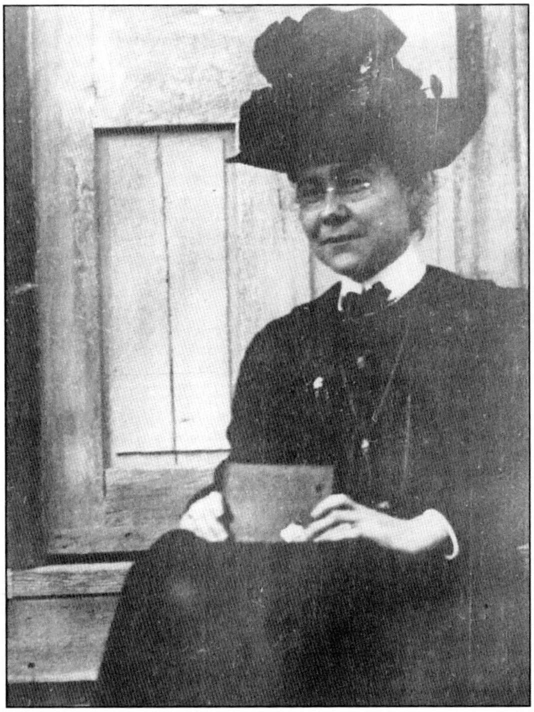

Martha Fitch was a familiar figure with notebook in hand at meetings throughout northwestern Rhode Island. This photo was taken about 1915 at a Needlebook Club meeting. She reported all the news from fires to butterfly sightings. Mattie was a news correspondent for the *Pascoag Herald*, *Providence Journal*, the *Windham County Observer*, and other Boston and Chicago newspapers. She was also a writer of children's stories, and served as a librarian at the Glocester Library.

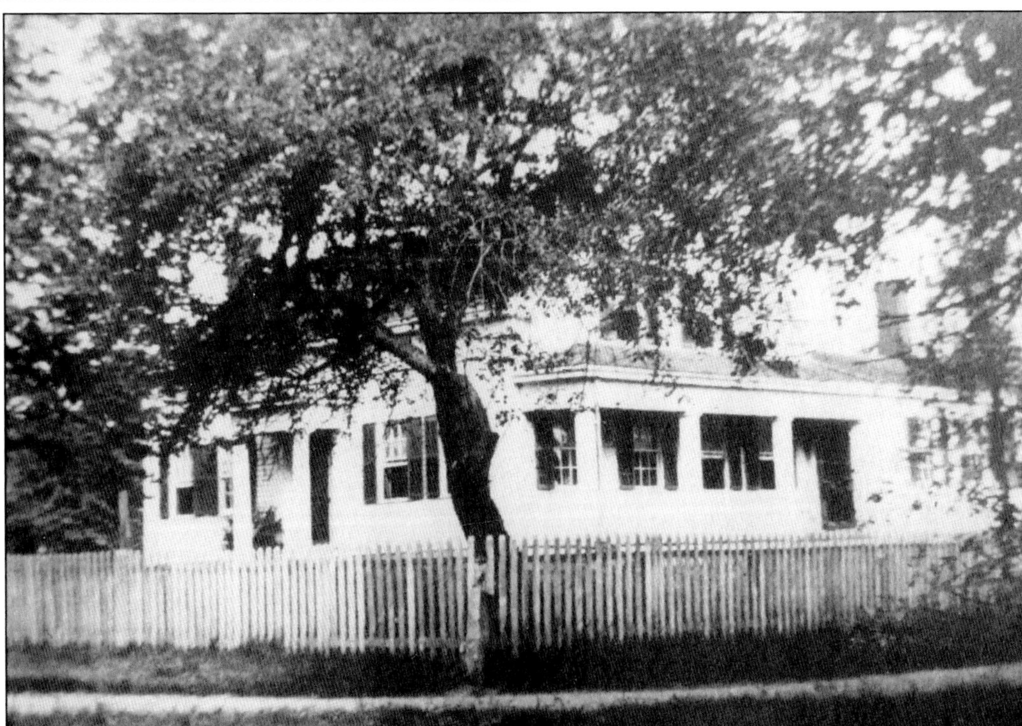

Originally an Eddy house, during this era it was home to Martha Fitch and her brother, Leon, on School Street (Dorr Drive) in Chepachet. The house looks much the same today, although the tree has been replaced by a spruce tree and the picket fence is gone.

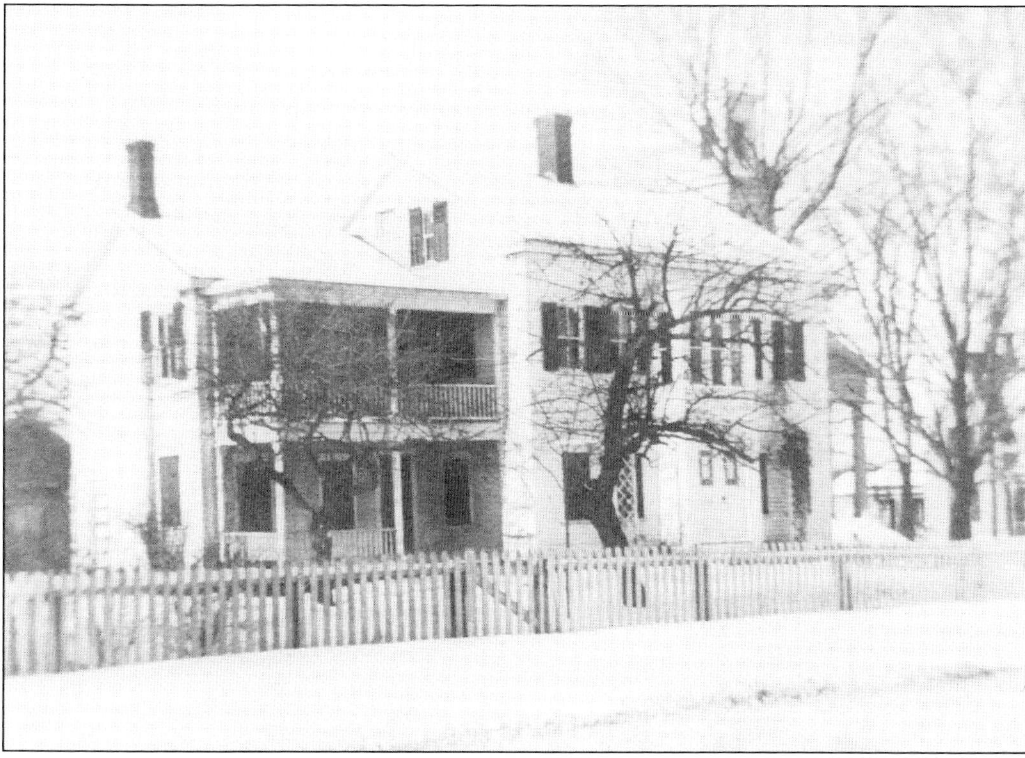

Manning Angell's house is next to Chepachet Union Church. Mr. Angell was a tailor who had a tiny shop in front of his house to the left just out of view in this early-1900s photo. The house is now the Chepachet Union Church parsonage. The original parsonage can be seen at right.

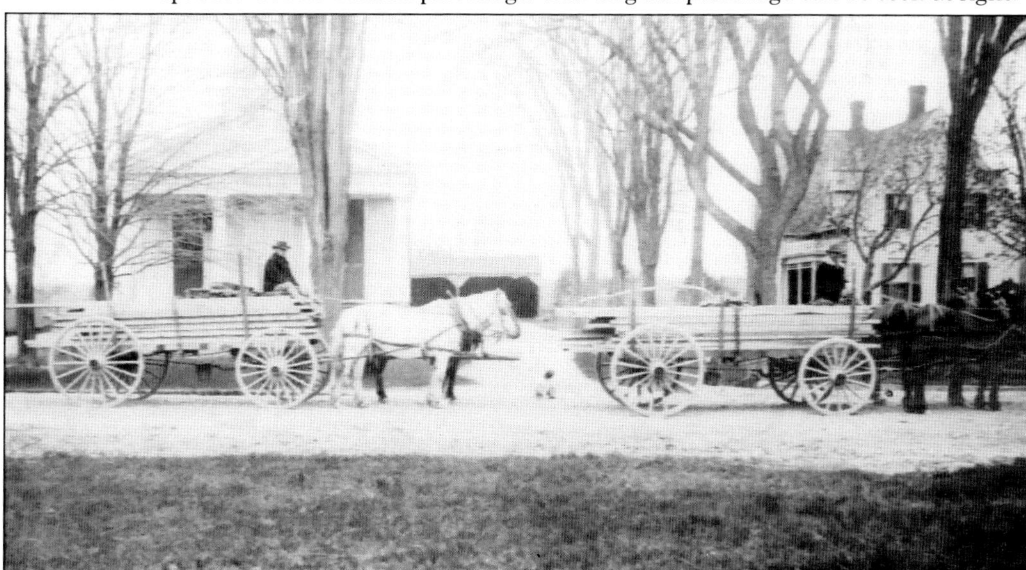

Chepachet Union Church was originally the Evangelical Congregational Church built in 1846 by Cyrus Eddy and Jesse Potter for $3,605. The classic Victorian parsonage was built in 1892. Simeon Sweet's wagons posed with their wagonloads of lumber on Main Street in this turn-of-the-century picture. Notice the wagon shed behind the church.

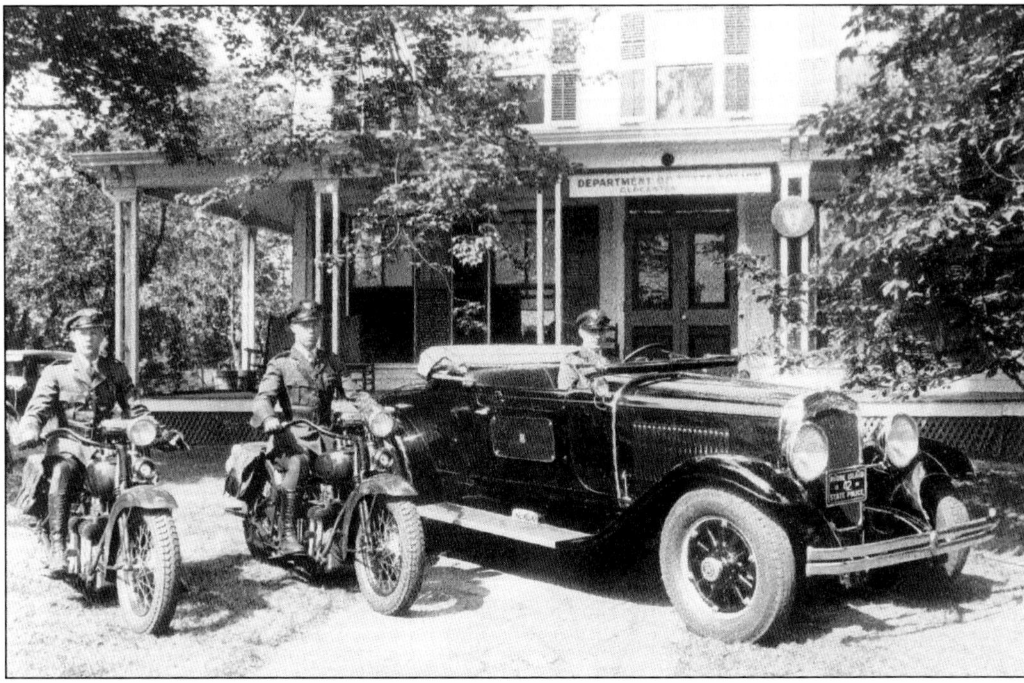

The first headquarters for the Rhode Island State Police in Glocester was in the Ben Steere house on Main Street at Douglas Hook Road across from Chepachet Grammar School. Glocester resident Ralph Bonat is on the left in this 1940s photo. On this site today is Chepachet Union Church's Greenhalgh Hall.

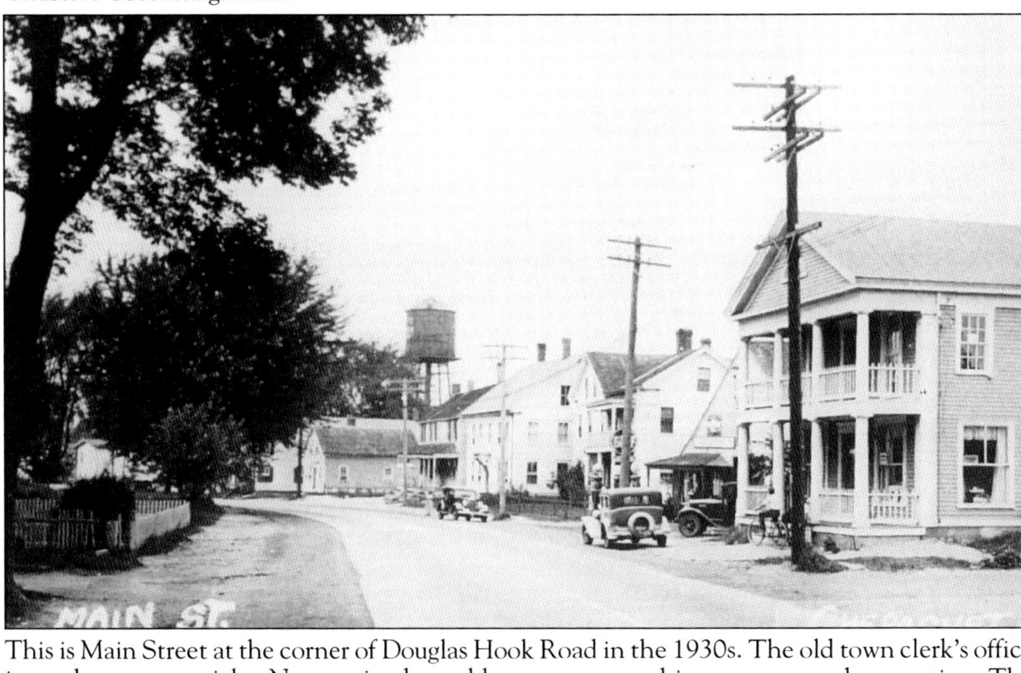

This is Main Street at the corner of Douglas Hook Road in the 1930s. The old town clerk's office is on the extreme right. Next to it, the stable was converted into a store and gas station. The house beyond was then occupied by the Rosenbergs. These buildings are no longer standing. On this site is the parking lot for the new Chepachet Post Office and CVS.

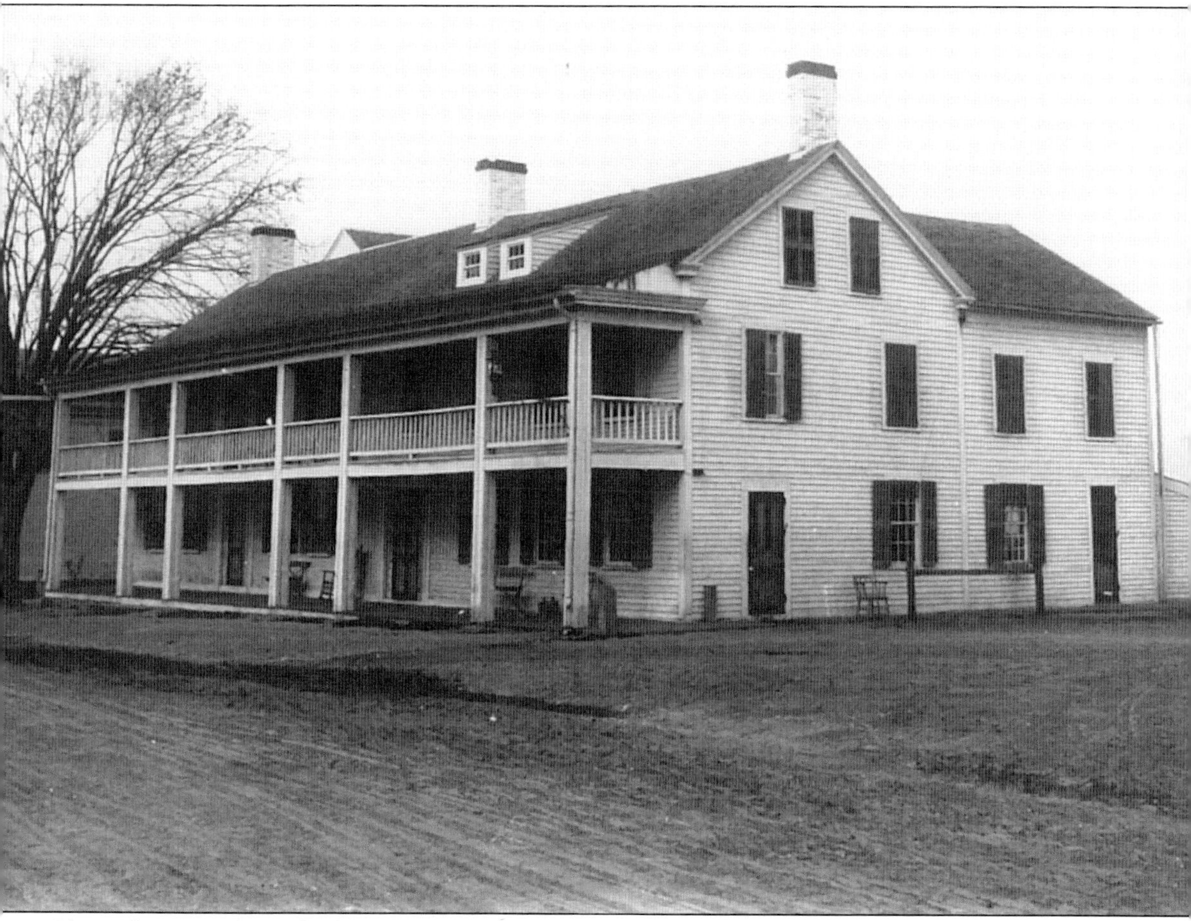

Chepachet Hotel was built in 1813 as a home and law school for Attorney Samuel Atwell. It stood next to the old town clerk's office on Main Street and Douglas Hook Road. In later years, it hosted town meetings, church services, dances, and entertainments, as well as the weary traveler. Renowned for its fine native fish and game dinners, it became a mecca for early auto tours and designated station #1, R.I. Auto Club by 1902. It burned in 1913 along with its enormous stable and the Neff house and barn, which would be the present site of the library. This is an 1880s photo from a glass negative.

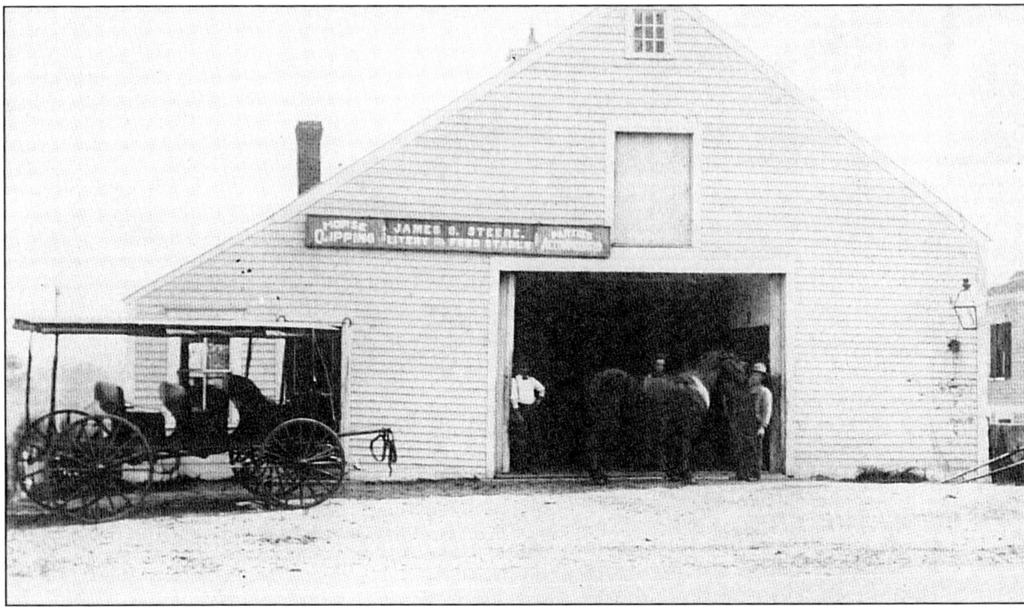

The sign says it all: "Horse clipping—James B. Steere, Livery & Feed Stable—Parties Accommodated." Mr. Steere conducted his business here from 1909 until 1923 next to the town clerk's office. John Flood is leaning against the door. Jim Steere is second from the right. The stage was run to the Oakland train depot by George Davis.

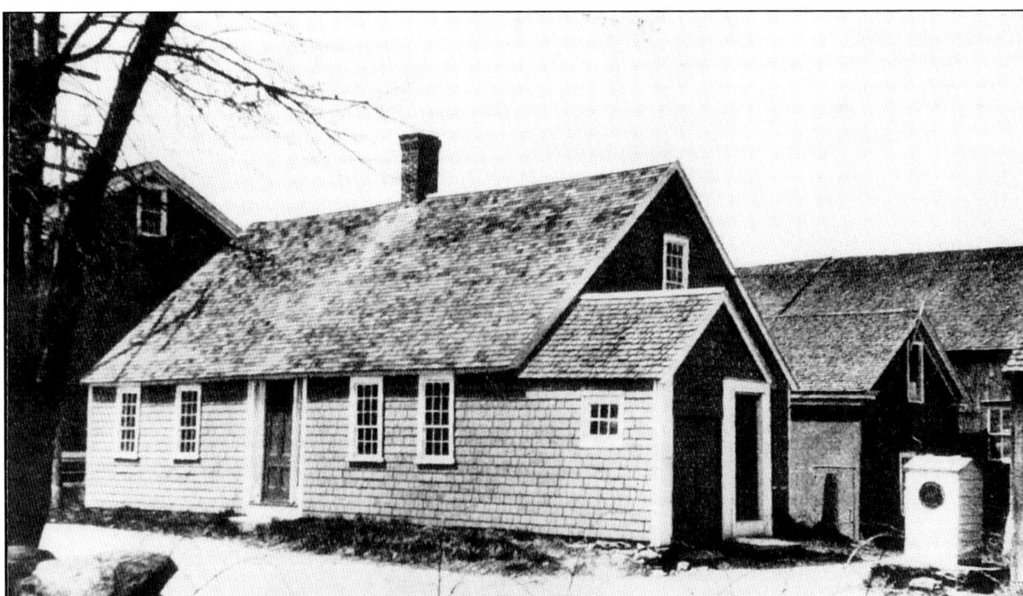

The 18th-century home of Lt. Governor Daniel Owen stood on Douglas Hook Road. With his water-powered triphammer, he manufactured and exported fine farm tools to England from iron ore found on his property. Mr. Owen was chosen president of the Rhode Island Constitutional Convention at South Kingstown and Newport in 1790, which finally accepted the United States Constitution—making Rhode Island the last state to do so.

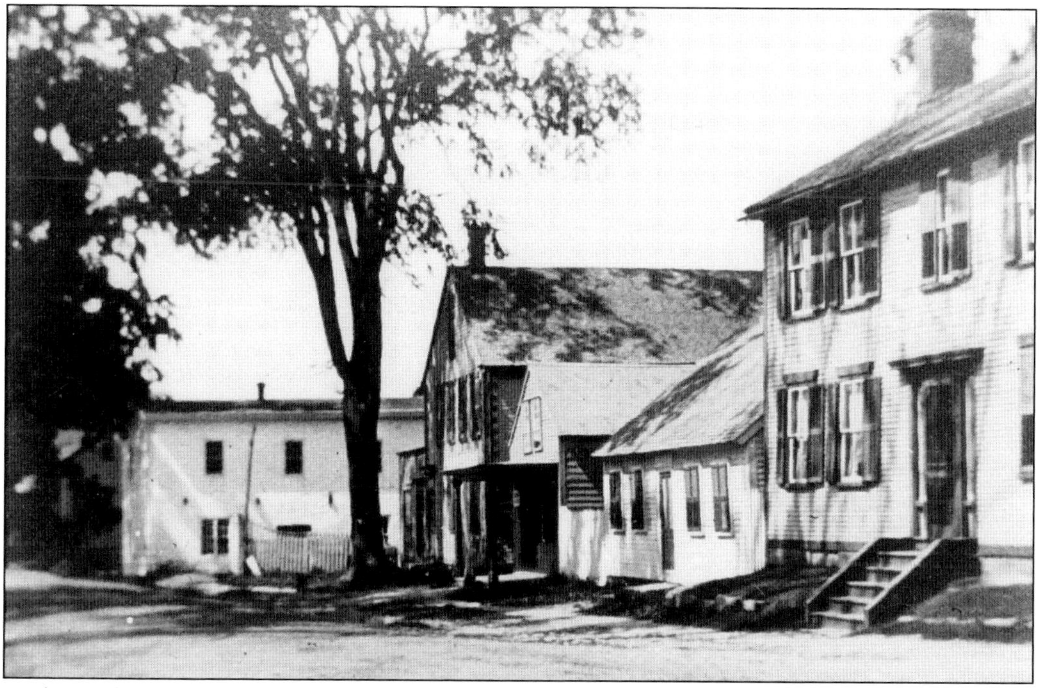

In this early-1900s photo of the east side of Main Street, the buildings are, from right to left, as follows: the old Cyrus Cooke house, George Davis's house and store, the Masonic Hall, and the Stone Mill—used as picker mill.

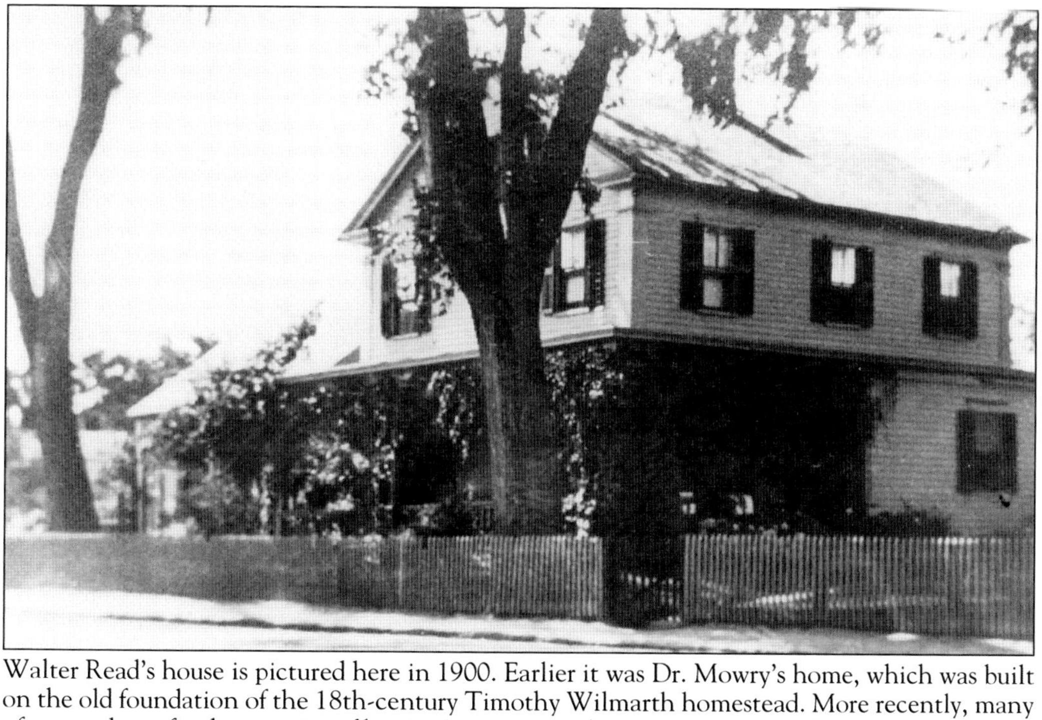

Walter Read's house is pictured here in 1900. Earlier it was Dr. Mowry's home, which was built on the old foundation of the 18th-century Timothy Wilmarth homestead. More recently, many of us may have fond memories of buying ice cream and penny candy at Arthur Trinque's Spa. It has been moved to Chestnut Hill Road to make room for the fire company.

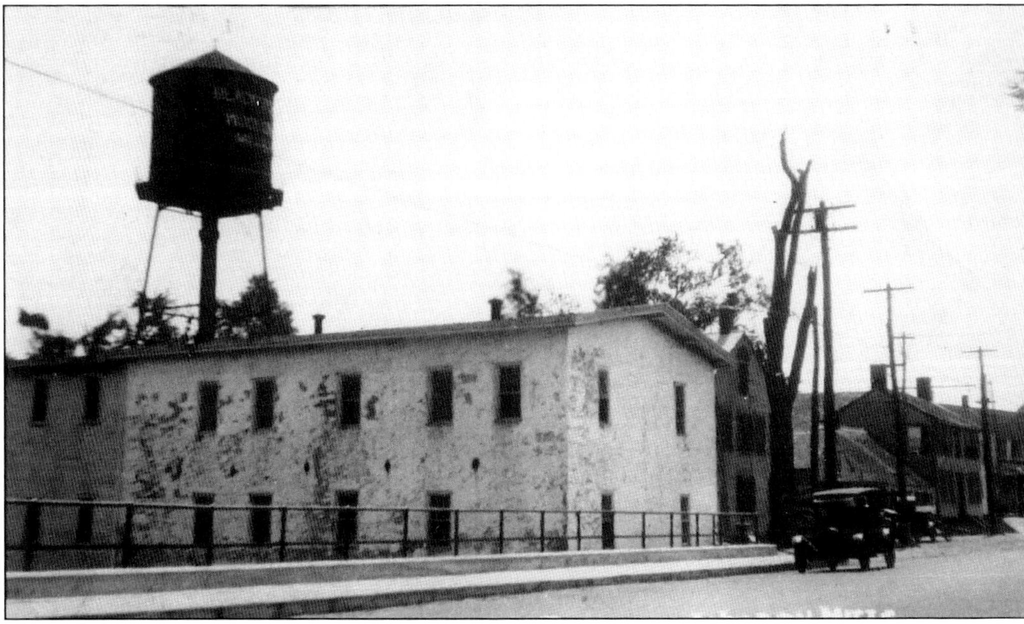

Bedford Woolen Mills operated from 1918 to 1927. An attempt to burn the mills for the insurance in 1923 failed thanks to alert neighbors who heard a car in the night—then an explosion. However, firefighters soon had it under control and the building suffered little serious damage. Notice the new bridge rail and sidewalk.

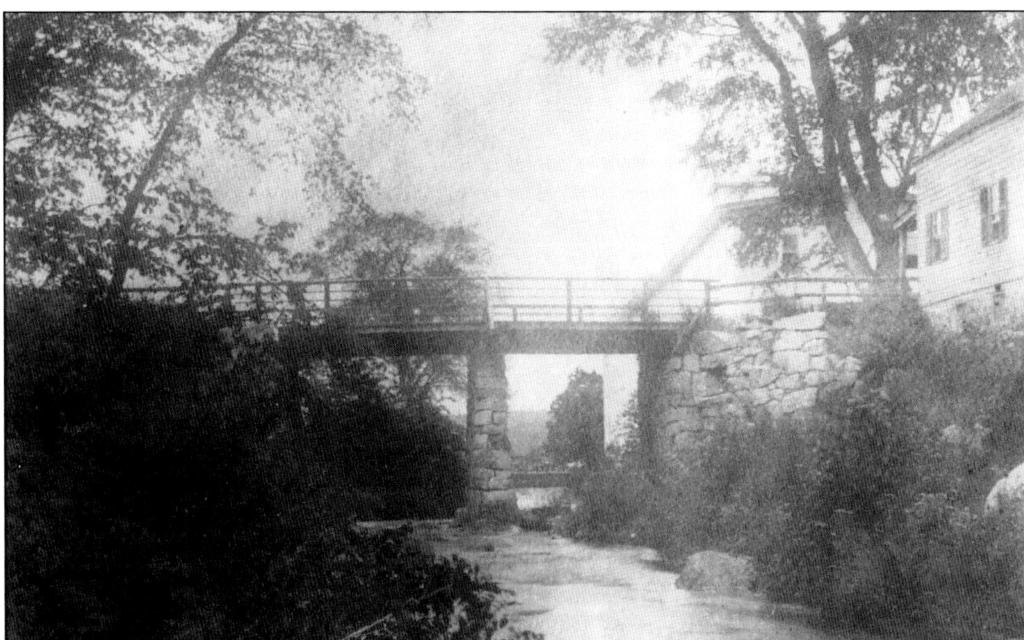

In the 1880s, the photographer shot this picture from the water's edge upstream facing east. This is the old bridge that was built after the freshet in 1867. To the extreme right is the Intermediate Cafe, which was decorated with hand-painted murals. Through the open windows in summer, the diners could hear the waterfall. The Stone Mill is on the other side of the bridge.

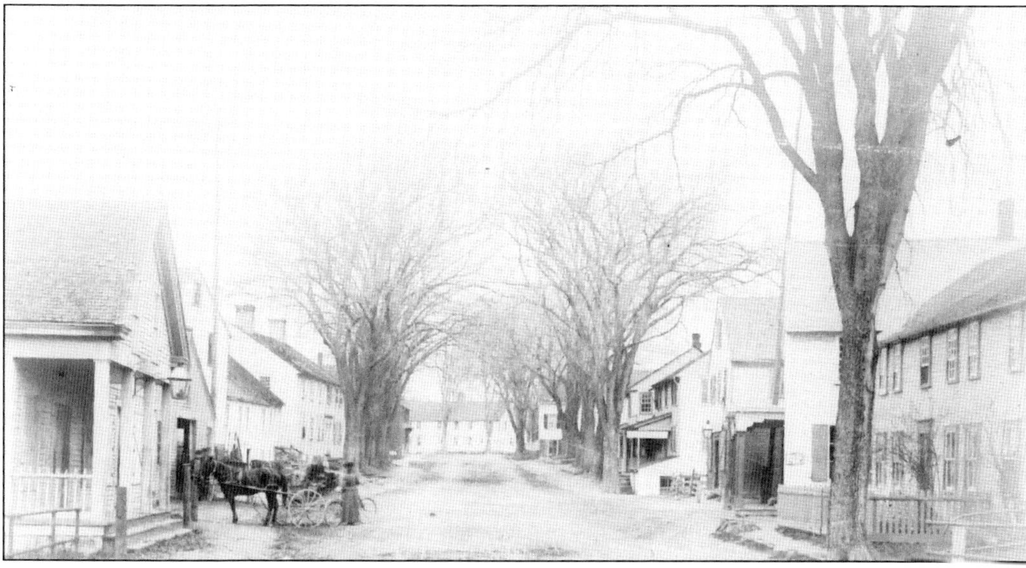

Looking northwest in the 1880s from Chepachet Bridge, this view shows Hawkins' Store on the left. The horse and wagon is standing at Hawkins' Blacksmith Shop. The old two-and-a-half-story Dr. Bowen house with its twin chimneys is beyond. At the head of the street is the old Kimball Hotel, built in 1732. The second building from the right is Walter Read's Store. The house with the porch sign is the Central Hotel. The towering elms have all been lost to Dutch elm disease.

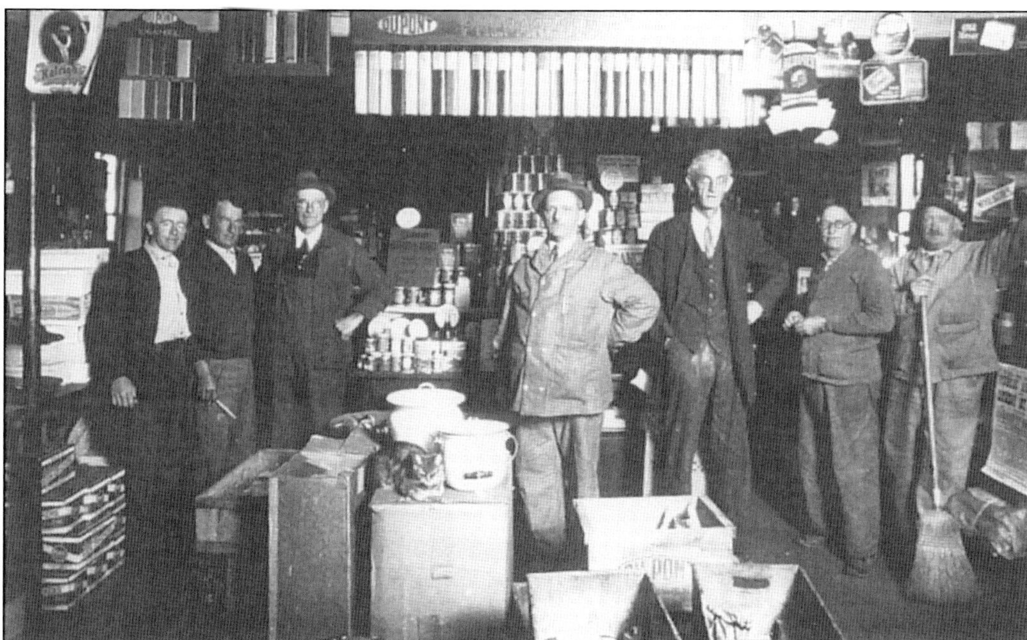

Familiar faces at Brown & Hopkins' Store in 1942 were, from left to right, as follows: Fred Halbig, customer; Fred Marseilles, clerk; William Hopkins, co-owner; James Brown, co-owner; Fred Greenhalgh, clerk; Steve Davis, clerk; and Jimmie Stott, clerk. The store was built in 1799 as a hat shop and residence. It was known by several names throughout its long history—Ira Evans's, Horace Kimball's, and Walter Read's, to name a few.

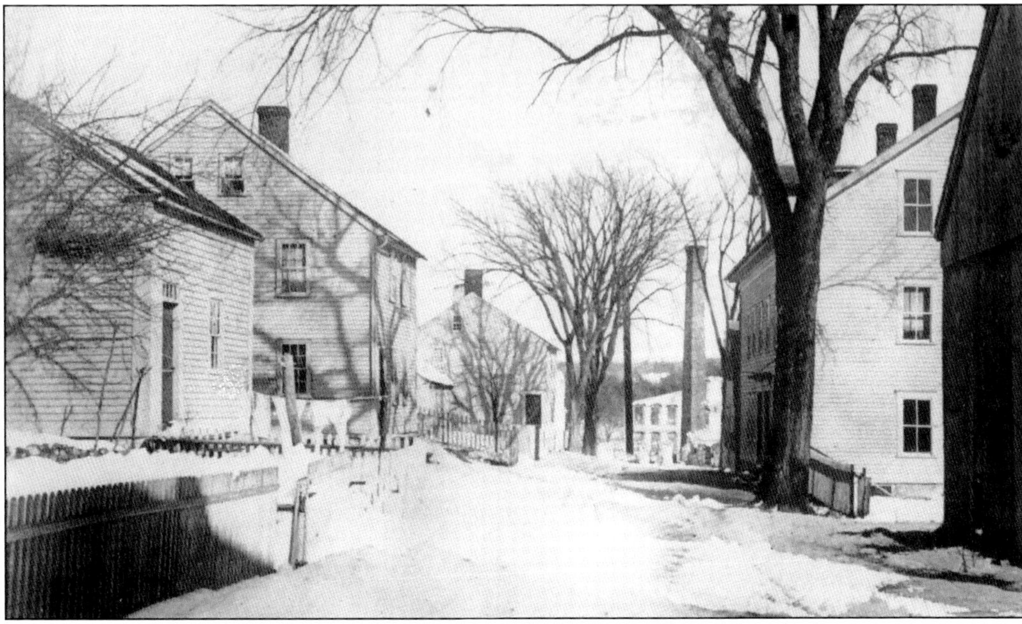

Tanyard Lane off Main Street once led to Owens Tannery, where the elephant was taken after being shot on the bridge in 1826. In this 1897 photo, the burned ruins of White's Mill can be seen in the distance. Today the tannery owner's house has been restored and is a private residence.

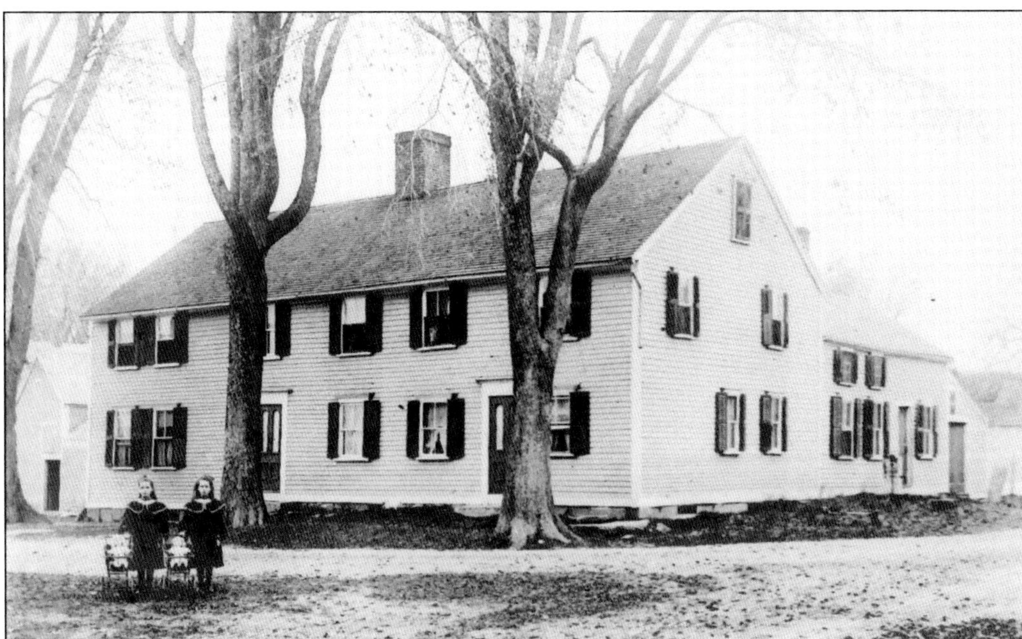

Harnessmaker Tom Cabana's twin daughters, Rosy and Flora, stand in front of the old Kimball Hotel about 1902 with their twin doll strollers. Several stores have occupied the first floor of this building, Nicholson & Thackray and the First National Store among them. A Texaco gas station stands on this site today at the intersection of Putnam Pike (Rt. 44) and Victory Highway (Rt. 102).

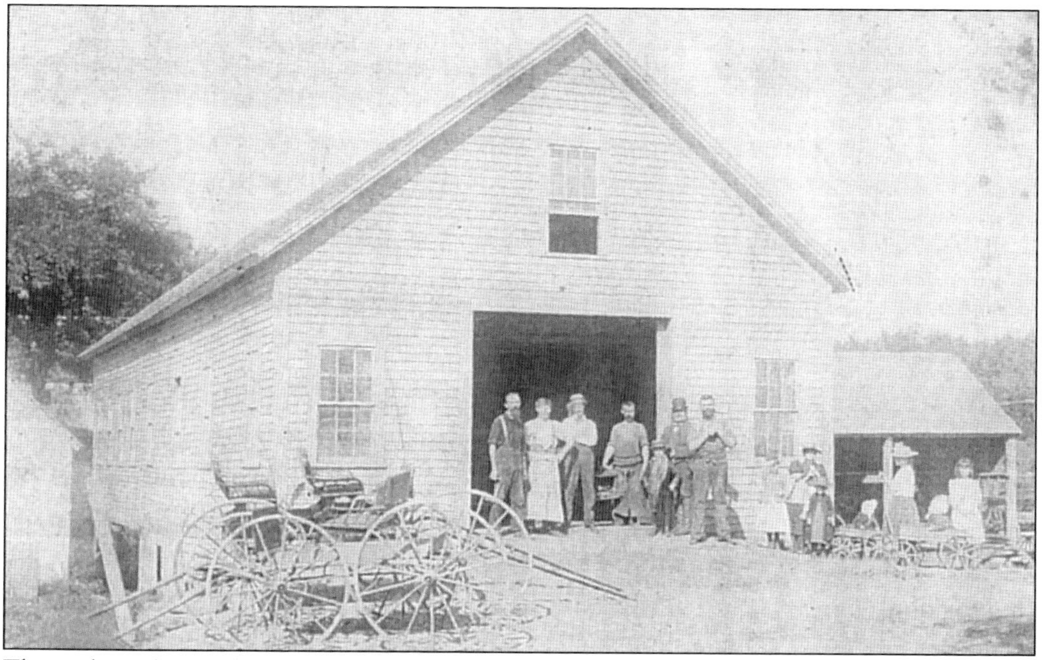

This is the only view known of Felix Slavin's Wheelwright Shop on the Oakland Road between Trinque's house and the American Order of United Workers (AOUW) Hall, taken in the 1890s. Today, an auto parts store is on that site. The back end of the Baptist church would be behind the tree on the left.

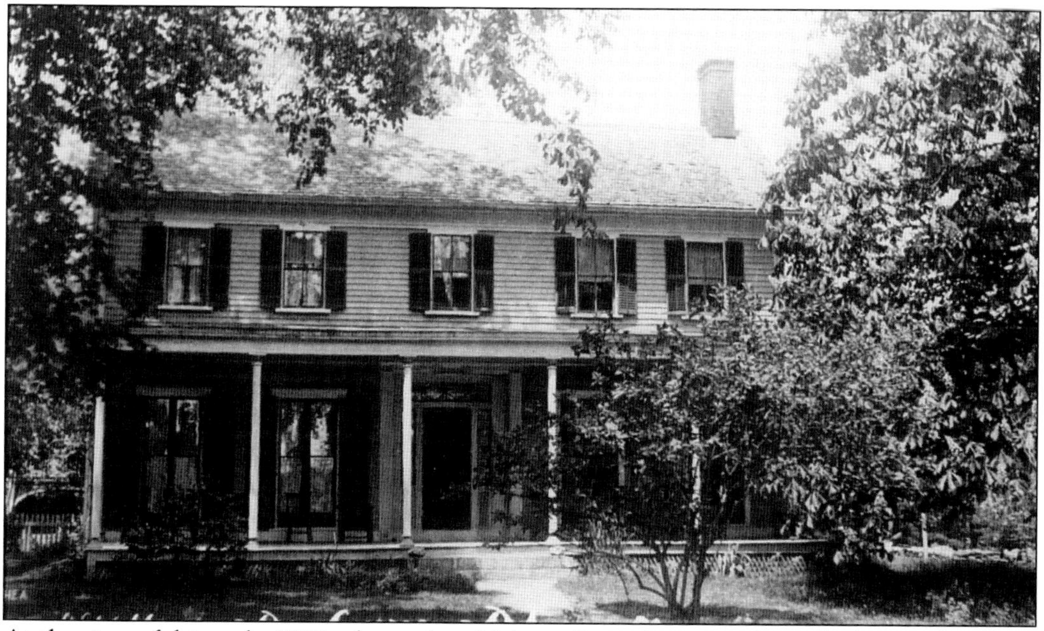

At the time of this early-1900s photo, the old Anan Evans homestead was the home of William Hopkins, who soon would become partners with his neighbor, James Brown, in the Brown & Hopkins' Store. Will's daughter Ella later ran a boardinghouse here called the Elms. This house is at the intersection of Pascoag Road (Money Hill Road, Rt. 100) and Oakland Road (Victory Highway, Rt. 102).

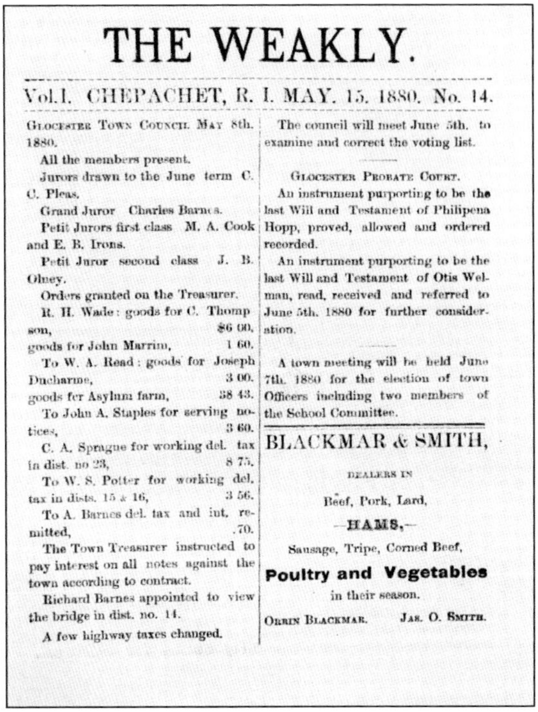

THE WEAKLY.

Vol. I. CHEPACHET, R. I. MAY. 15. 1880. No. 14.

GLOCESTER TOWN COUNCIL MAY 8th. 1880.

All the members present.

Jurors drawn to the June term C. C. Pleas.

Grand Juror Charles Barnes.

Petit Jurors first class M. A. Cook and E. B. Irons.

Petit Juror second class J. B. Olney.

Orders granted on the Treasurer.

R. H. Wade: goods for C. Thompson, $6 00.
goods for John Marrim, 1 60.

To W. A. Read: goods for Joseph Ducharme, 3 00.
goods for Asylum farm, 38 43.

To John A. Staples for serving notices, 3 60.

C. A. Sprague for working del. tax in dist. no 23, 8 75.

To W. S. Potter for working del. tax in dists. 15 & 16, 3 56.

To A. Barnes del. tax and int. remitted, .70.

The Town Treasurer instructed to pay interest on all notes against the town according to contract.

Richard Barnes appointed to view the bridge in dist. no. 14.

A few highway taxes changed.

The council will meet June 5th. to examine and correct the voting list.

GLOCESTER PROBATE COURT.

An instrument purporting to be the last Will and Testament of Philipena Hopp, proved, allowed and ordered recorded.

An instrument purporting to be the last Will and Testament of Otis Welman, read, received and referred to June 5th. 1880 for further consideration.

A town meeting will be held June 7th. 1880 for the election of town Officers including two members of the School Committee.

BLACKMAR & SMITH,
DEALERS IN
Beef, Pork, Lard,
—HAMS,—
Sausage, Tripe, Corned Beef,
Poultry and Vegetables
in their season.
ORRIN BLACKMAR. JAS. O. SMITH.

The Weakly was written and published by Frank Potter, son of Dr. Albert Potter, in a small barn north of their home. This little single-fold newspaper measuring 5.25-by-7.25 inches was available every week for about three years.

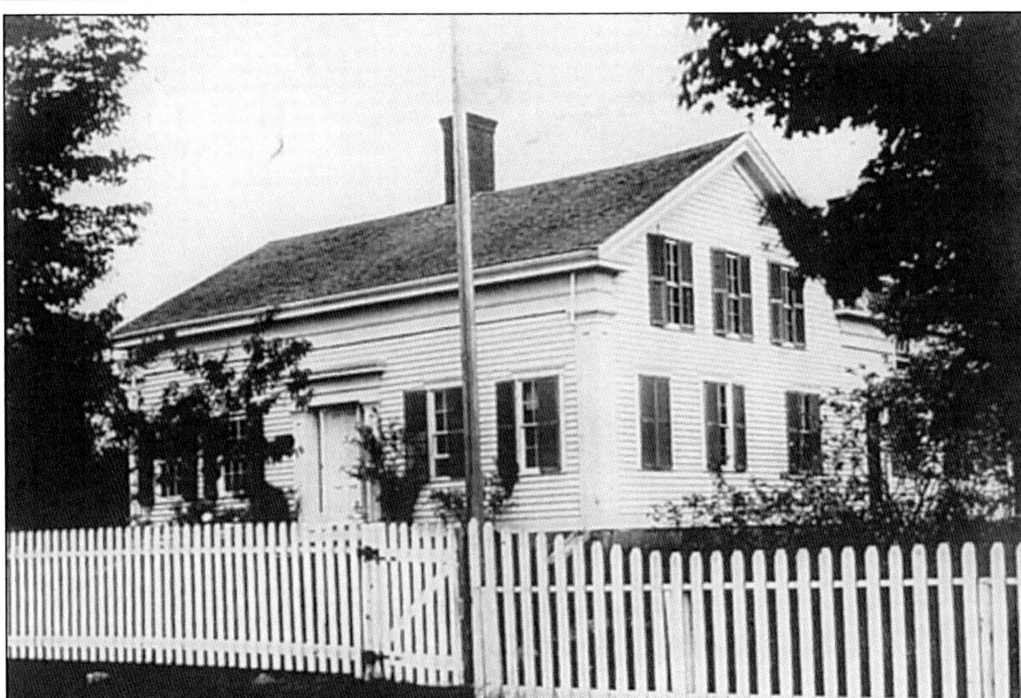

Dr. Albert Potter, a Civil War surgeon, continued his practice here at his Chepachet home until his death in 1902. His grandson Edgar moved here after he completed his medical studies and continued the practice of medicine until his death in 1965. The house was moved north of its original site to make way for Old Stone Bank on Victory Highway (Rt. 102).

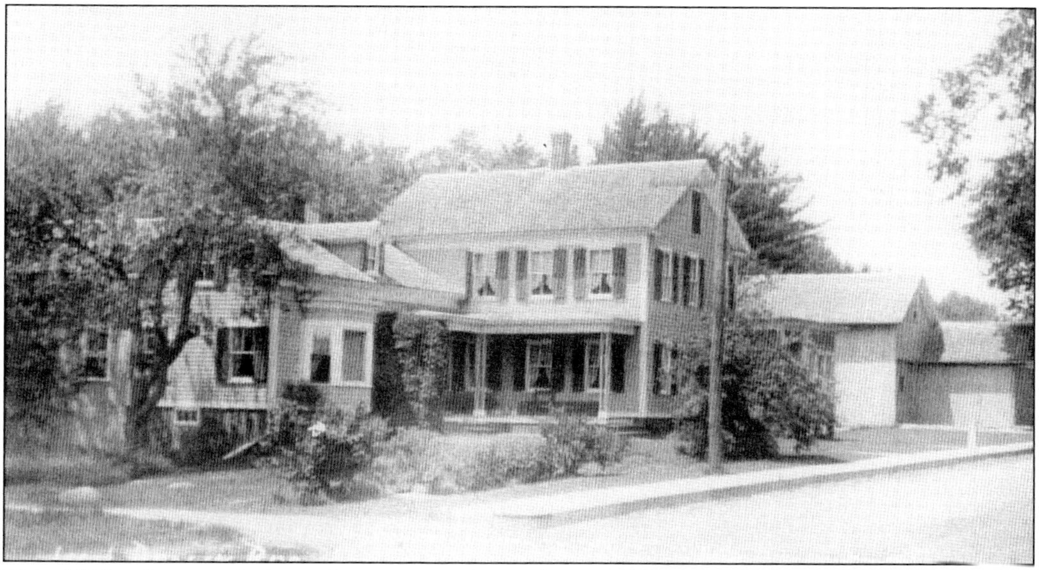

This 1920s photocard shows James Brown's residence on the west side of the intersection of Pascoag Road (Rt. 100) and Oakland Road (Rt. 102). Previous to Brown's ownership, Dr. George Harris, who was Dr. Albert Potter's nephew, made it his home and medical office. Notice the pole is an electric service pole from John Steere's electric plant.

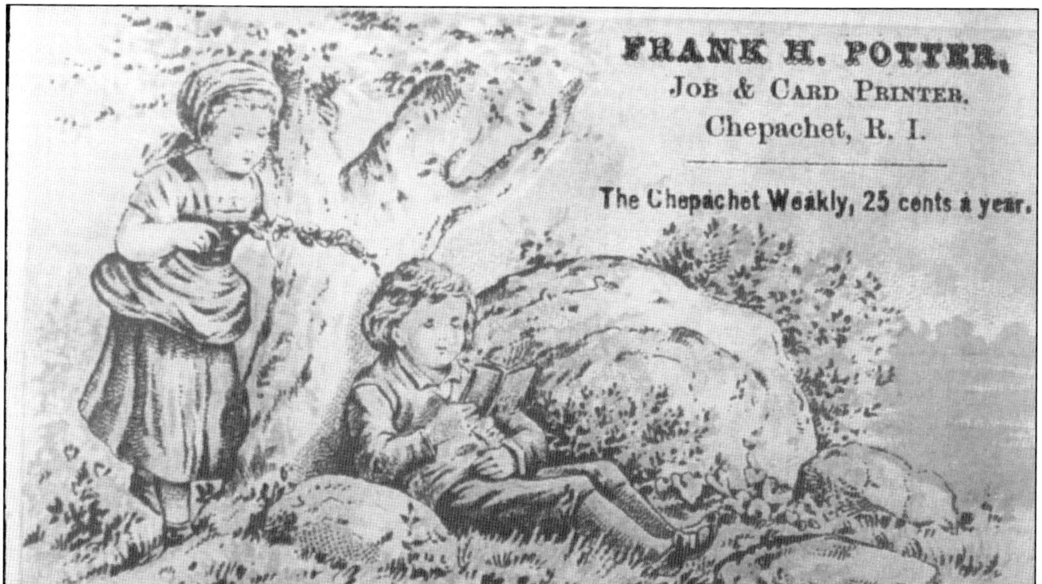

Frank Potter, Job & Card Printer, passed out his business cards wherever he went. This is one of several color designs that he created. The *Chepachet Weekly* was only 25¢ a year.

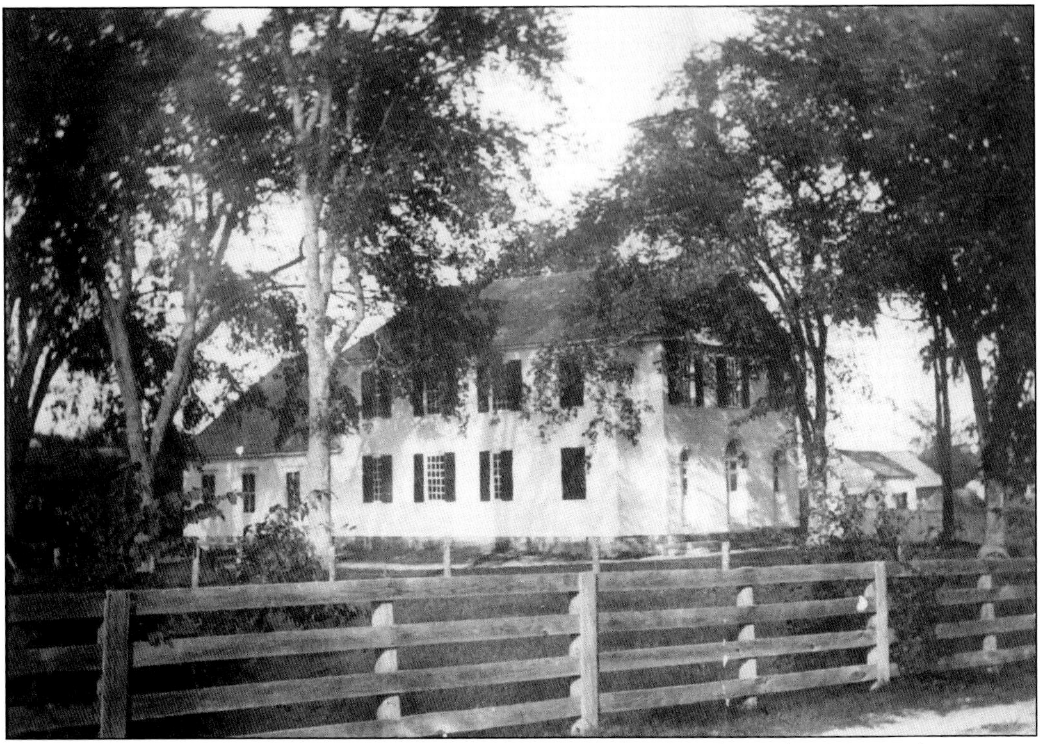

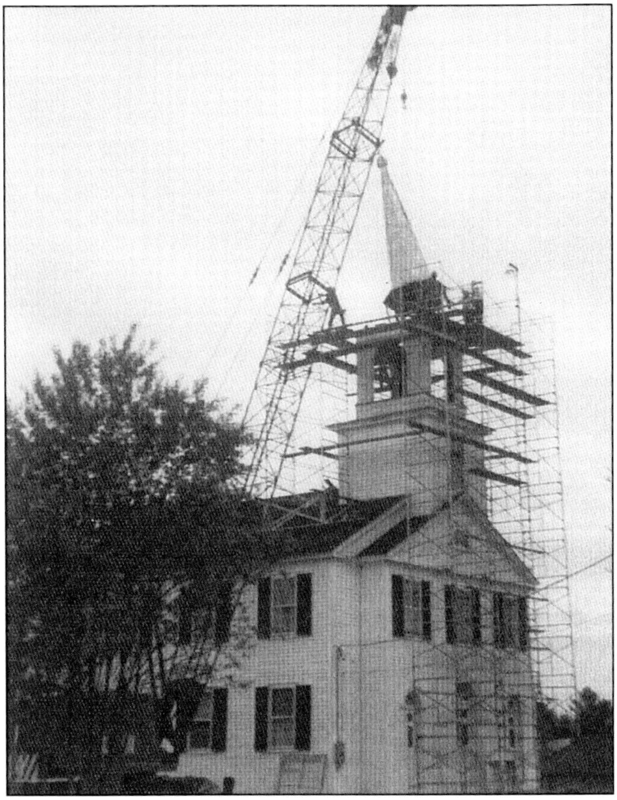

The Chepachet Meetinghouse on Putnam Pike was built in 1821. This is an 1880s view. The white steeple is difficult to see against the brilliant sky. This is the oldest church in Glocester.

During the summer of 1978, the Chepachet Freewill Baptist Church steeple was restored. The workers are in the process of taking the steeple down to work on it in the side yard.

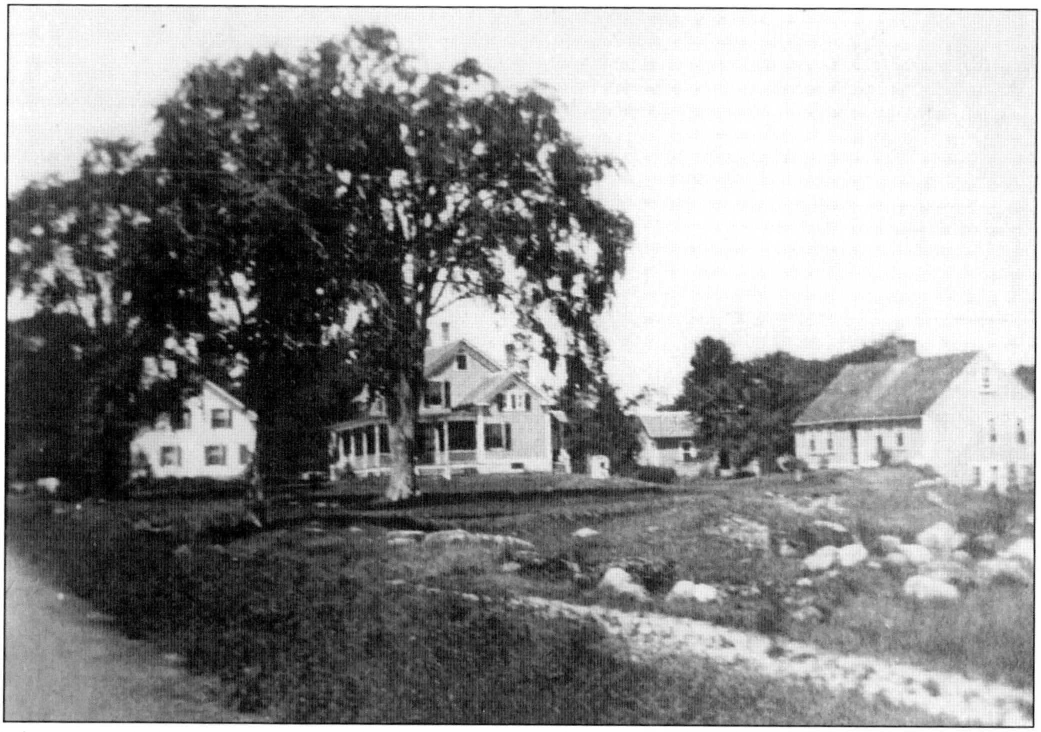

This turn-of-the-century view is looking west on the north side of Putnam Pike. The old Asa Kimball house (built about 1757), which, at that time, was the Keach residence, is on the right. In the center is Ernest and Emma Hopkins' "new" house. Beyond is the Baptist parsonage. All these remain to this day.

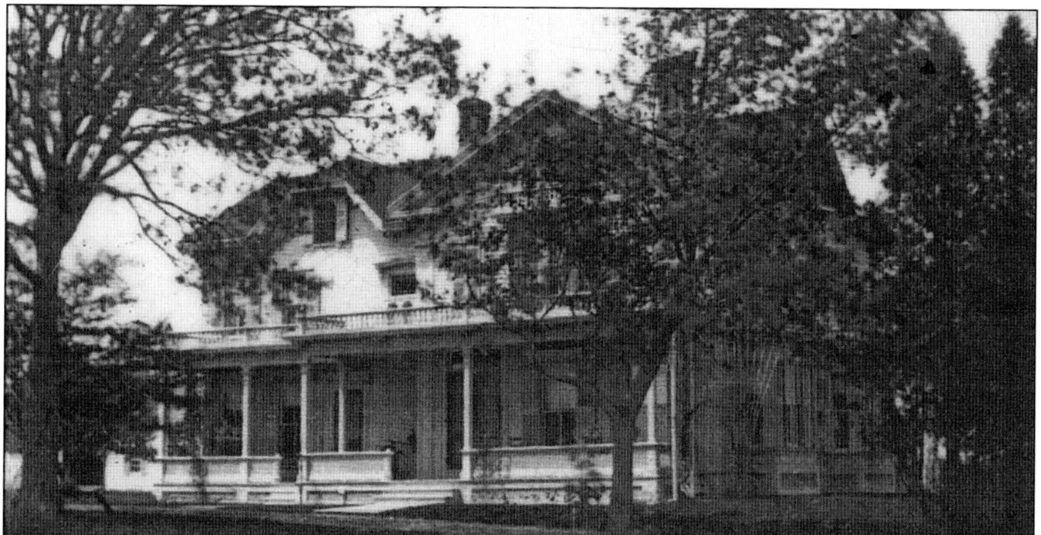

This was the grand estate of Congressman George Huntington Browne, and, in this 1890s photo, Congressman Warren O. Arnold. It is said that the estate had a horse-drawn coach and a coachman dressed in top hat and tails. Peacocks strutted around the estate throughout the year. This is now the St. Eugene's Catholic Church rectory.

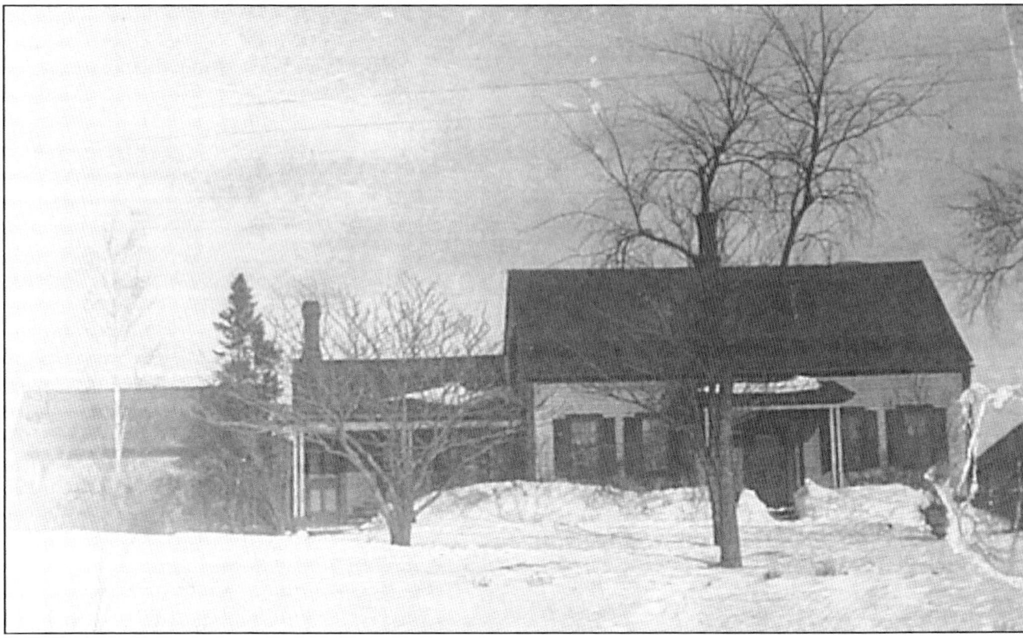

This worn 1930s photo is the only old picture of J. Curtis Hopkins's house at Prospect Hill on Chestnut Hill Road. Mr. Hopkins was an orchardist and greenhouse horticulturist, as well as an accomplished cornet player and conductor of the Oakland Band.

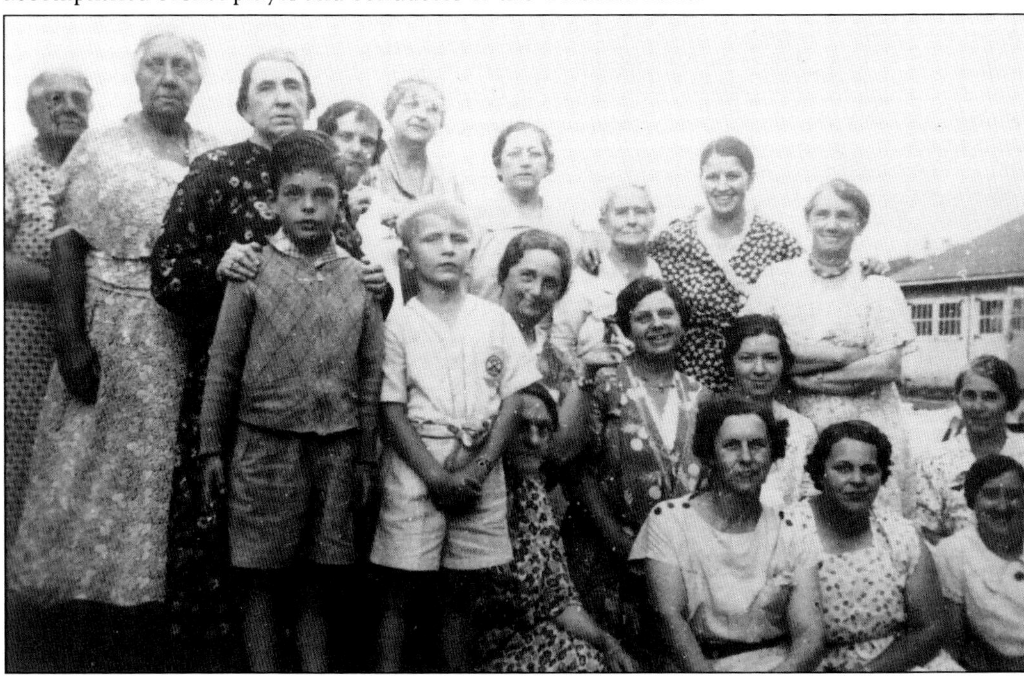

The Needlebook Club met at Hopkins's Prospect Hill Farm in 1940. Attending were, from left to right, the following: (front row) Jennie Chase, Edith Greenhalgh, Ellen Townend, and Abby Paine; (middle row) Richmond Kent, Andrew Townend, Cora Kent, Esther Blackinton, ?, and June Blackinton; (back row) ?, Mrs. Snow, Maude Farnum, Amy Buxton, ?, ?, Cora Eddy, Celia Paine, and Ella Hopkins.

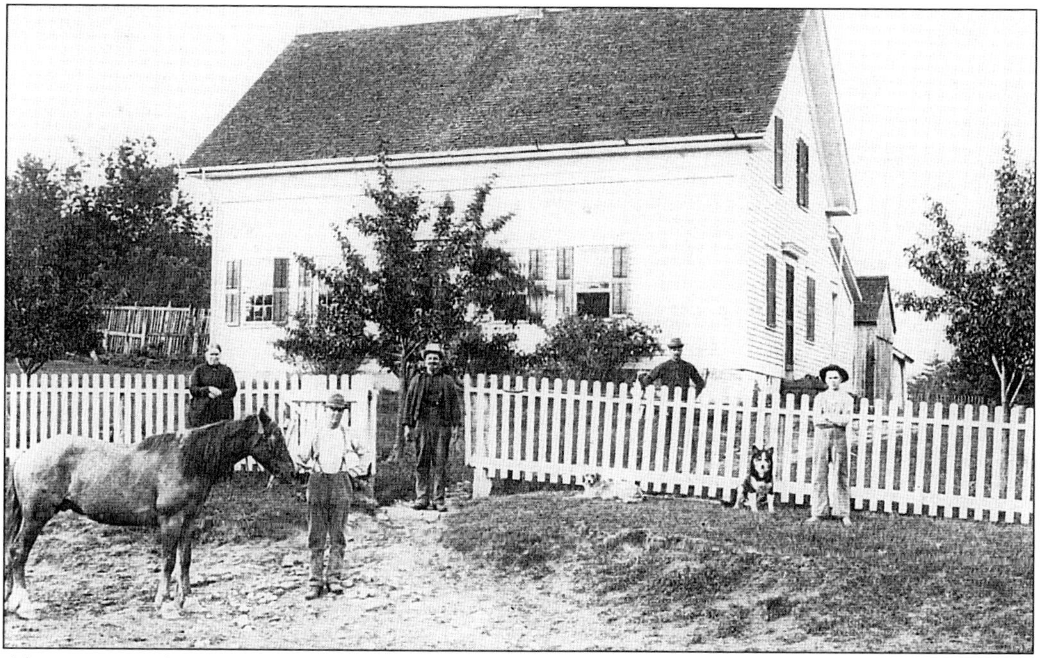

About 1888, the Steere family posed for the cameraman at George W. Steere's farm near Chepachet River, east of Chepachet. They are, from left to right, as follows: Martha S. Steere, Benjamin Steere Jr. (holding the horse), George W. Steere Sr., George W. Steere Jr., and John P. Steere Sr. (with the dogs).

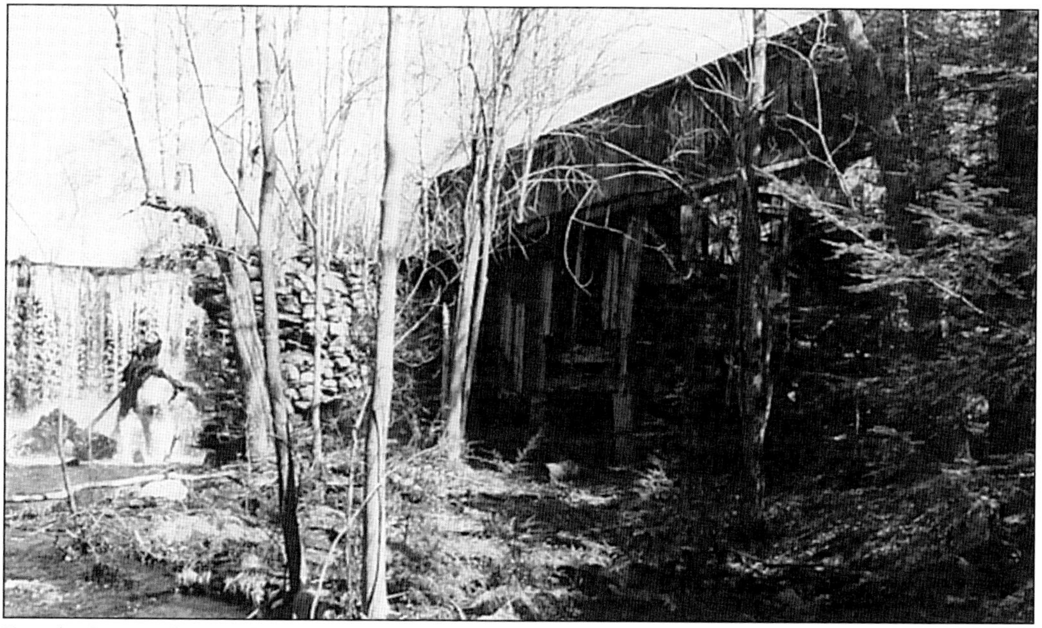

Enoch Steere dammed up Sucker Brook and built the first sawmill here in 1774. His son Anthony raised the height of the dam to get more power. One of the last sawmills in Rhode Island to run on waterpower, this mill has sawn over 25 million board feet since 1910. John Steere generated electricity from this site beginning in 1922, and he eventually served over 110 households in Glocester and Burrillville before Narragansett Electric bought him out in 1931.

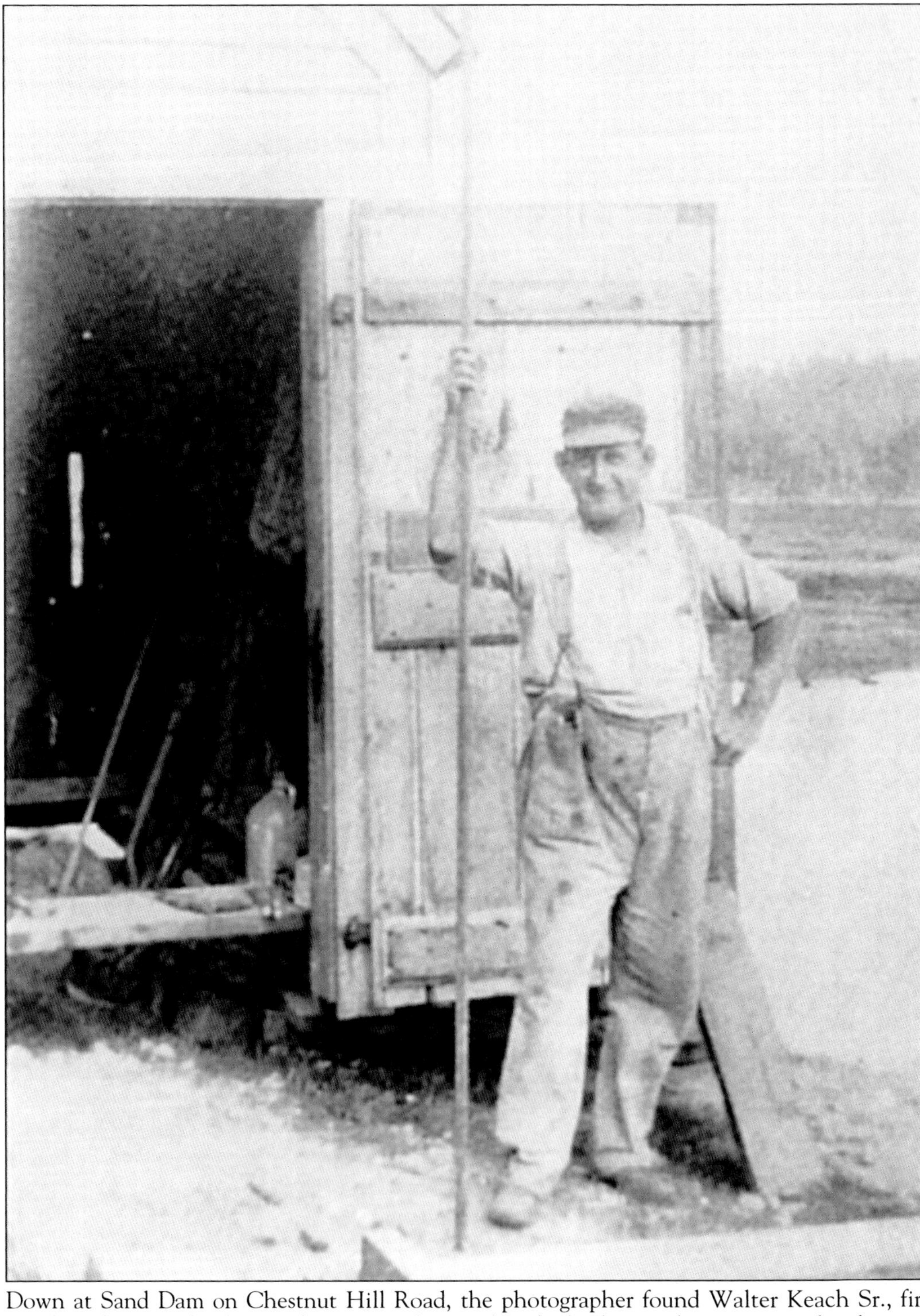

Down at Sand Dam on Chestnut Hill Road, the photographer found Walter Keach Sr., fire chief, working on the dam in the 1920s. The pond in the background appears very low because the water had been let out to inspect the dam. The top of a long ladder extending to the base of the dam is just out of sight to the right.

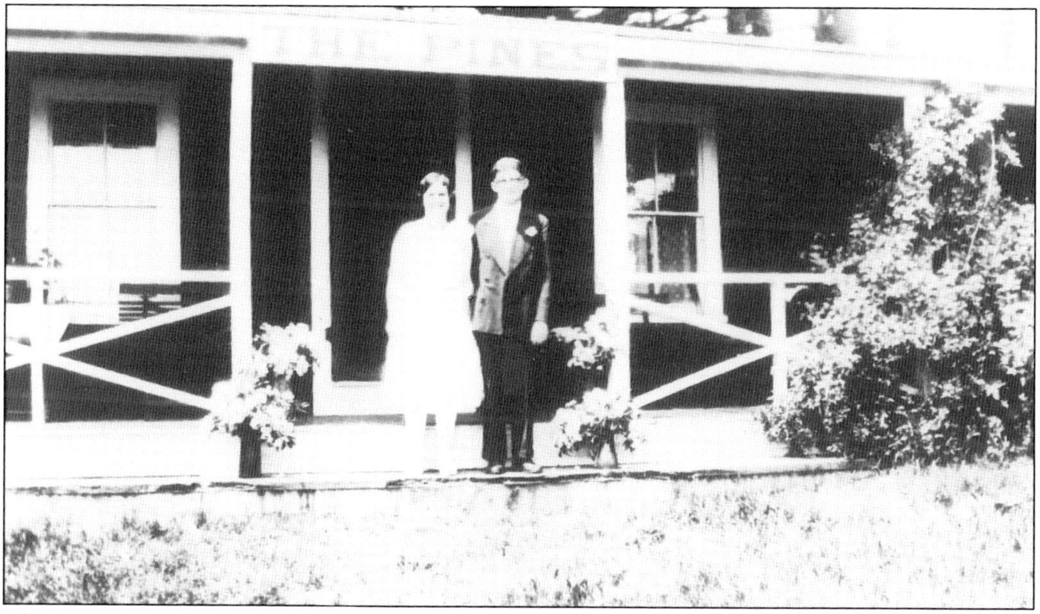

This photo was taken on Reverend Elden and Beatrice Bucklin's wedding day in the late 1920s. They made their home at "The Pines" for several years before moving to the Chepachet Union Church Parsonage, where he served as pastor. "The Pines" was on the Oakland Road (Victory Highway) on the present site of the C. Place Trucking Company.

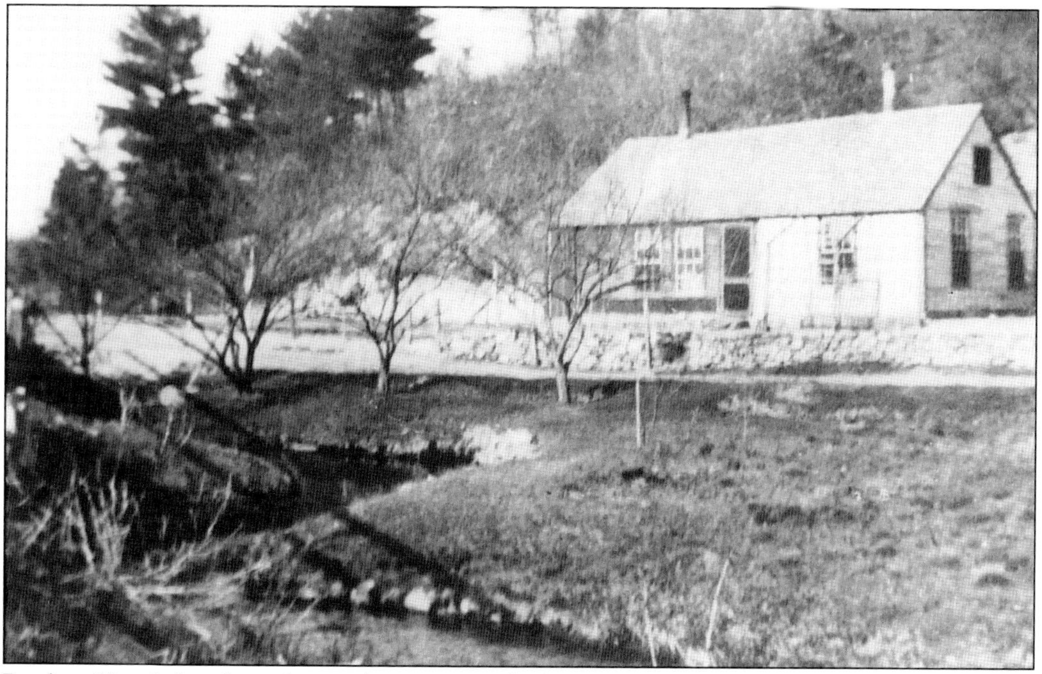

Reuben Keach lived on the road to Harrisville (Steere Farm Road). He frequently was able to catch fish for dinner from Sucker Brook, which zigzagged through his front yard. He called the narrow lane that ran in front of his house "Lover's Lane," but now it has been renamed Cross Road.

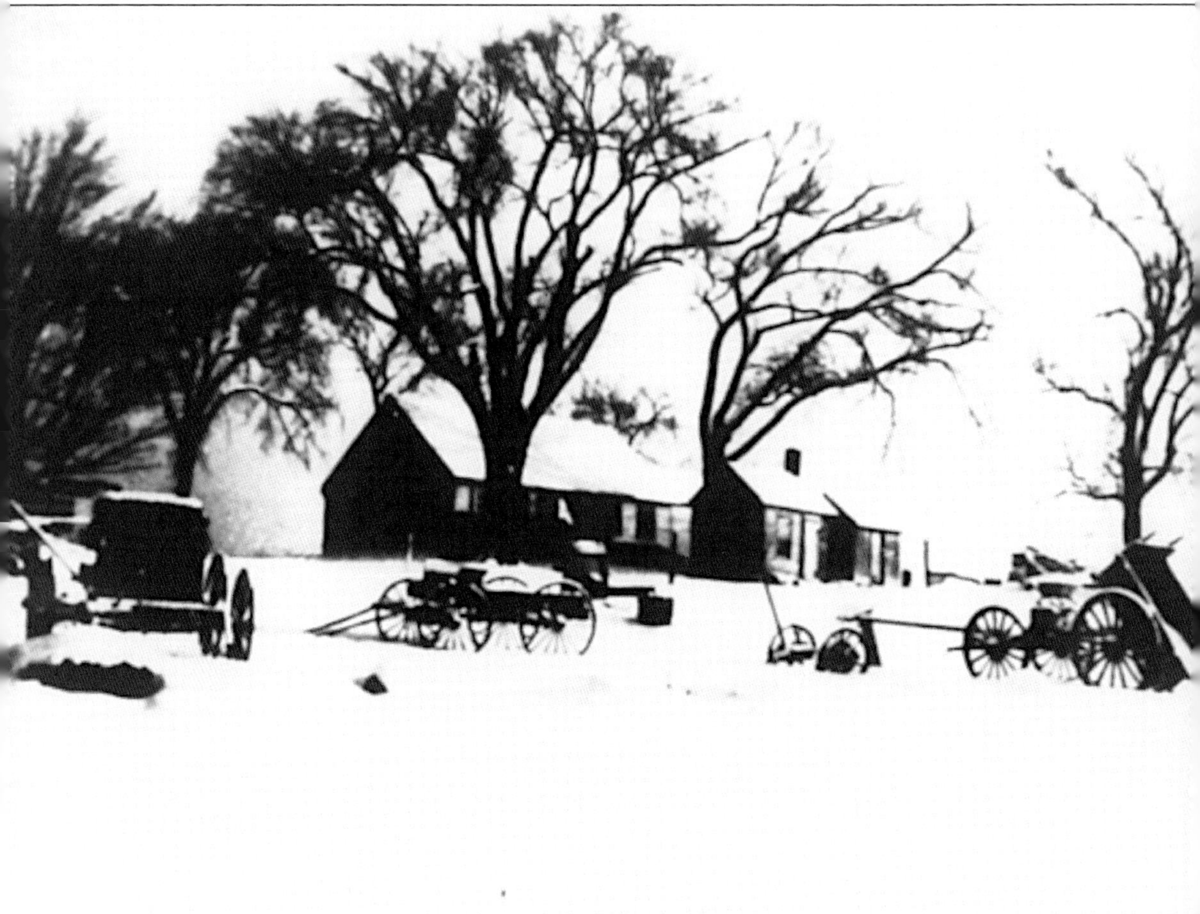

This snowy scene in the early 1900s is the old Lee farm, where one could look east over the fields right down into the village of Chepachet. Both this farm and the house at the corner of Adelaid Road and Putnam Pike were once owned by the Smiths; it is more recently known as the Marceau residence.

Five

Harmony and East Glocester

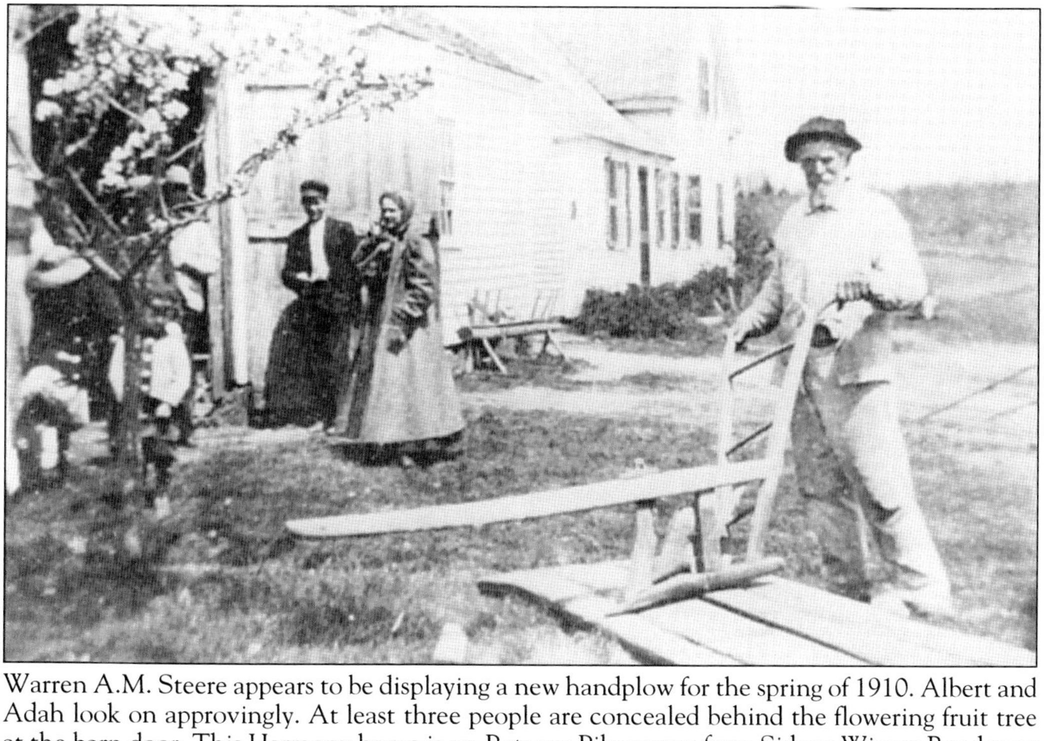

Warren A.M. Steere appears to be displaying a new handplow for the spring of 1910. Albert and Adah look on approvingly. At least three people are concealed behind the flowering fruit tree at the barn door. This Harmony home is on Putnam Pike across from Sidney Winsor Road near the shore of Waterman Lake.

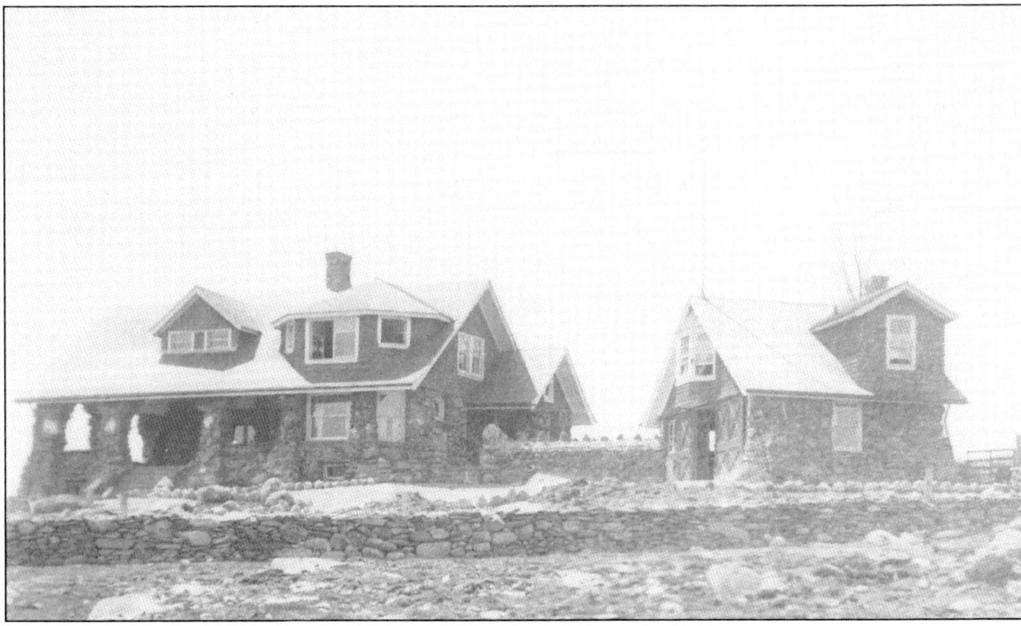

This photo of Dr. Frederick Hamilton's "Boulder Lodge" atop Brown's Hill in Harmony must have been taken about 1914 while his nephew, Austin Corbin, and Parkman Jacoy were developing the grounds. A nine-hole golf course, which began with the first tee on the hill, was a part of the plan, some of which today is the Glocester Country Club.

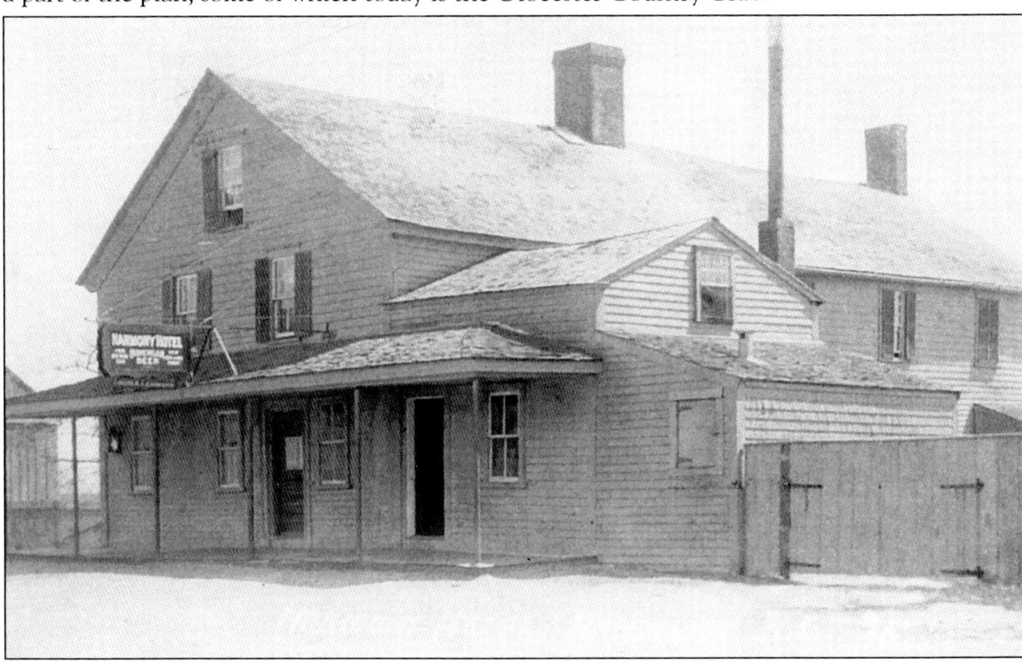

Harmony Hotel on Putnam Pike is listed on the 1790 map as belonging to Elisha Walker. It had a second-floor ballroom with an arched ceiling. At the time of this early-1900s picture, it may have been owned by Harris. By the 1920s it was Albert Shedyak's hotel. Harmony Fire Company's Reo truck was housed in the hotel barn in 1925. Today this is the site of the Harmony Fire Station.

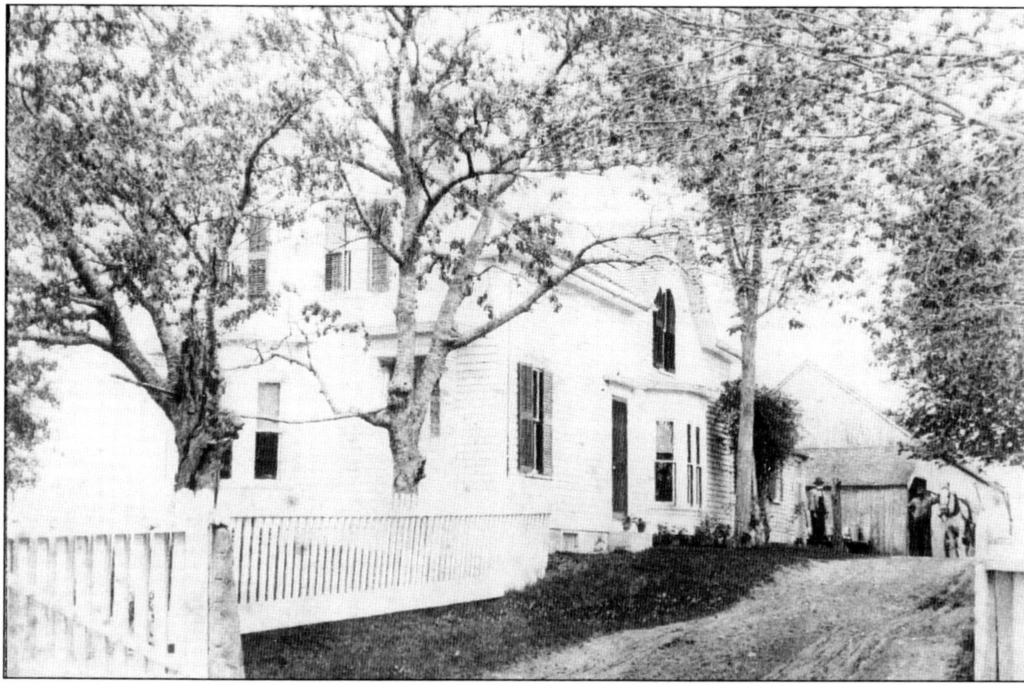

Andrew Winsor Brown is standing next to a horse on his farm on Cooper Hill Road, Harmony. Henry Tibbitts Brown is standing on the steps. Careful restoration has brought this torn turn-of-the-century photo back to nearly original condition. The farmhouse is now the residence of Russell and Ann Burlingame.

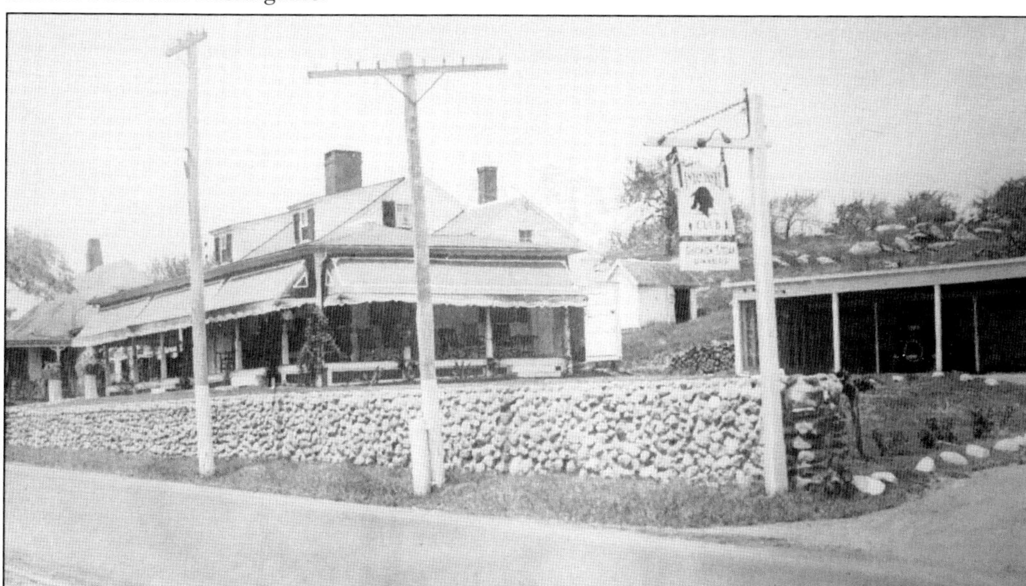

"In-Yan-Yan-Ke" is said to be a Native American term meaning "stony ground." The land was purchased in 1720 from Obadiah Lewis by Hezekiah Tinkham. By 1894, this property on Putnam Pike had two dwellings, a blacksmith shop, a wheelwright shop, and a barn. In 1912, Albert Eastman named it the "In-Yan-Yan-Ke Club," complete with restaurant, tearoom, game room, and other private meeting rooms. Lucius B. Steere was the handyman and gardener.

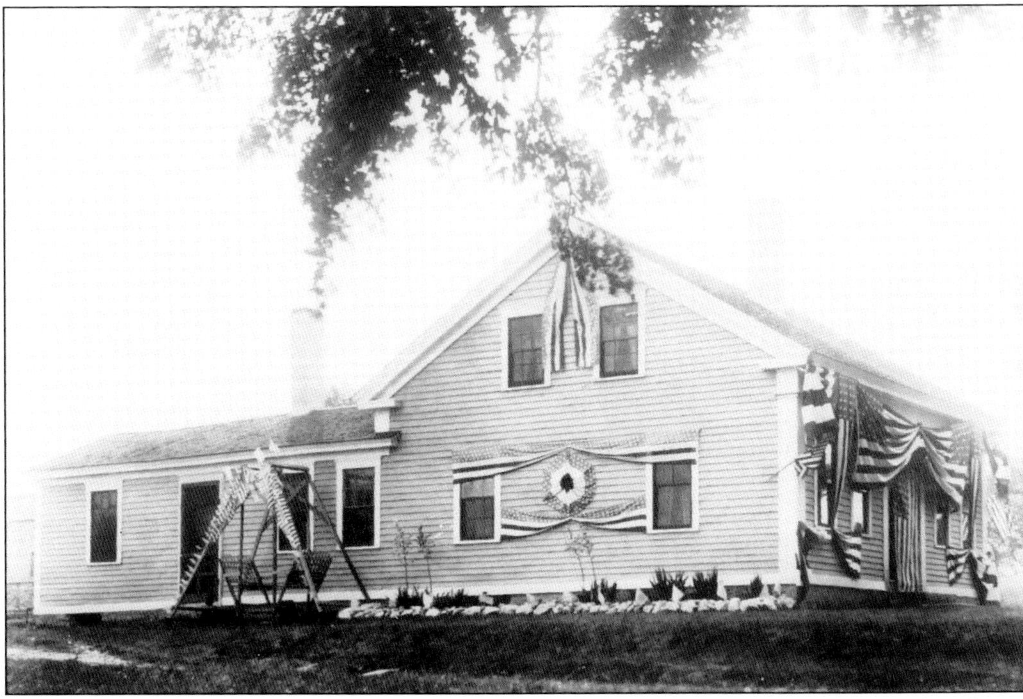

This is the home of Henry and Ruth W. Hall, east of Edgewood Drive on Putnam Pike, draped with bunting to celebrate Trolley Day, July 25, 1914. The Halls were owners of the stagecoach line from Harmony to Centredale. The loss of this house to fire in 1922 resulted in the formation of the fire company at Harmony.

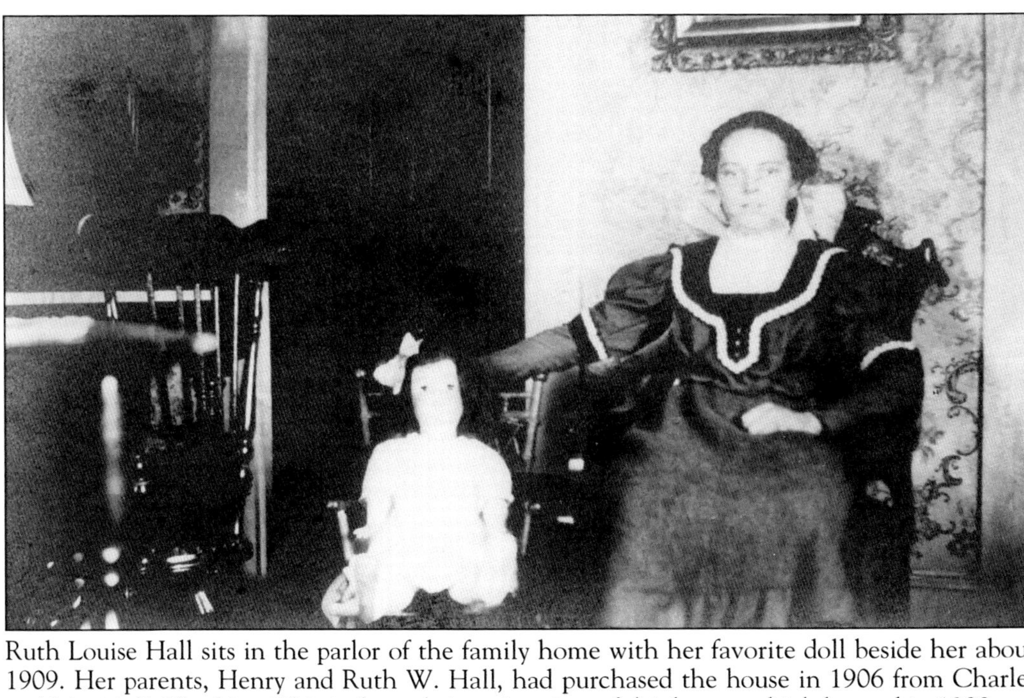

Ruth Louise Hall sits in the parlor of the family home with her favorite doll beside her about 1909. Her parents, Henry and Ruth W. Hall, had purchased the house in 1906 from Charles and Mariah S. Hawkins. This is the only interior view of this house, which burned in 1922.

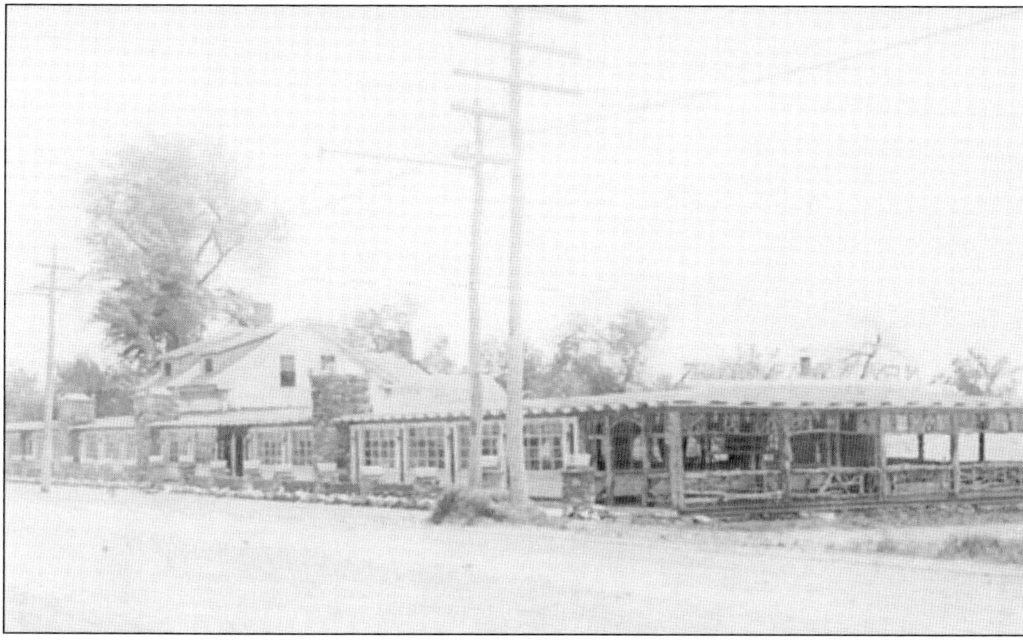

Twin Elms Farm was begun by Maxon and Bertha Gilbert in 1922 with a roadside stand on Putnam Pike that gradually expanded to a 280-foot-long rustic restaurant and dance hall. While popular bands played, chicken dinners were served to capacity crowds. A ball field and 1/2-mile-long toboggan slide on an adjacent hill was created for the patrons enjoyment. Twin Elms burned on August 28, 1941.

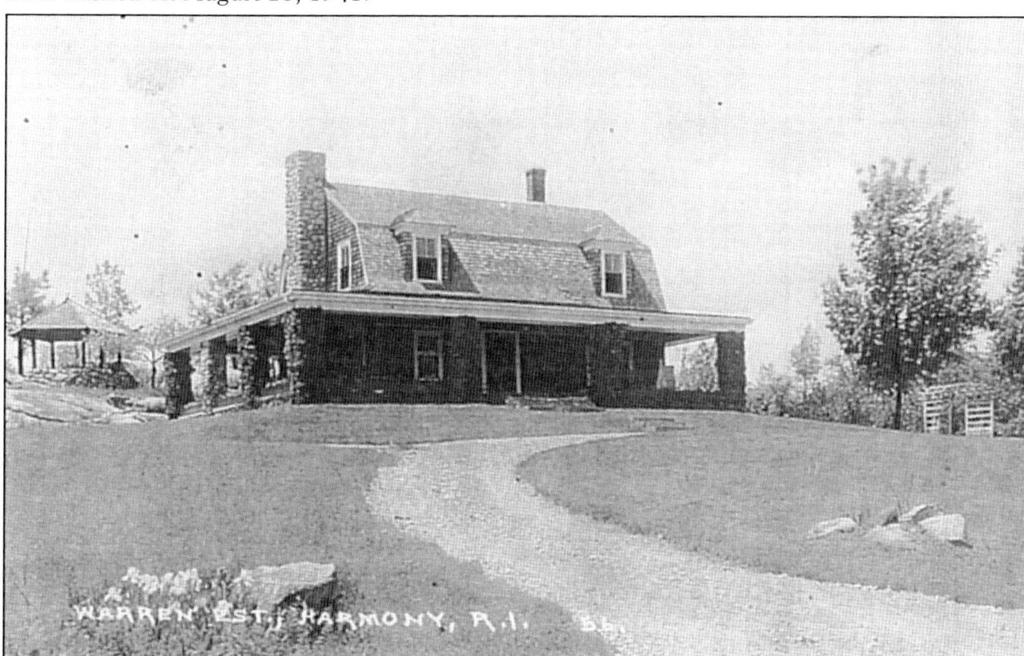

This early-1900s photocard shows the Warren estate on the west side of Sawmill Road in Harmony. Other names associated with this property are Chase, Zuck, and W.P. Jacoy, who ran the Harmony Hotel from 1864 to 1881.

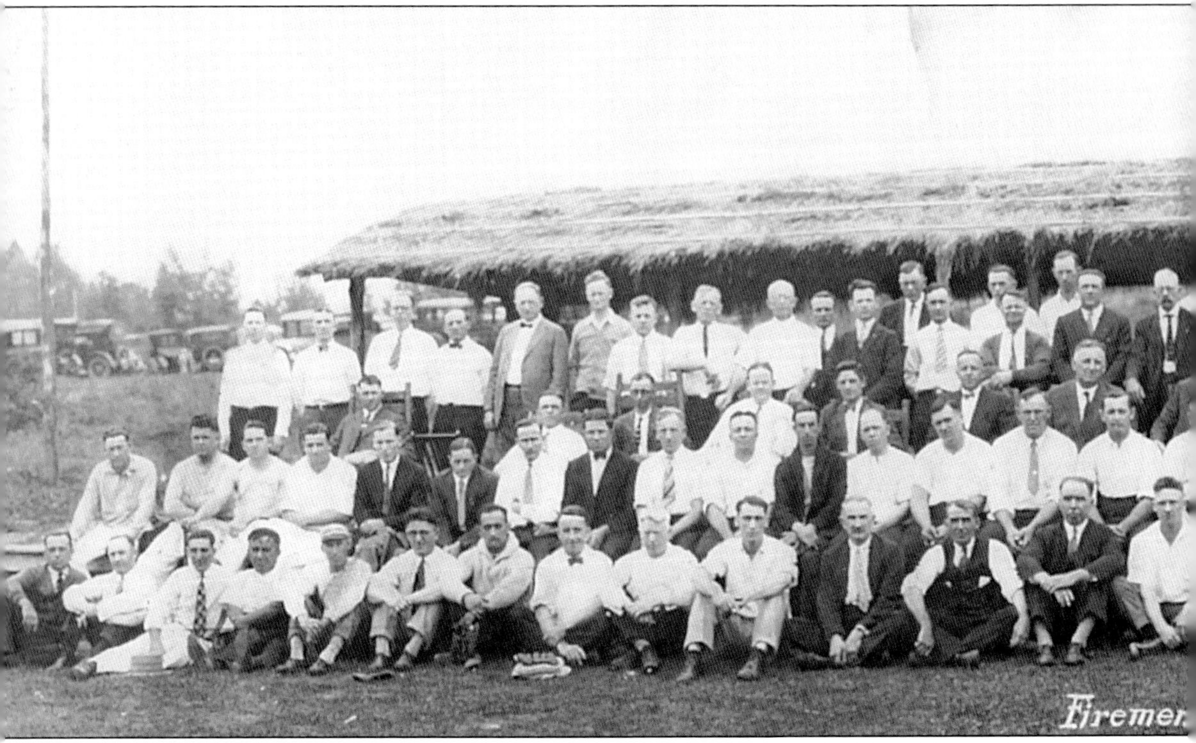

One of the first Northern Rhode Island Firemen's outings was held at Twin Elms Farm on Putnam Pike in Harmony. Some familiar faces are, from left to right, as follows: (first row) Mike Russell, Peter Rivers, Chief Walter Keach Sr., and Benny Steere; (second row) Leon Chase and George Greenhalgh; (third row) Albert Trinque, James Maher, and Dennis

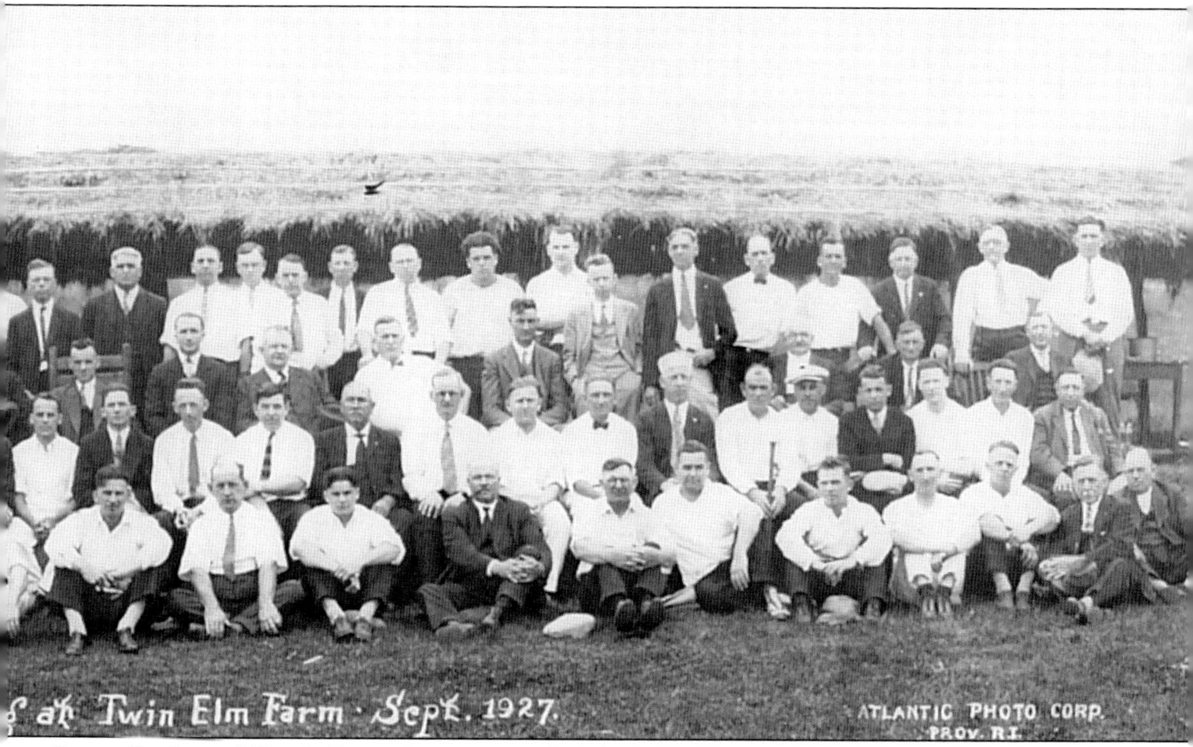

Ryan; (back row) Frank Davis, James Greenhalgh, George Clough, and Roy Converse. The cooperative efforts of these fire companies have saved countless properties and lives. We are grateful for their selfless acts of courage under extraordinary and, at times, life-threatening conditions, throughout the years.

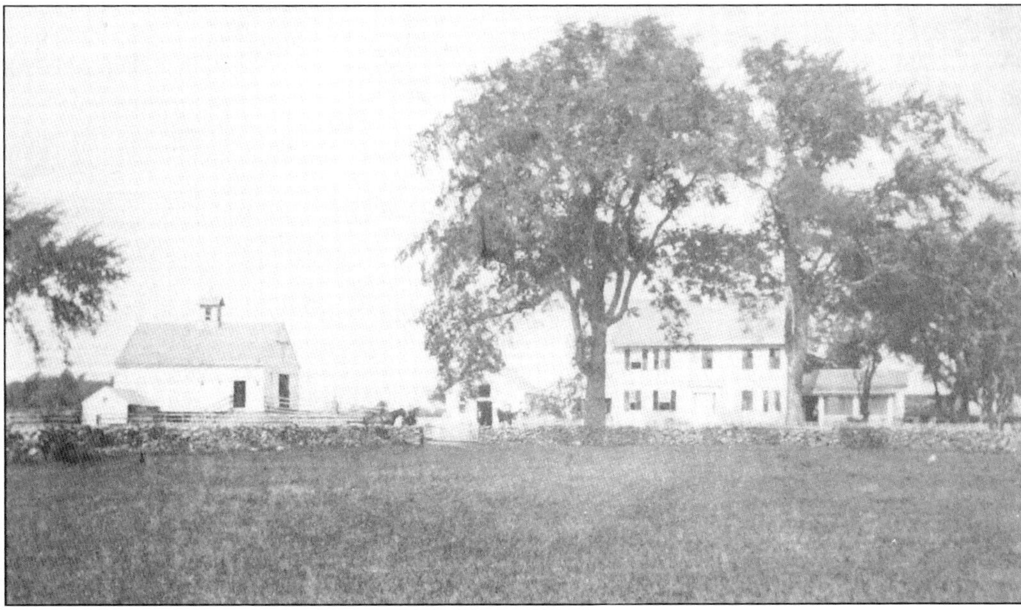

The old Wheaton Whitaker farm was on Snake Hill Road west of Waldron's Corners. It was recalled that a big tree there accommodated a fine tree house with steps going around the trunk. It is believed that this grand two-and-a-half-story colonial home burned in the 1930s when the Barker family lived there. This is an 1870s stereoscopic view.

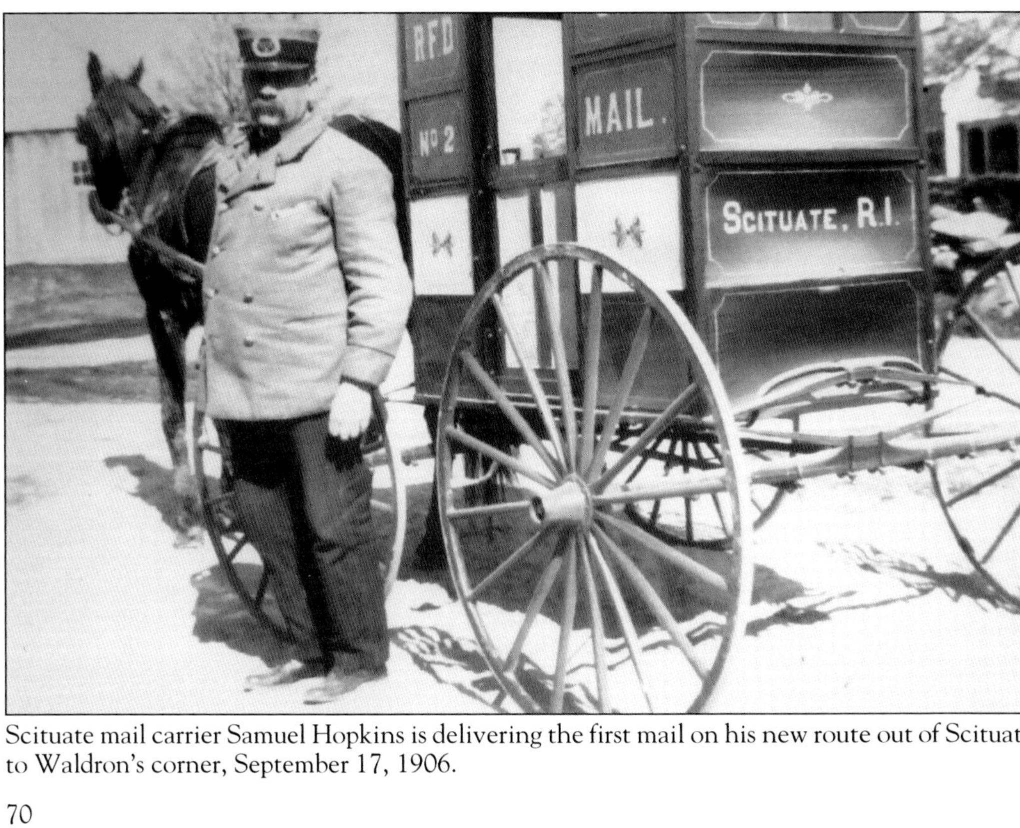

Scituate mail carrier Samuel Hopkins is delivering the first mail on his new route out of Scituate to Waldron's corner, September 17, 1906.

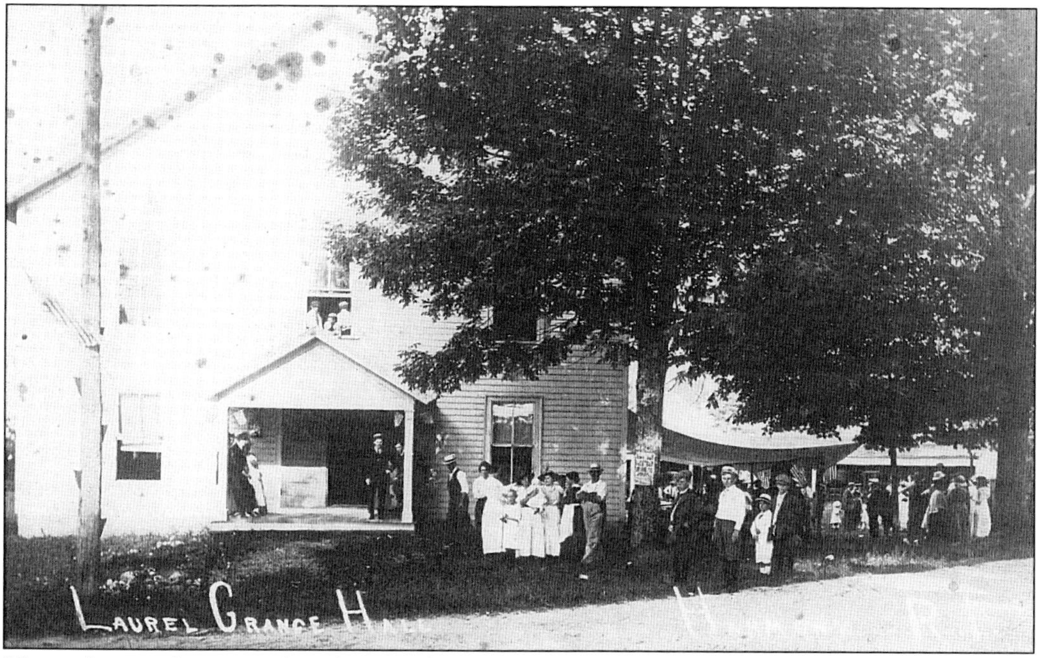

The gathering shown on this photocard is at the new Laurel Grange, which was built in 1914 at Waldron's Corners in Harmony. No indication was given whether it was the opening celebration or one of many clambakes that they put on to defray the cost of the building.

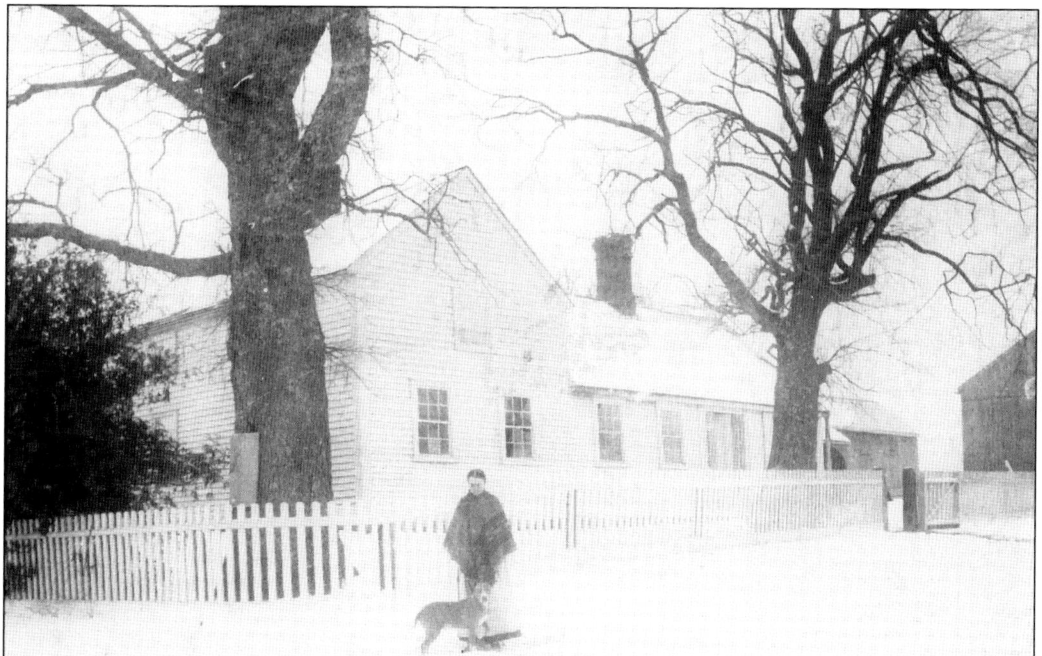

Patience Steere, the daughter of Seth H. Steere, was walking with her dog in front of her home at Waldron's Corners (Sawmill Road and Snake Hill Road) when the photographer captured this picture in the early 1900s.

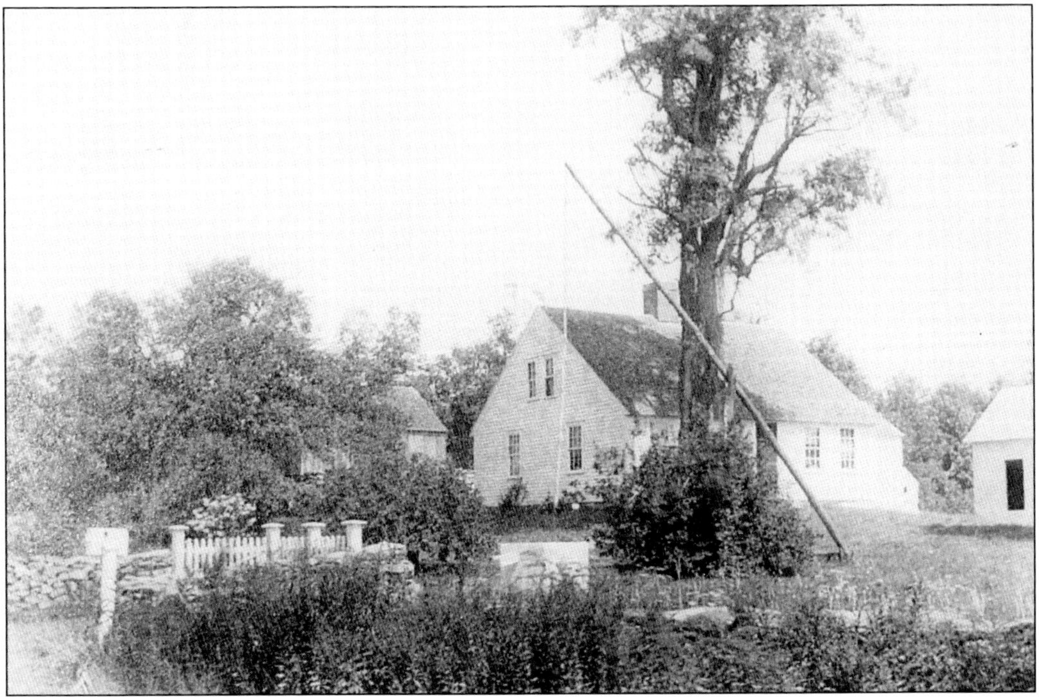

This house on Snake Hill Road is the old Barnard Hicks homestead. In the late 1800s, it was home of Charles Hunt Steere and family. His daughter Mary was still living here when this picture was taken. Notice the well sweep in the front yard.

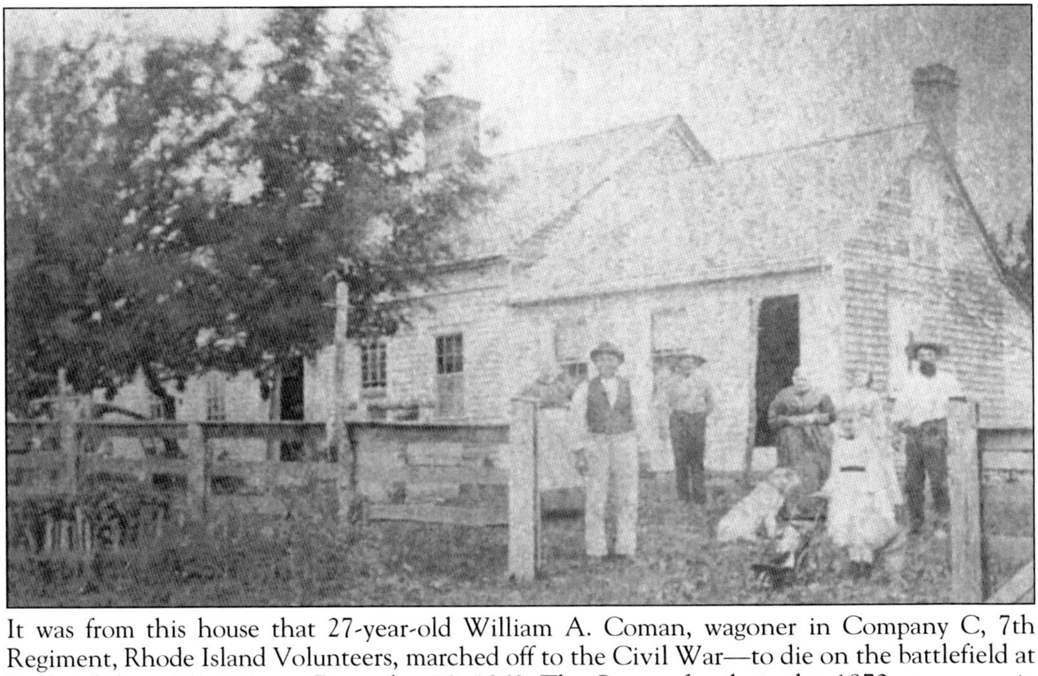

It was from this house that 27-year-old William A. Coman, wagoner in Company C, 7th Regiment, Rhode Island Volunteers, marched off to the Civil War—to die on the battlefield at Fredericksburg, Virginia, on December 19, 1862. The Coman family in this 1870s stereoscopic view are, from left to right, Maria Coman and her husband, David; (in back) John, grandmother, ? Zaloti, and Stephen Coman (standing near the post).

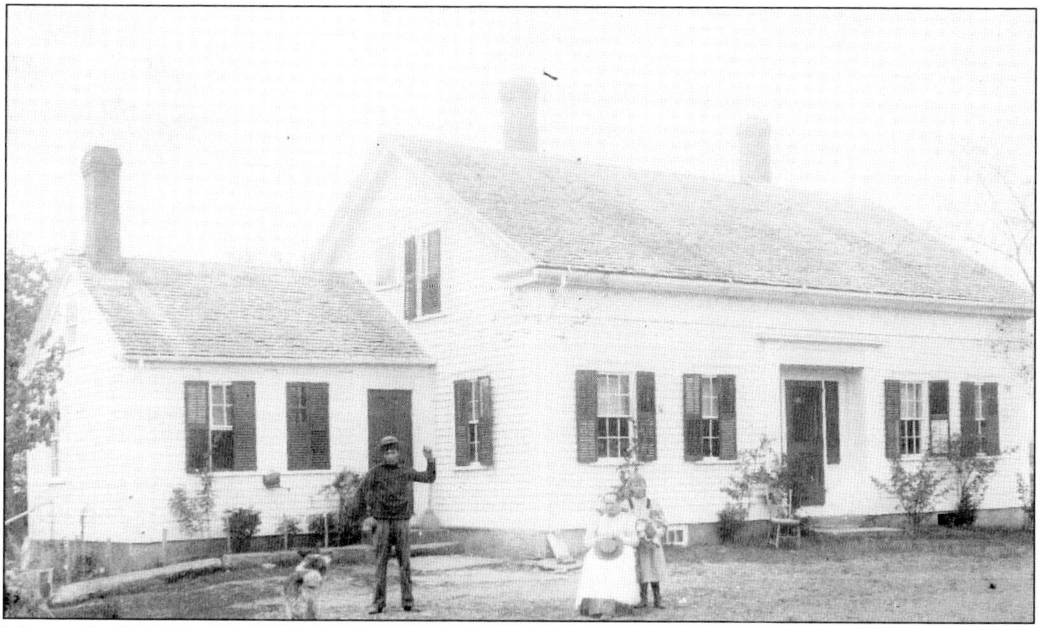

Mason Ballou's farm on Farnum Road west of Mapleville Road still has many original features today. In this early-1900s photo are Edward Inman, Mrs. Mason Ballou, and Lila Ballou.

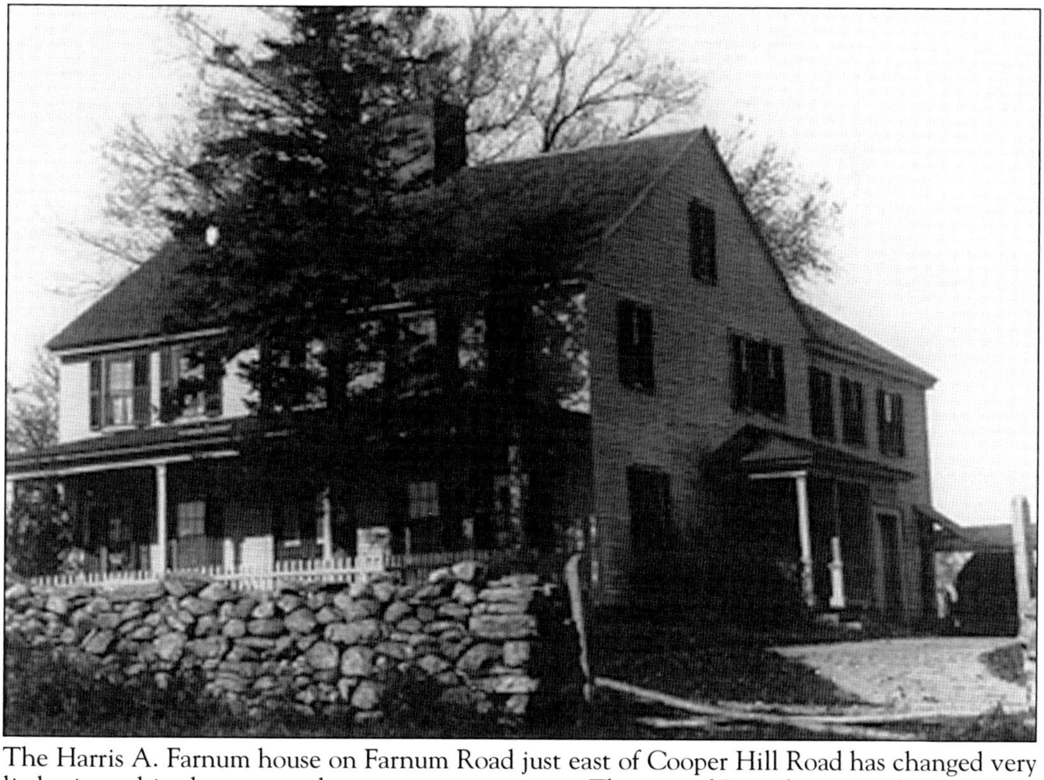

The Harris A. Farnum house on Farnum Road just east of Cooper Hill Road has changed very little since this photo was taken over a century ago. The city of Providence can be seen from this hill.

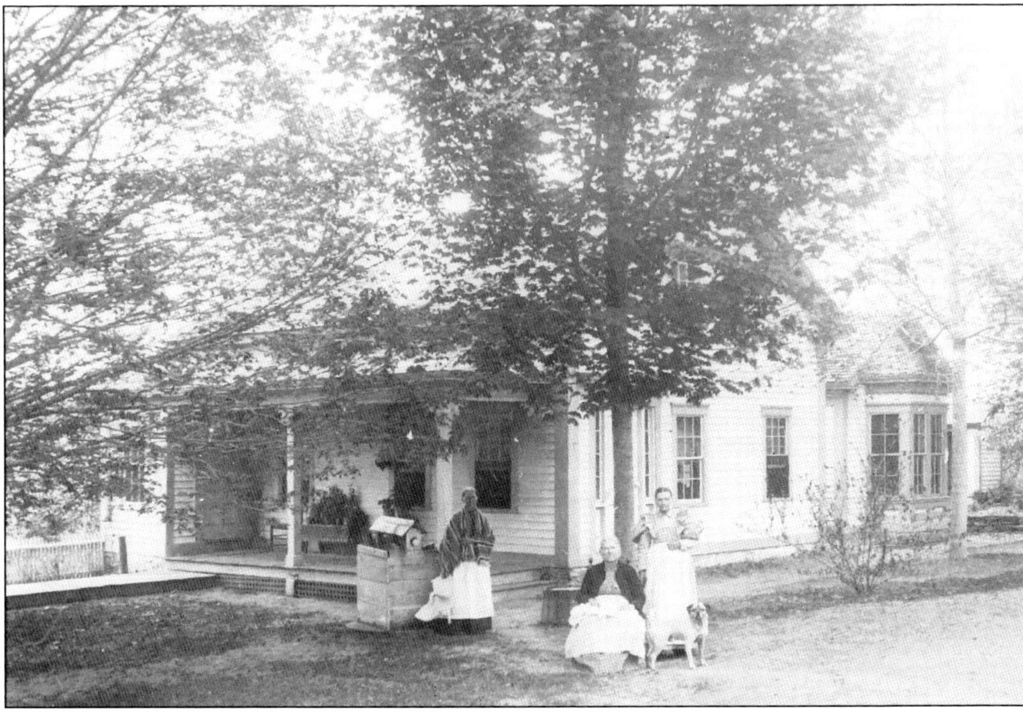

At the sharp corner of Eddy Road and Evans Road in East Glocester stands the home of James and Marietta Evans. Pure spring water was piped from a nearby hillside when the Wilburs lived here. The ladies are not named on this 1890s photo.

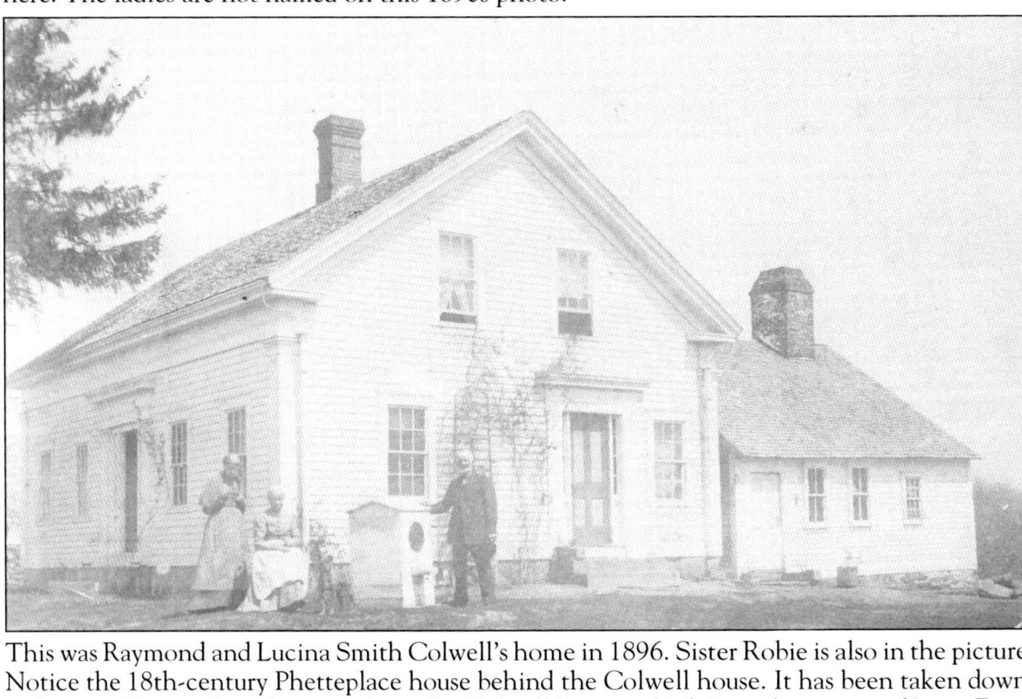

This was Raymond and Lucina Smith Colwell's home in 1896. Sister Robie is also in the picture. Notice the 18th-century Phetteplace house behind the Colwell house. It has been taken down, and new additions have been made to the Colwell house, which is at the corner of Long Entry Road and Tarkiln Road, East Glocester.

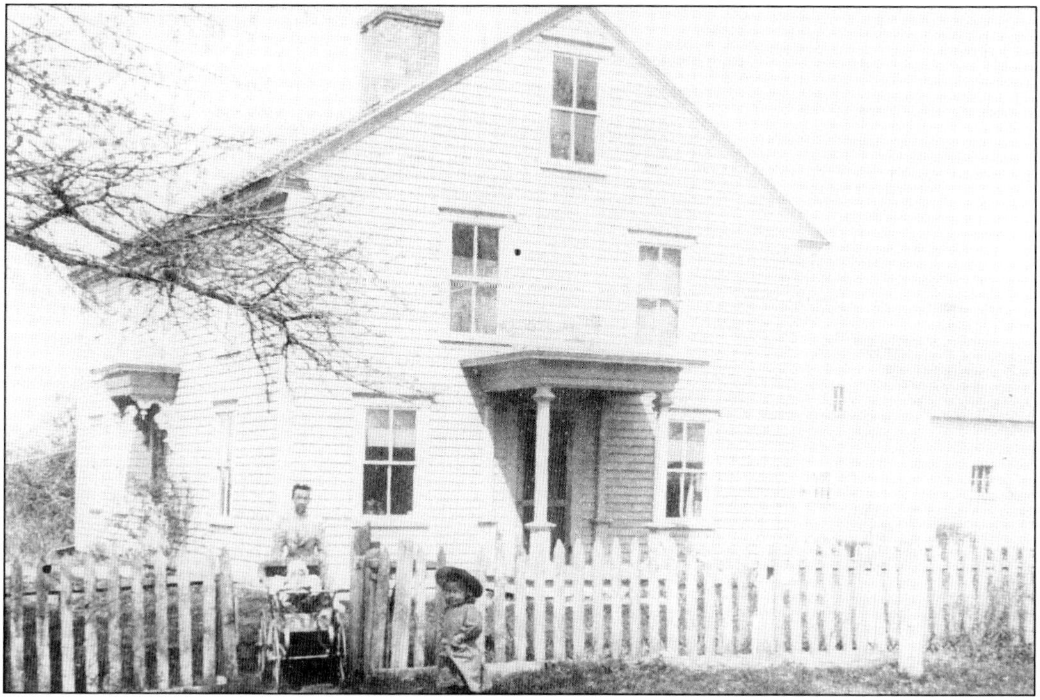

Emily Colwell's house "on the hill" near Mapleville Road, East Glocester, was owned by the William Steere family when this picture was taken in the 1890s. The overhangs over the doors have been removed and the door toward the street is now a window. This house is on Long Entry Road.

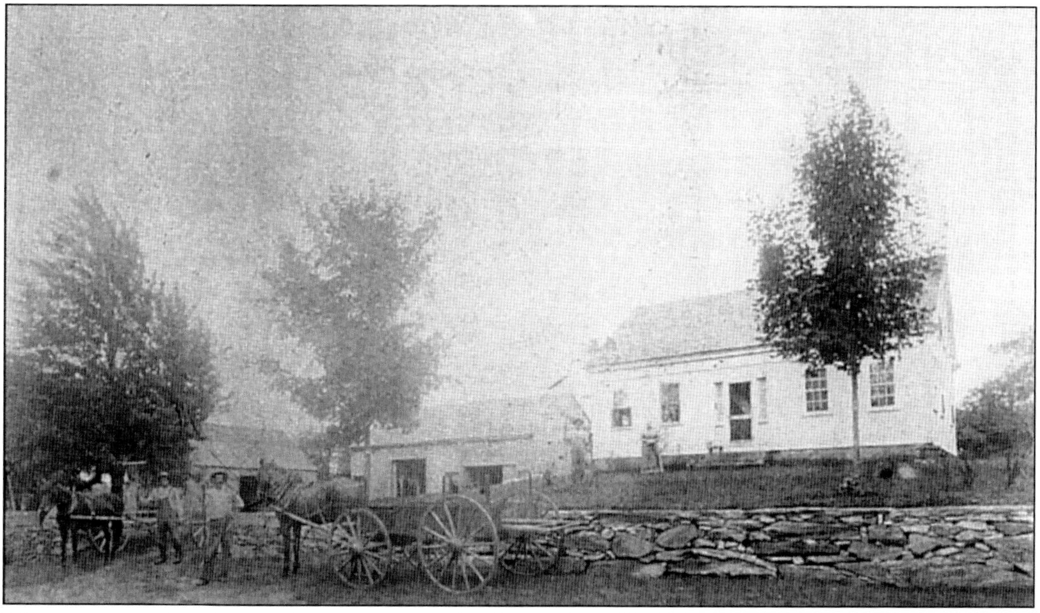

The photographer found the Clemence family at their Tarkiln Road homestead farm on this summer's day in the 1880s. Reuben and wife, Elsa M., stand near the house, while Richard and Daniel, carpenters by trade, are busy with horses and wagons at the gate. This house, still lived in by a descendant, was built for Reuben about 1840.

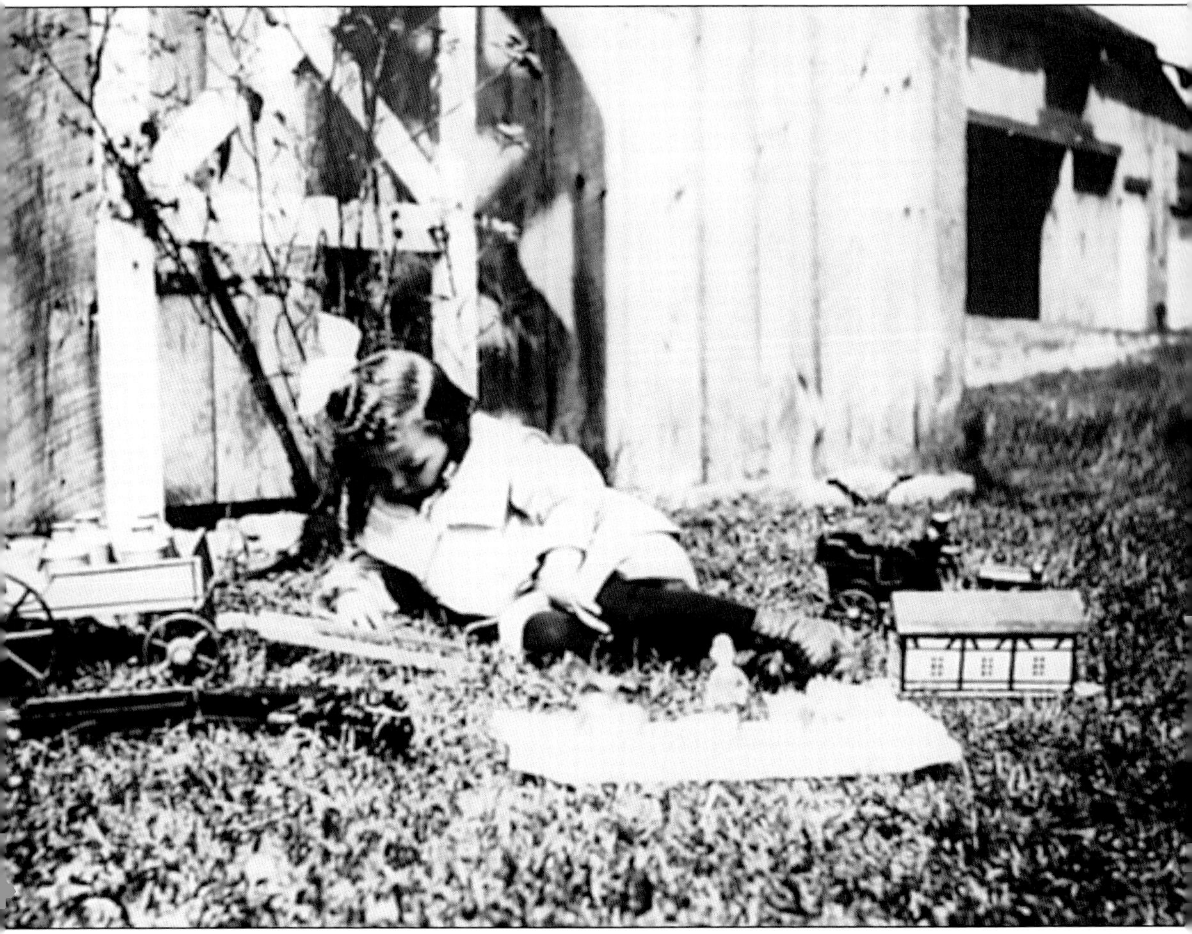

Young Wilton Newman found a special place in the sun near one of the barns at the Reuben Clemence homestead to play with his favorite toys. This photo was taken about 1909. These barns are gone today, but the house remains and is still his home.

Six

Hawkins' Village and West Glocester

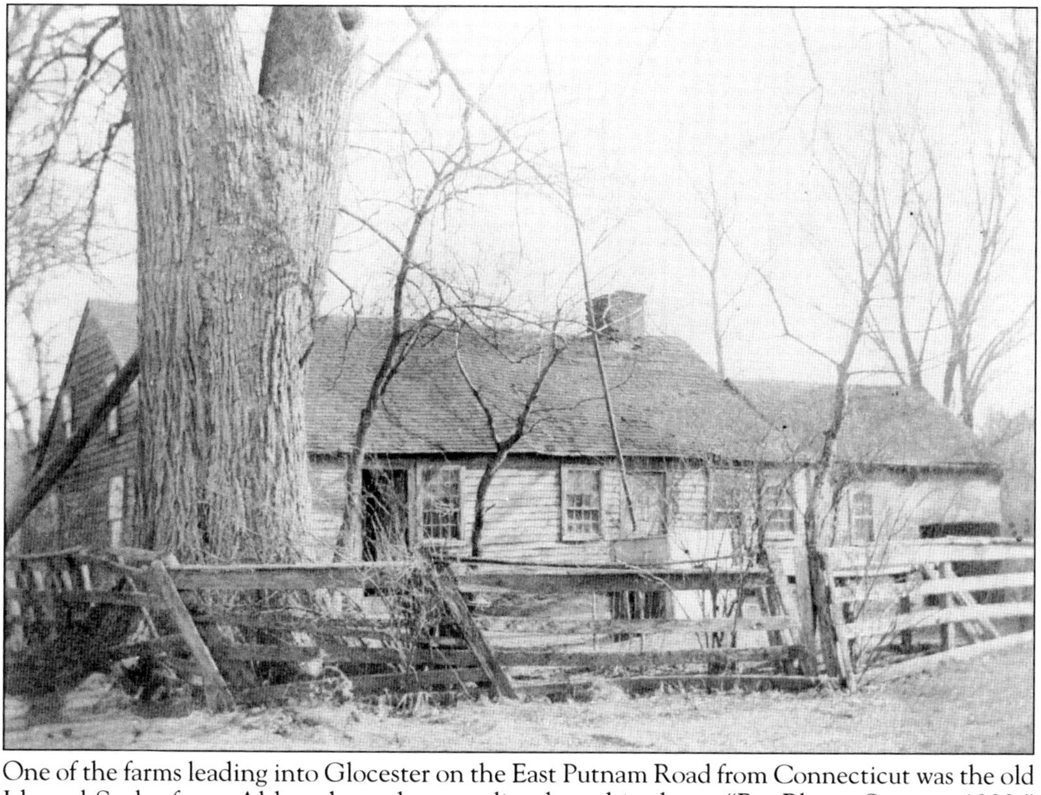

One of the farms leading into Glocester on the East Putnam Road from Connecticut was the old Ishmael Sayles farm. Although no date was listed on this photo, "Big Blow—Summer 1900s" was the inscription on an accompanying picture when the big tree fell across the front yard.

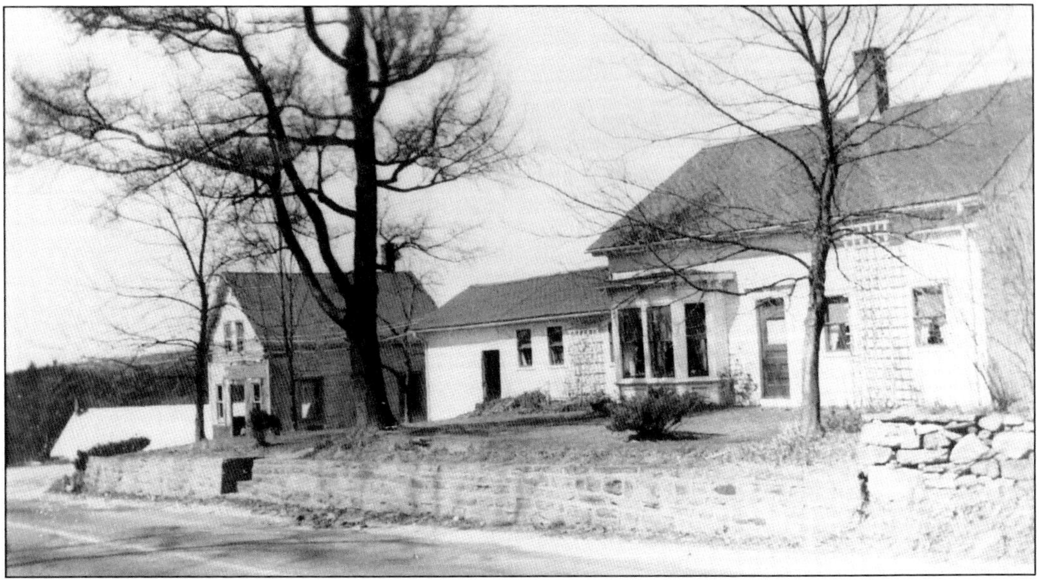

About 1918, Hawkins' Village still had front yards lined with stone walls and shaded by trees. The hardtop road was then only 12 feet wide. Hawkins' Mill's roof can be seen just past the store and post office.

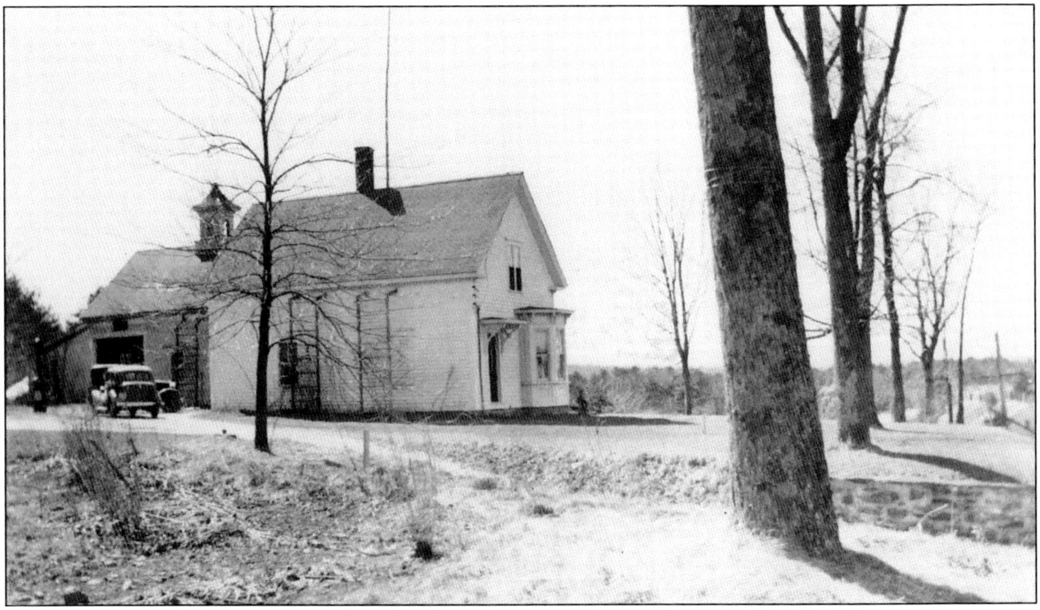

Walter Hawkins's car stands in the driveway of the Hawkins/Houghton house. Down in the valley can be seen the rooftops of the two big mill tenements. Hawkins's electric pole can also be seen. Electric service for this house was drawn through a pipe under the road.

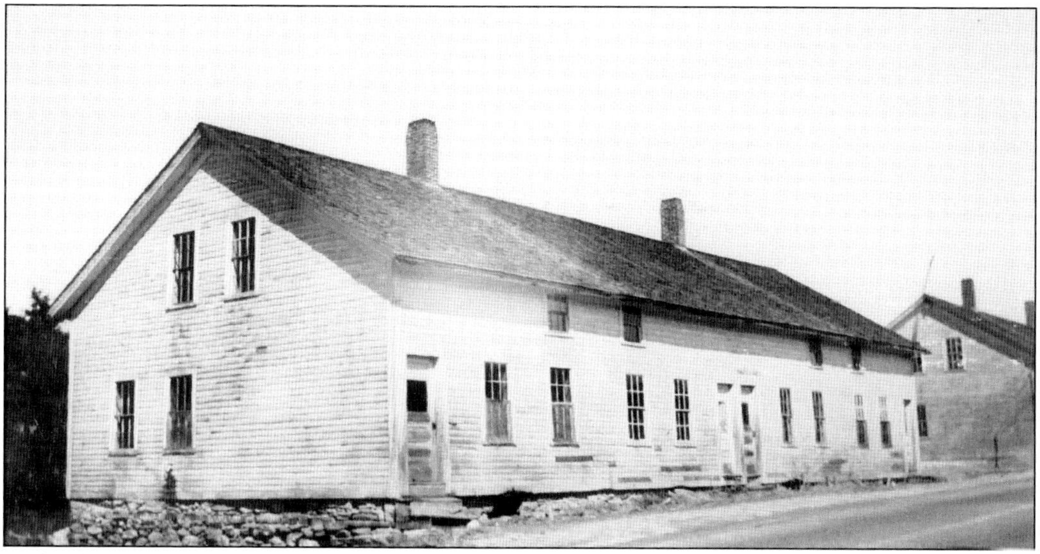

Eight families lived in these Hawkins' Mills tenements on Putnam Pike only "a stone's throw" from the Connecticut line. The Bakers, Sheldons, Halls, and Brodies were some of the families who lived there. By 1938, when the road was widened to four lanes, these buildings had been demolished.

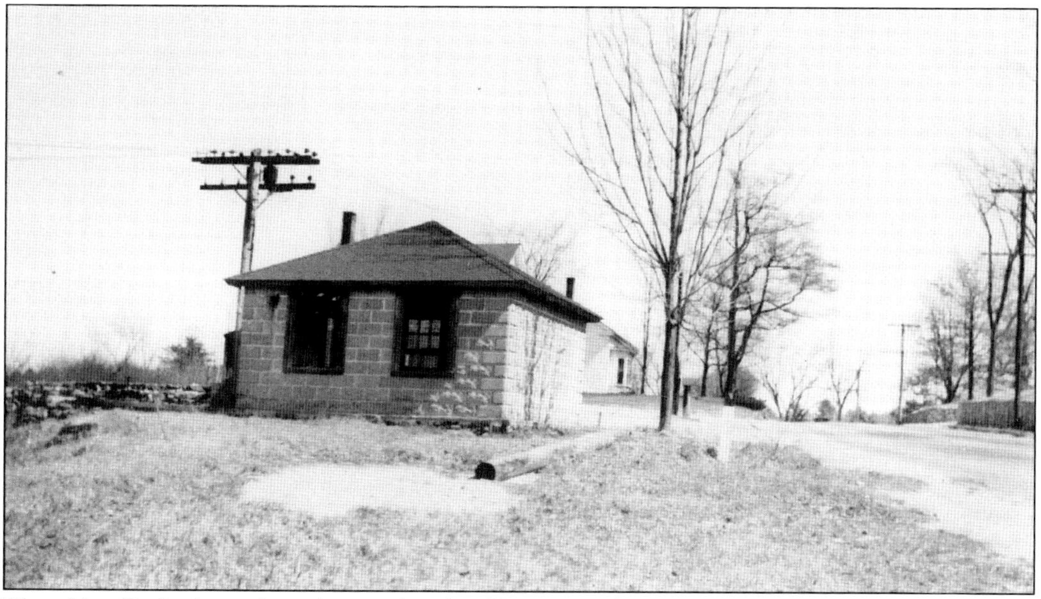

The old milk shed stands at the north side of Putnam Pike—seemingly with no purpose—since the barn was taken down. It was a "catchall" for the mill after that. Only the store roof is visible, and the Hawkins house can be seen in the distance.

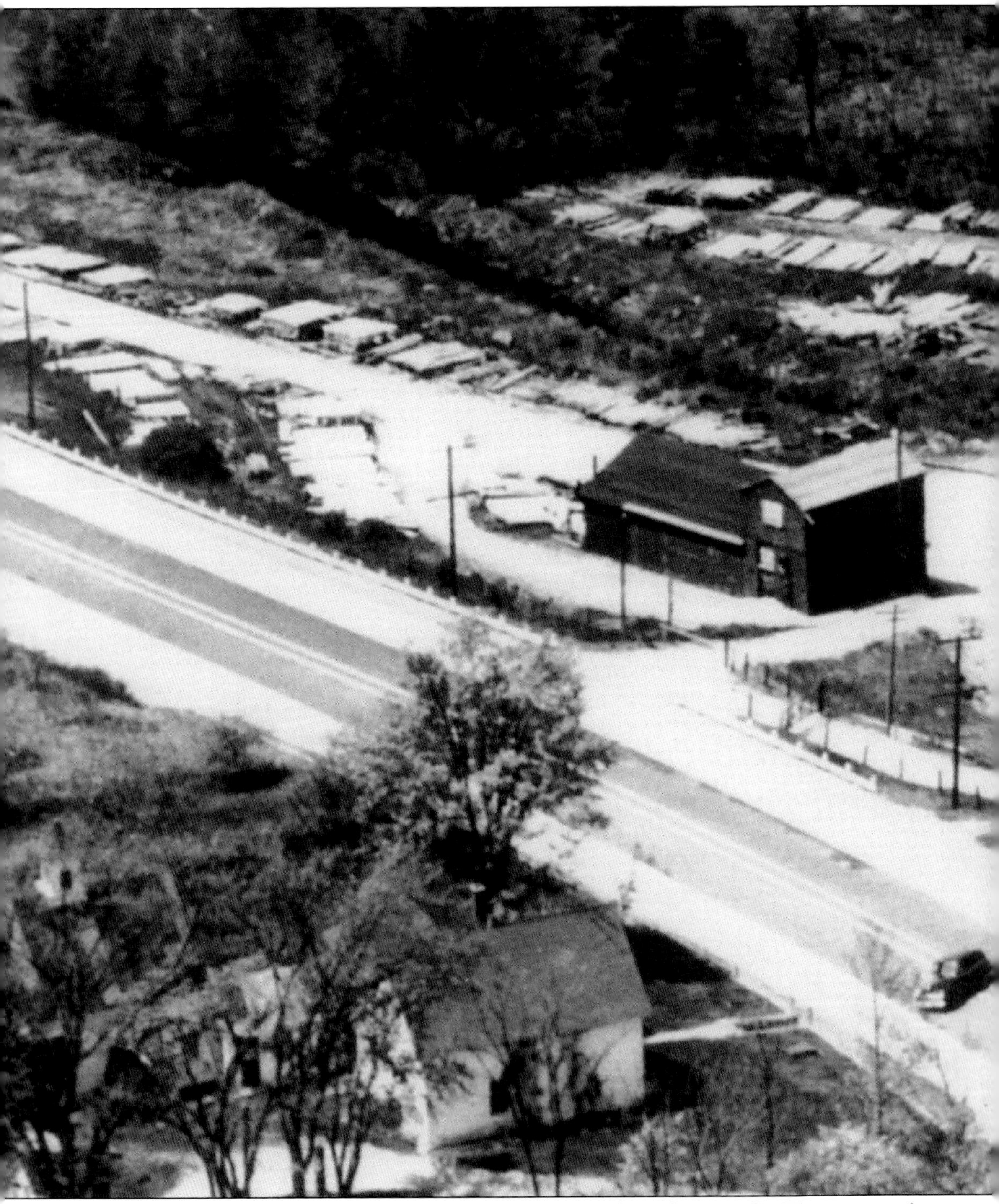

A pilot was paid $10 to take this photo in the 1940s of Hawkins' Mills. This view is facing northwest. The Hawkins/Houghton house and barn are in the lower left corner, and the Hawkins' house and store are on the lower right. The mill pond is beyond. The dark building with the white roof on the left is the planing mill, and the lower extension is the baler shed.

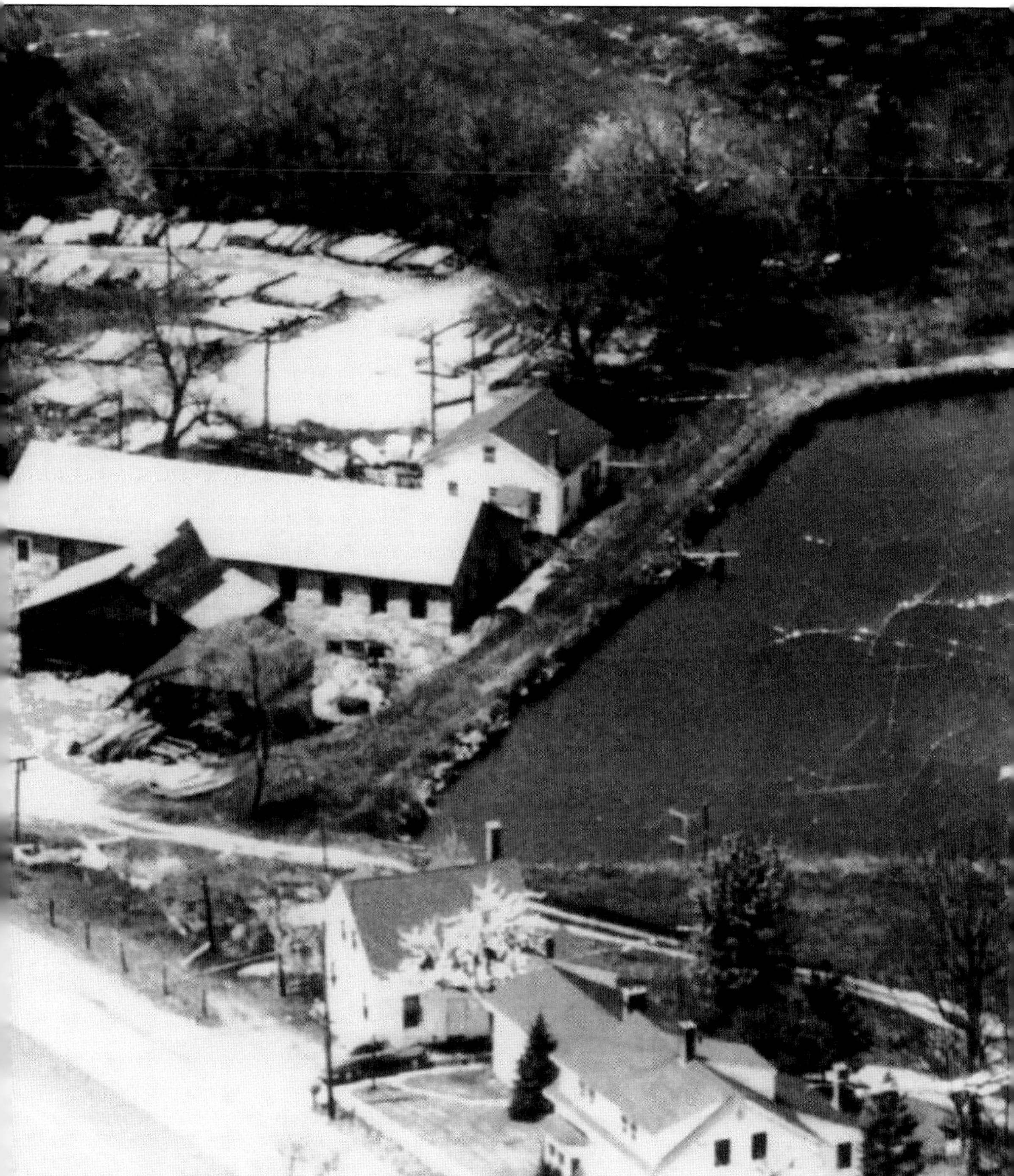

The building in front of the main mill on the right housed the main planer, which shaved wood to various thicknesses for a variety of uses. The white building behind the main mill housed a diesel generator, the electric company, and a mechanics shop. A C.P. Bradway water turbine generated power at the dam near the main mill.

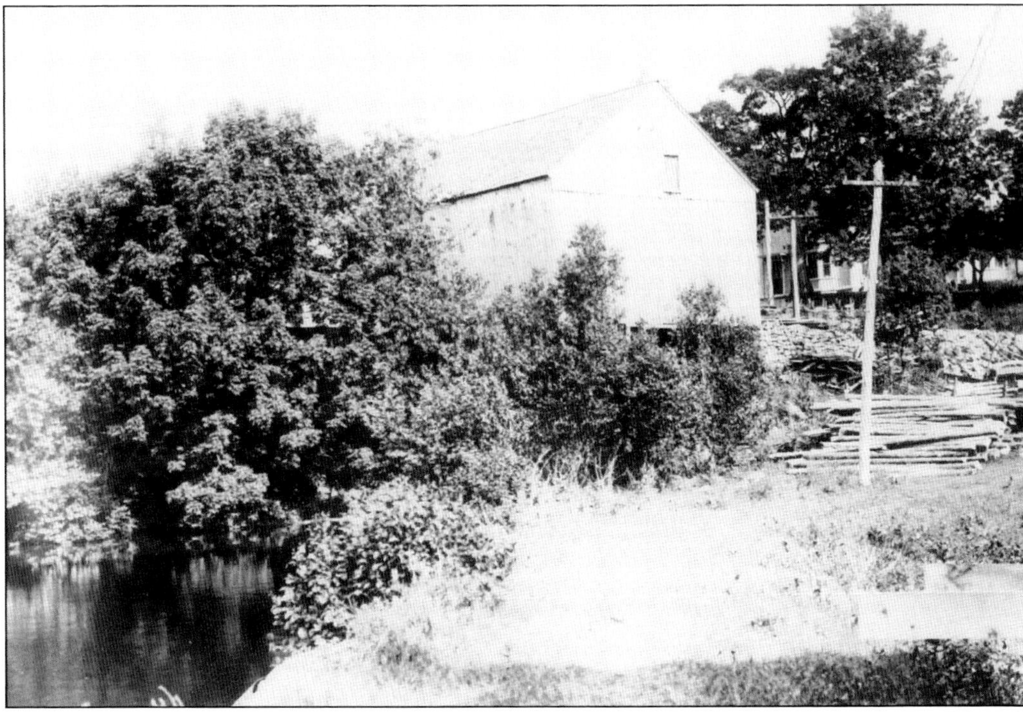

The photographer stood on the mill pond dam facing the road to take this picture of the old barn. On that portion of the dam extending to the road was a short length of railroad track used to transport lumber to the mill—the only railroad in Glocester.

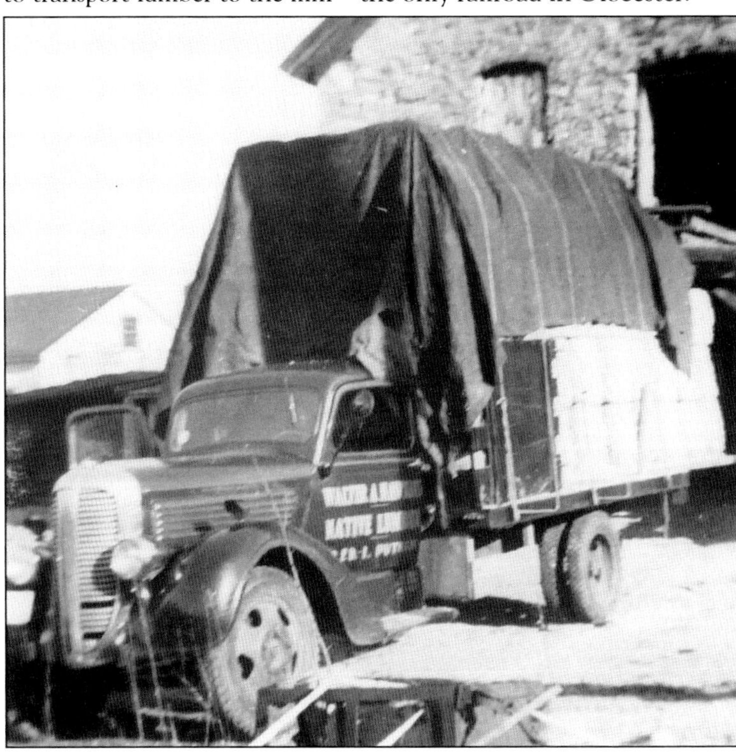

The lettering on the truck door reads as follows: "Walter A. Hawkins, Native Lumber, RFD 1, Putnam." The mail came via the Star route out of Putnam, and he supplied so much lumber in Connecticut that Hawkins simply put Putnam on the truck instead of West Glocester, Rhode Island—and it was shorter, too.

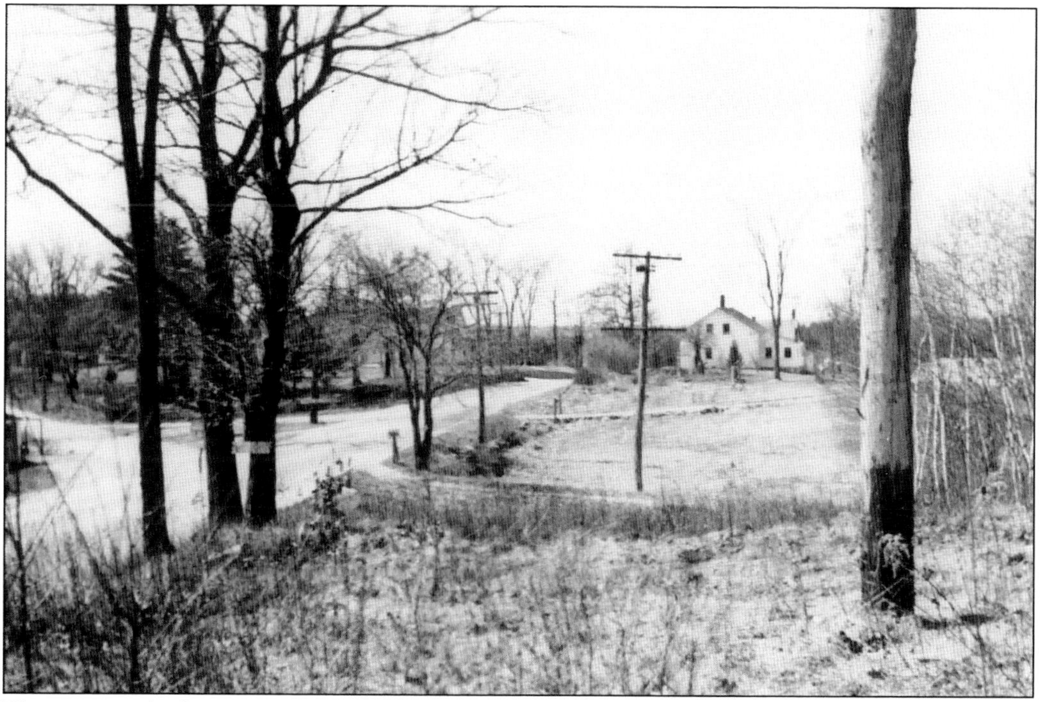

This view is looking west toward the Hawkins's houses and the intersection of Putnam Pike and East Putnam Road. On the very left edge of the picture at the intersection can be seen the "Little Brown Hut" lunchroom run by Eva Peal.

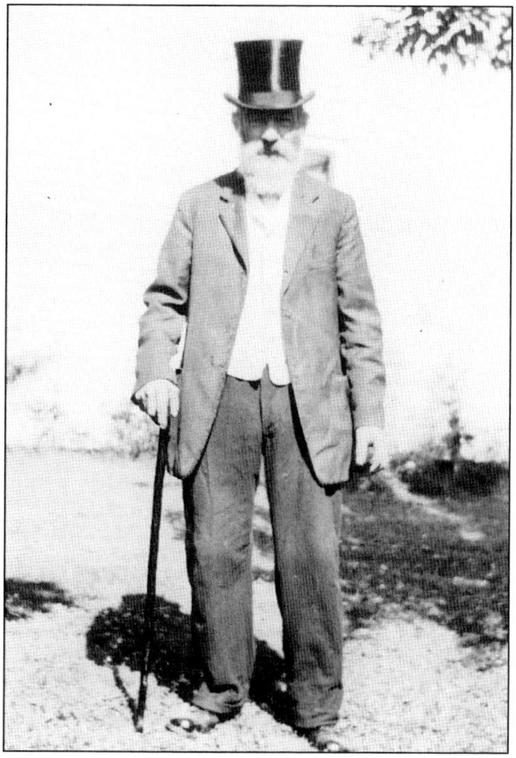

George Hall, age 80 in this picture, worked for Torrey Brothers in the potato fields all summer and cut wood in winter for Hawkins' Mills. His job was to take wood from the planer and place it on rollers that carried it away from the planer.

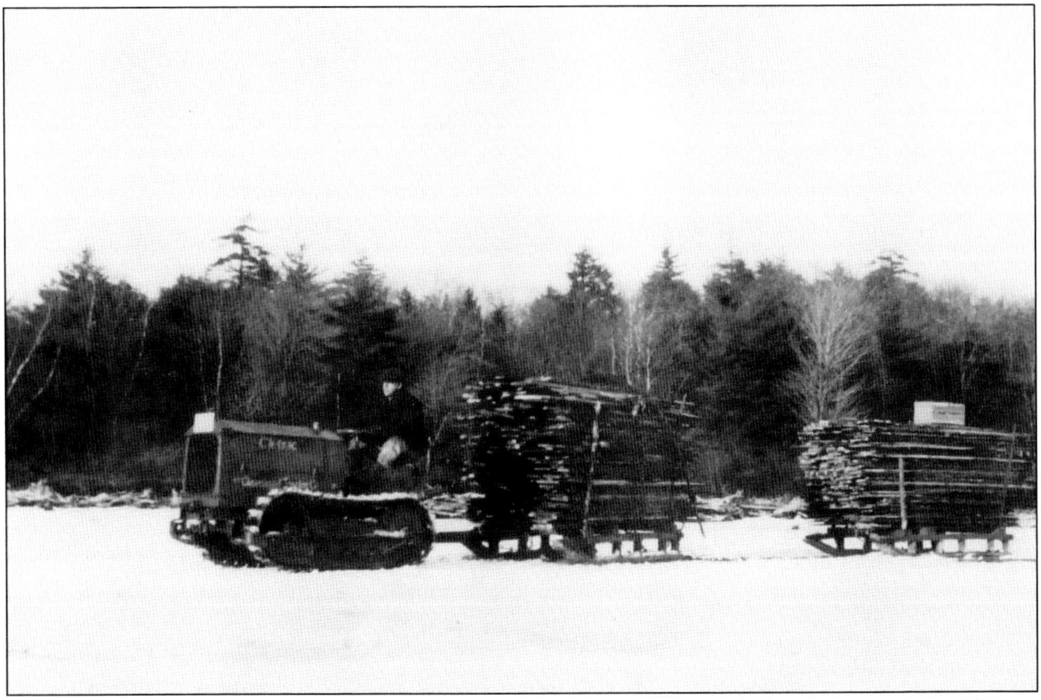

Tractor loads of wood were hauled on sleds across the ice at Bowdish Reservoir from Wilbur Pond to Hawkins' Mills.

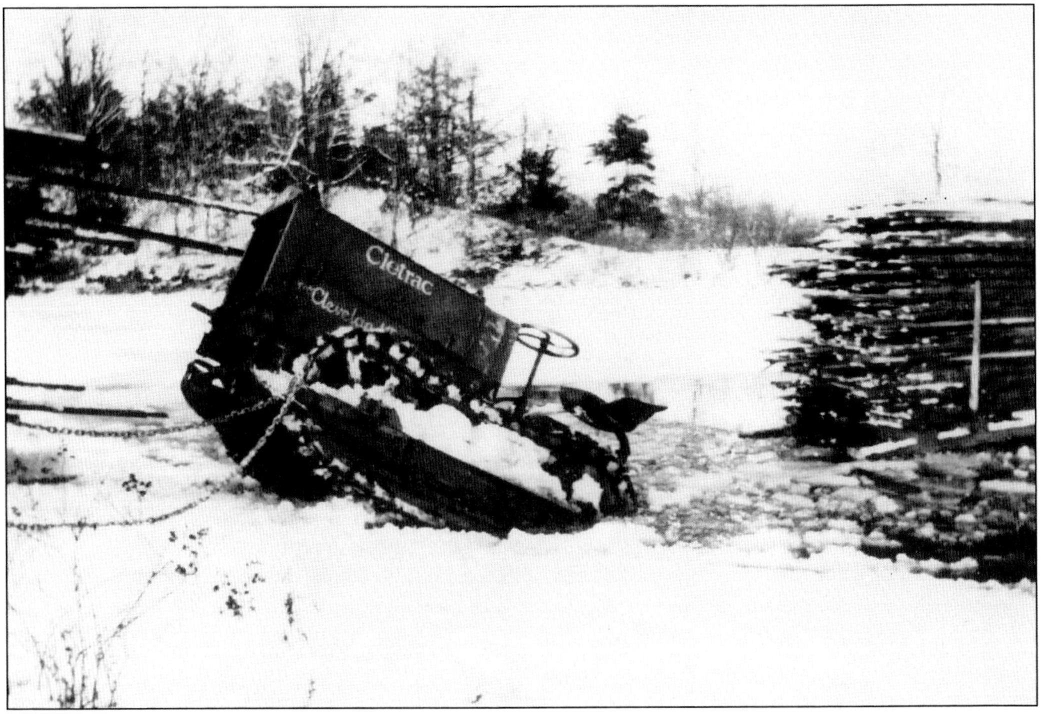

The Cleatrac "took a bath" this time, but the men from the mill chained the tractor out and brought all the wood back, too.

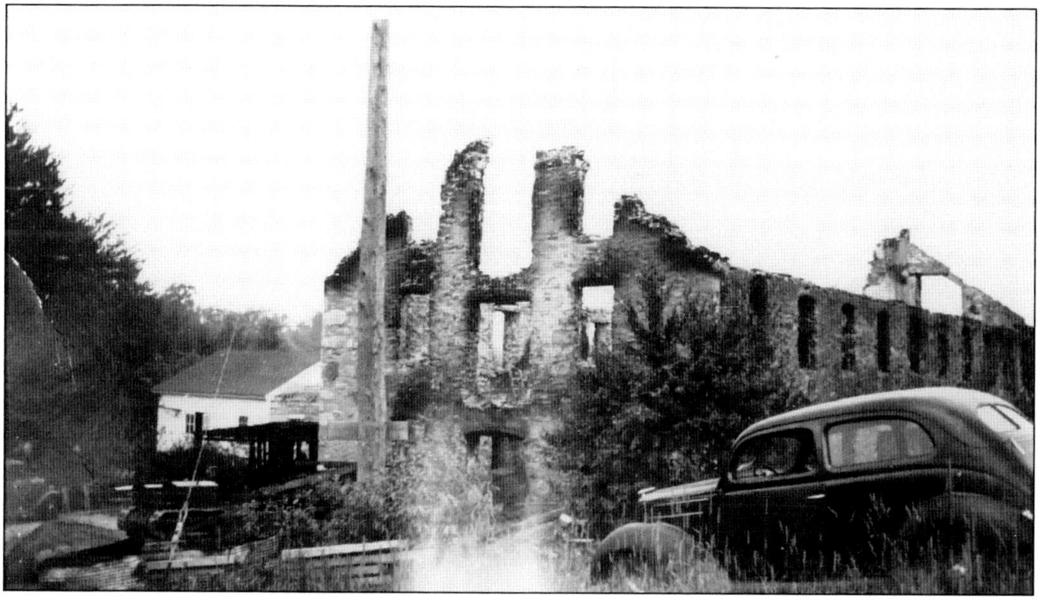

The efforts of fire companies from Chepachet, Putnam, and Thompson could not quell the consuming flames that devastated Walter Hawkins' sawmill on July 4, 1946. The morning fire began in planer shavings and spread through a blower to the upper stories. Lost were 10,000 board feet of finished pine, hemlock, and spruce ready for shipment, and 1,500 bales of shavings. A 1902 blaze left a similar scene from which they had rebuilt.

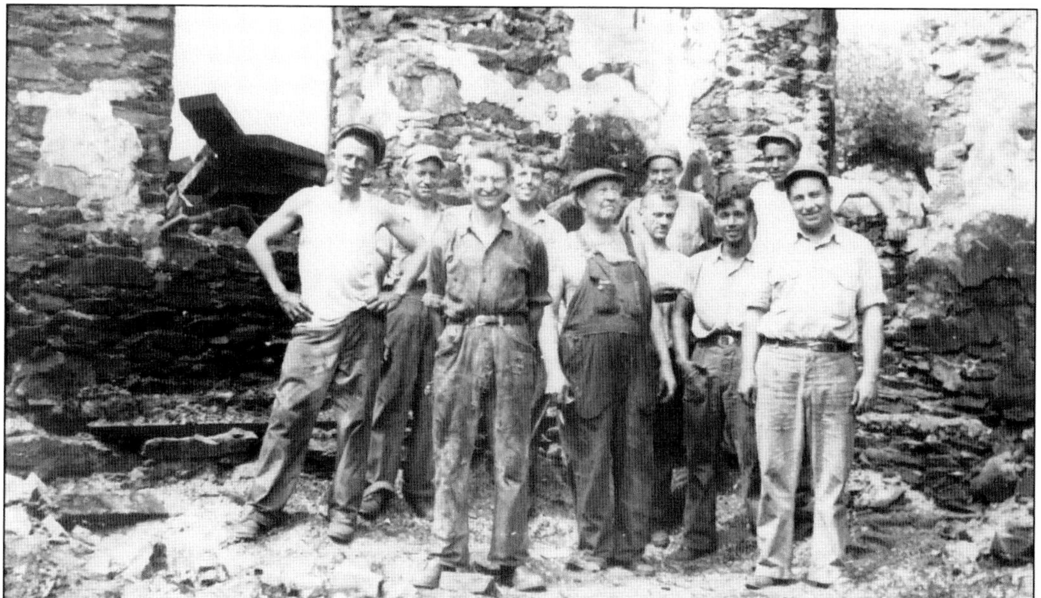

This photograph was taken the day after the fire at Hawkins' Mill. The cleanup gang's smiling faces prompted by the photographer would turn grim and blackened by the end of that day. Among those in the picture are Randall Law, Tom Adams, Francis Keach, Conrad Montie, and Norman Montie.

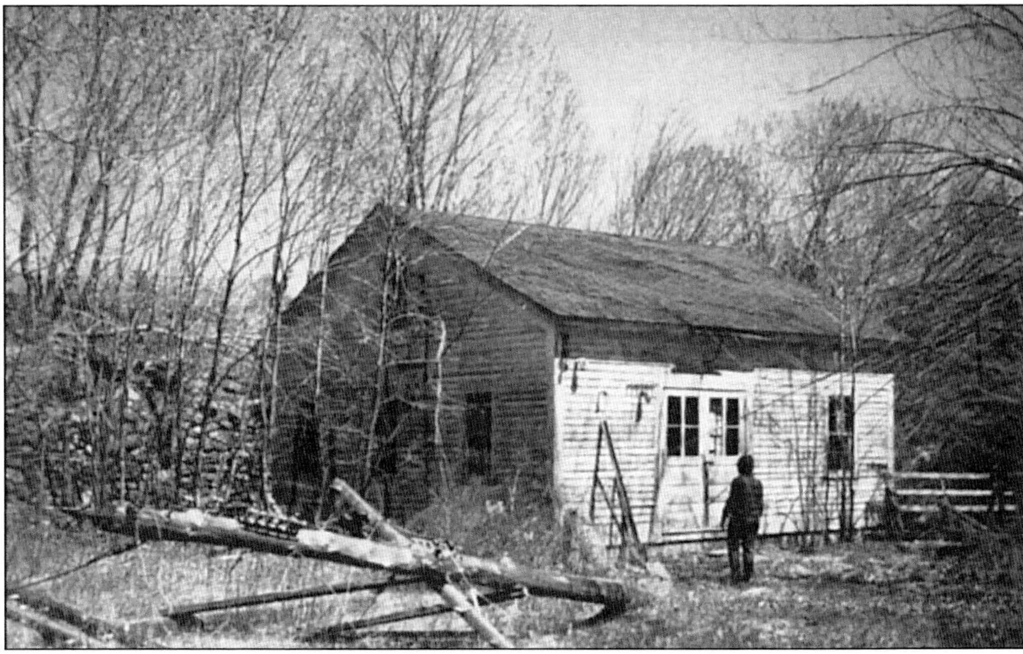

Walter Hawkins began generating electricity here to power the Hawkins's homes in 1912. By 1921, he extended electric service to neighbors as far as Bowdish Reservoir and continued until 1934, when three men attempted to manage it as West Glocester Light & Power Company with little success. The electric service was then taken over by Narragansett Electric in 1936. This 1970s photo was taken near the mill pond dam.

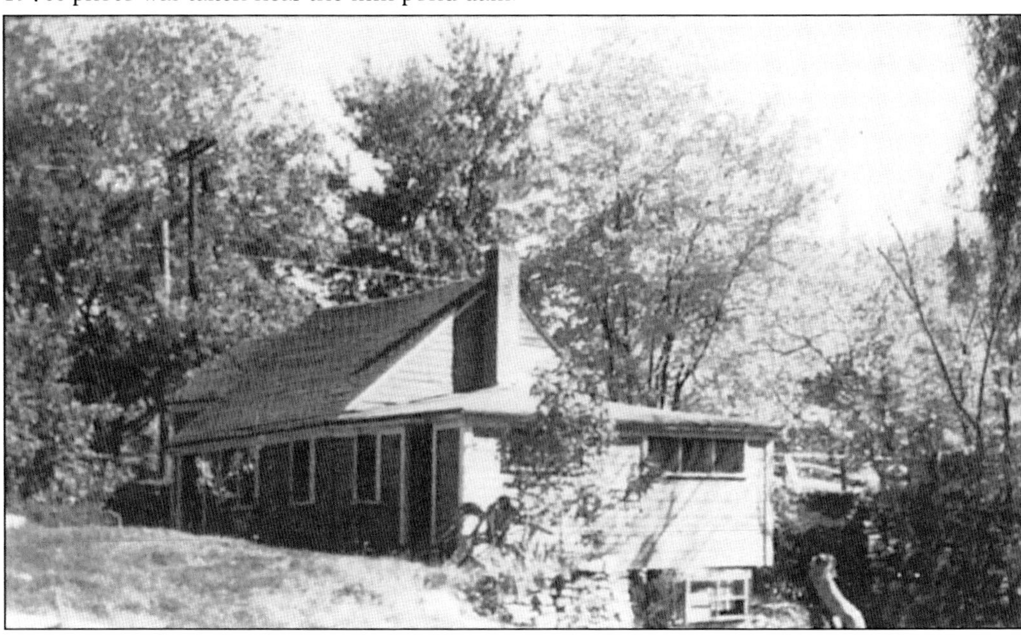

Arthur Boucher made his home for many years in Sheldon's old gristmill, pictured here in the 1970s on Gristmill Road in the Williams's Mills section of West Glocester. The little bridge over the falls can be seen to the right of the mill. On the opposite side of the road is a residence which began as a cooperage (at left just out of this picture).

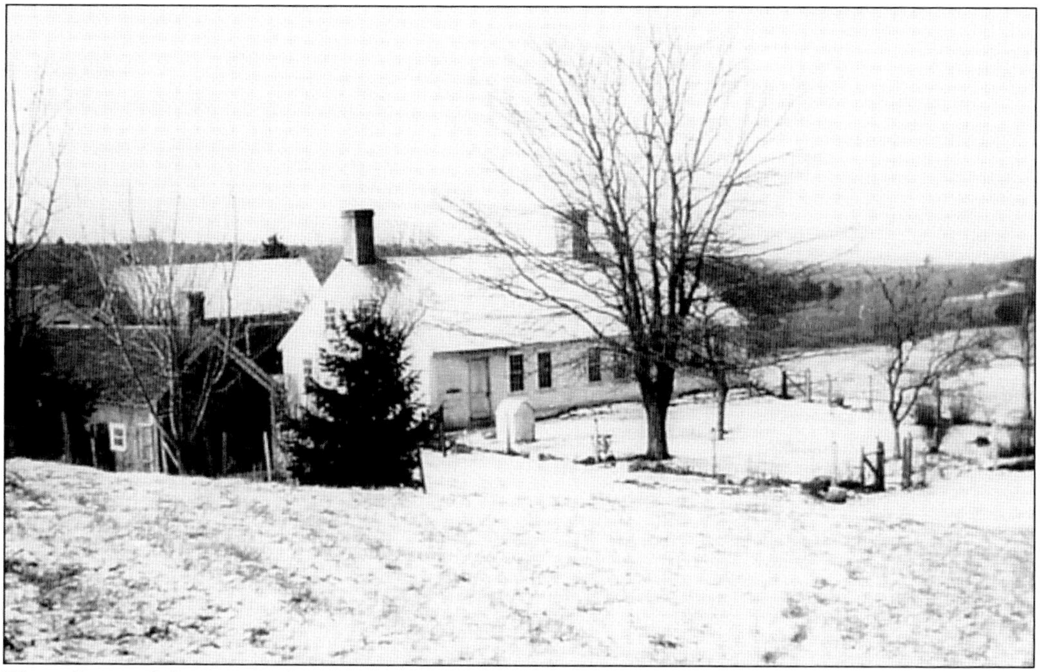

This photo of the Jeremiah Smith farm was taken about 1920. The house, built in 1791, is in the Shady Oak District south of Williams's Mills on the Reynolds Road (Rt. 94). It is one of very few 18th-century Glocester homes continuously inhabited by direct descendants.

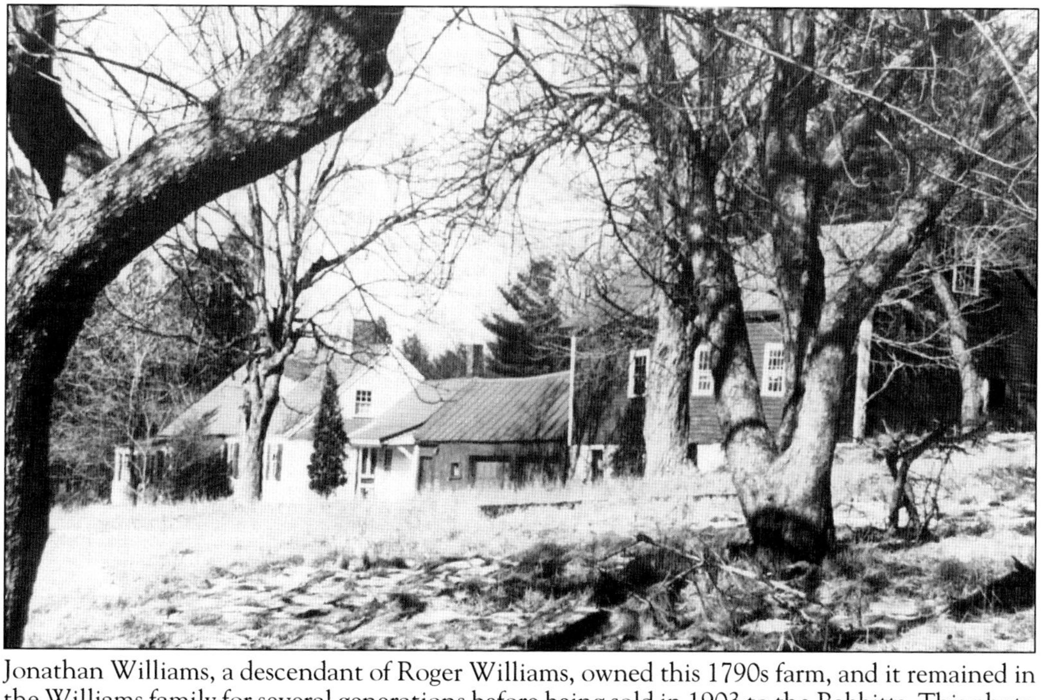

Jonathan Williams, a descendant of Roger Williams, owned this 1790s farm, and it remained in the Williams family for several generations before being sold in 1903 to the Babbitts. This photo was taken in 1968 just before the cow barn (at right) burned. The present owners purchased the farm a few months later.

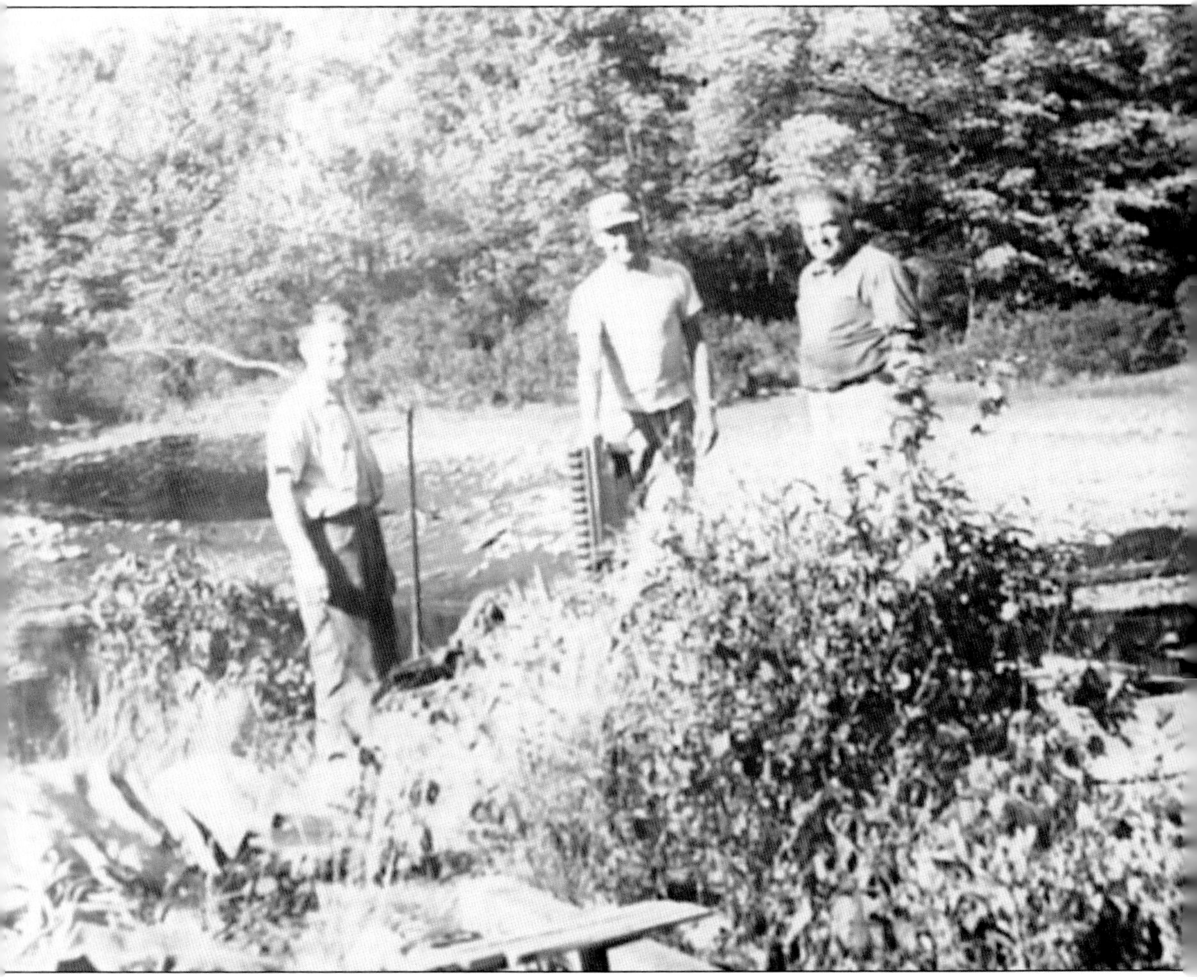

Replacing a gate at the Bowdish Dam in 1951 are Francis Keach, Jason Cutler, and Henry Hawkins. This was one of many responsibilities in owning a water right. The Hawkins family had several gates to maintain.

Seven

Cherry Valley and South Glocester

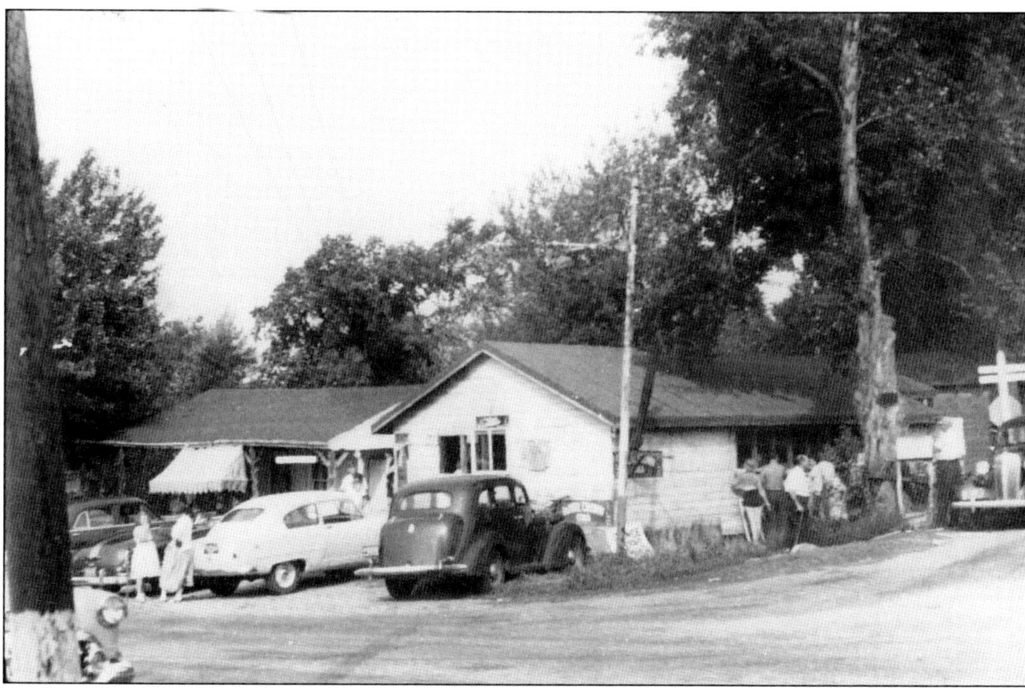

The Cherry Valley Store at the corner of Chopmist Hill Road and Snake Hill Road became even more popular when a dance barn was added on the south side in the 1940s. Every Friday they served clam cakes and chowder. Wilson Peckham came to fry the clam cakes, the fiddlers tuned up, and dancing continued most of the night.

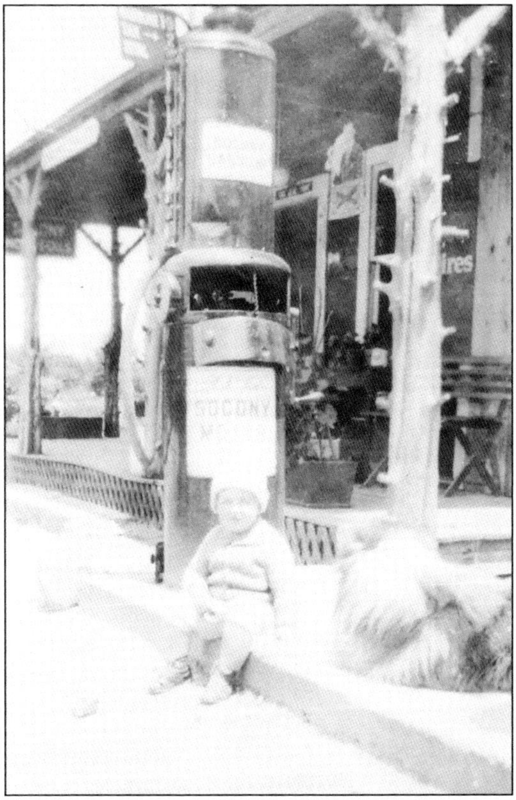

This photo of Charlie Sherman was taken about 1950 at the Cherry Valley Store. According to the sign, Socony gas was selling for 21¢ a gallon.

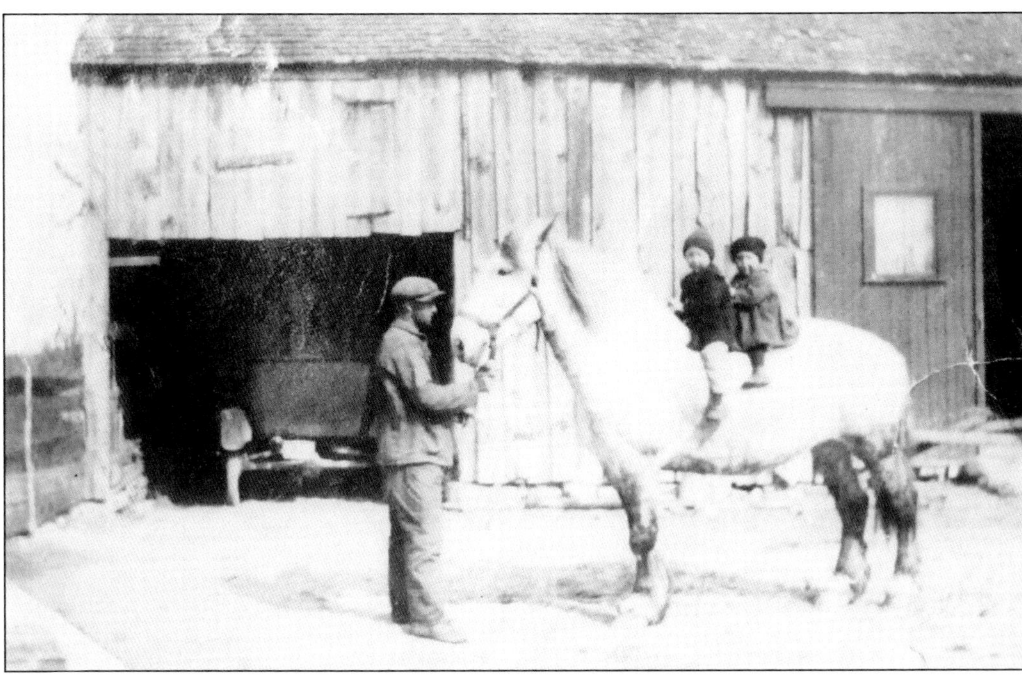

Will Sherman holds the horse while Charles and his sister Ruth get set for a ride. They are in front of Burgess's barn on Trap Schoolhouse Road about 1916.

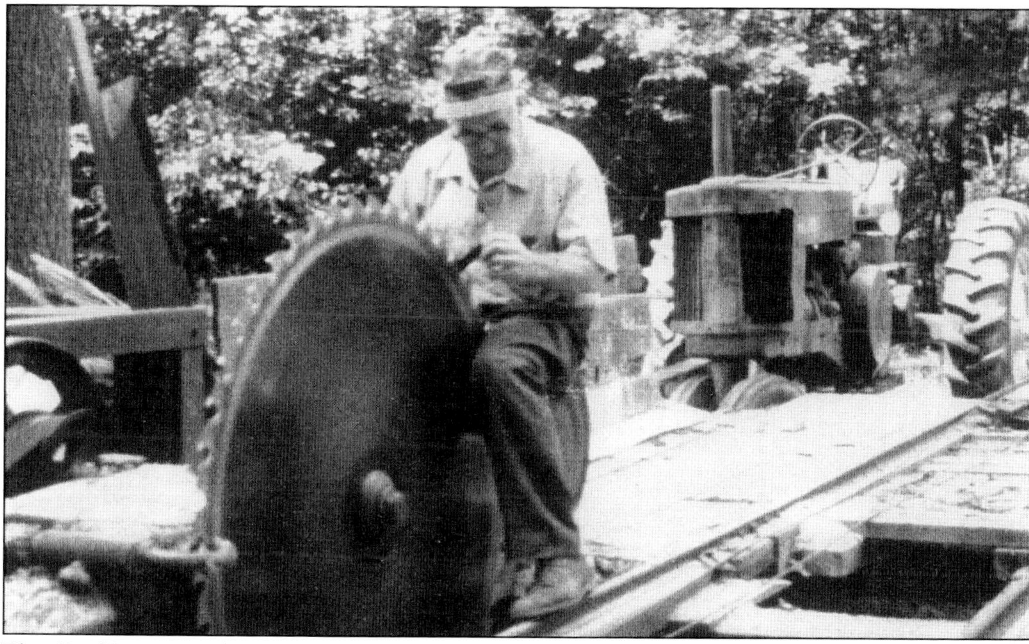

Elias Peckham was sharpening the circular saw at his sawmill up on Ham Hill on Chopmist Hill Road when his daughter took this photo in the 1960s.

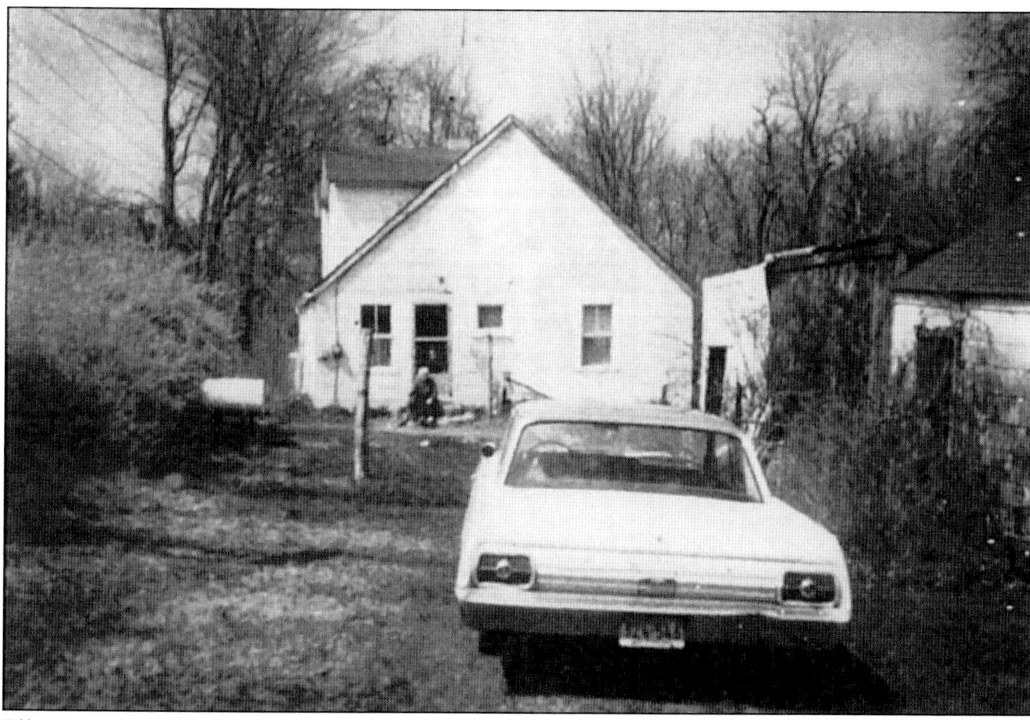

Ella Steere sits on the doorstep at her brother Philip's house on a warm spring day in the 1950s. The first Cherry Valley Store she operated was out of the little barn closest to the house. The large dormer windows on the second floor of the house were added in the early 1900s.

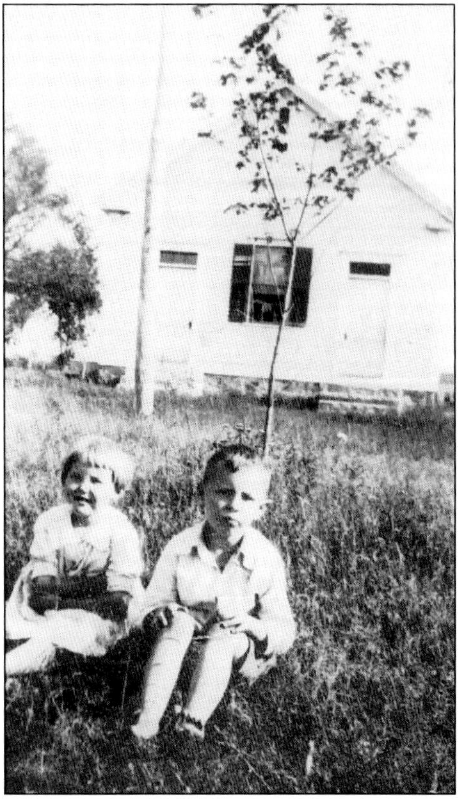

Ruth and Charles Sherman sit on the lawn in front of the second Cherry Valley School about 1920. In later years, Charles purchased the building from the town and made it home for his family—to whom it still belongs to this day.

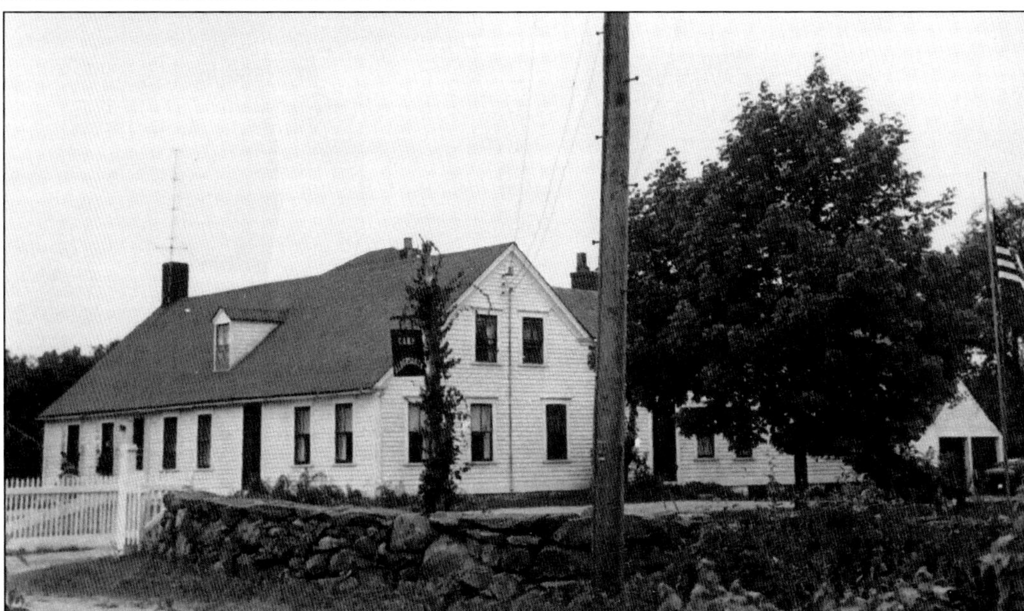

The old 18th-century Elisha Hawkins house became the residence of Horace Steere in the late 1800s. It became the Grace Church Camp, then the Aldersgate Methodist Camp. Although this 150-year-old dwelling burned in the 1940s, Camp Aldersgate continues today with more modern summer camping facilities.

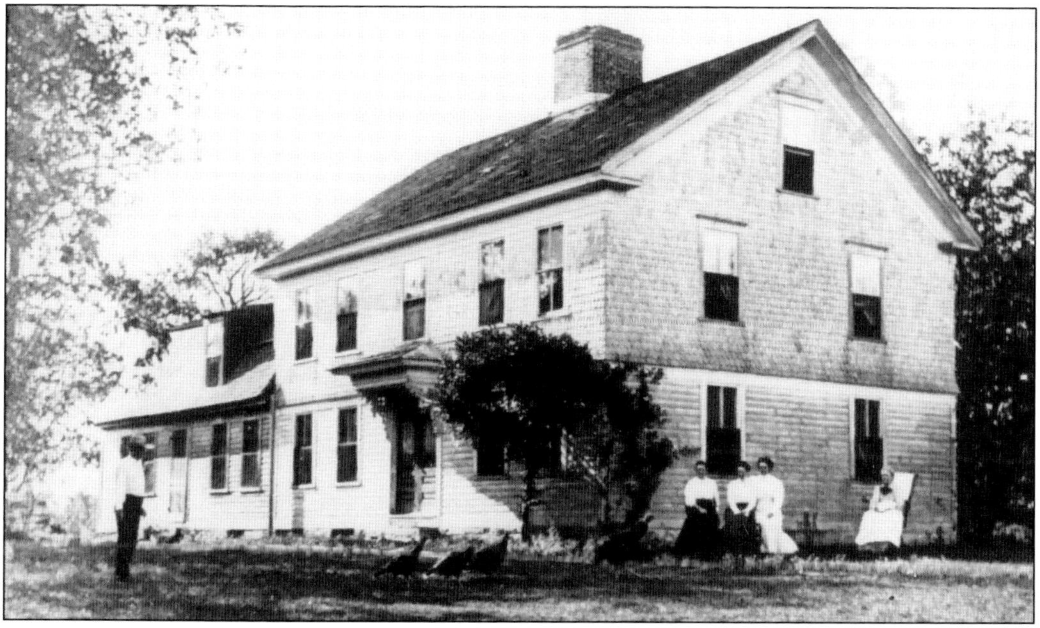

Although the people in the picture are not named, the photograph was taken in the late 1880s when the Burlingame family lived there. During the Revolutionary War, John Fenner kept a slave named Jockwhy here, who ran away. An ad described him and offered a $6 reward. Originally the house was built by James Brown about 1728 on the hill overlooking Cherry Valley.

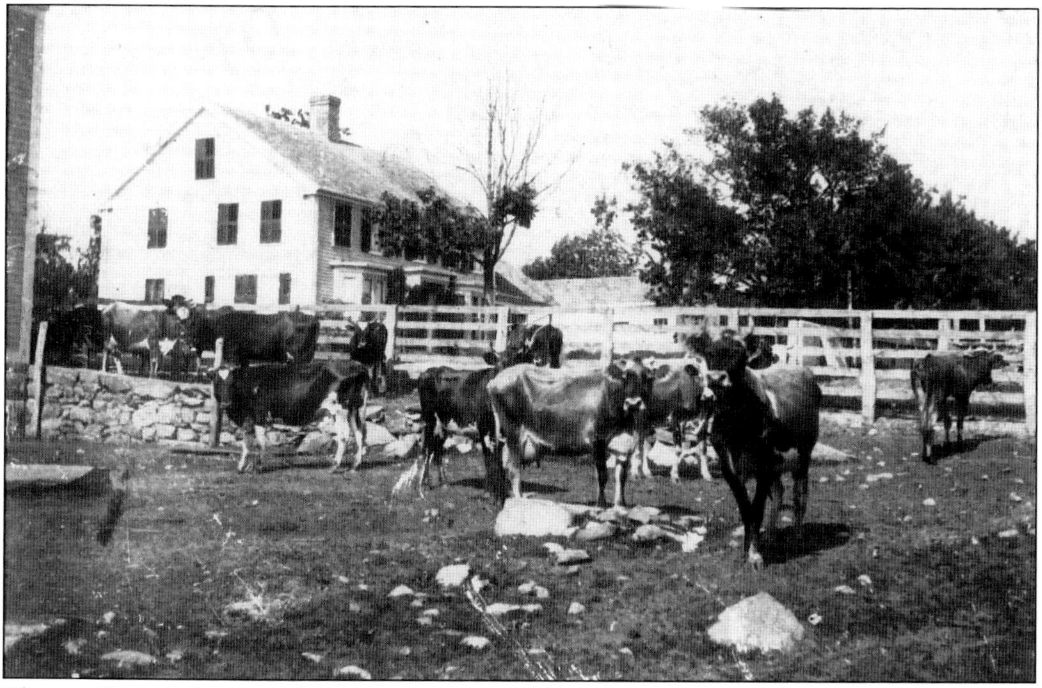

Thomas Steere's house and barn were separated by Chopmist Hill Road (beyond the fence). As a wagon path, it posed little hazard, but when widened for automobiles, the newly opened Victory Highway claimed Mr. Steere as its first auto/pedestrian fatality.

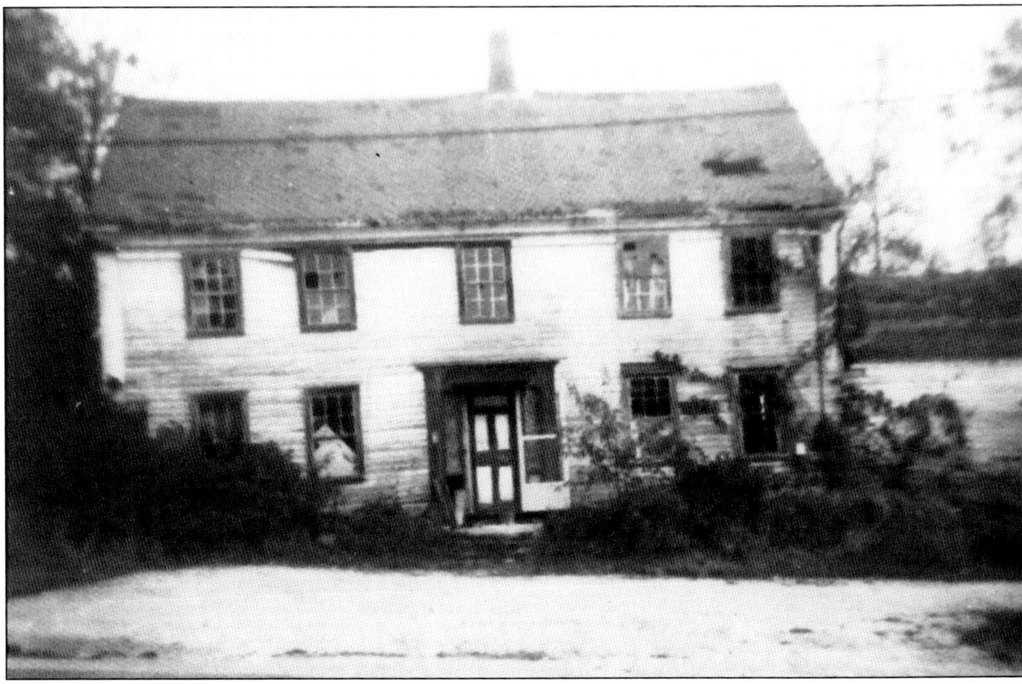

The old Joseph Winsor house stood across from the entrance to Stone Dam Road on Snake Hill Road. It belonged to C. Winsor in 1870, but by about the turn of the century, it became home to the Peckham family.

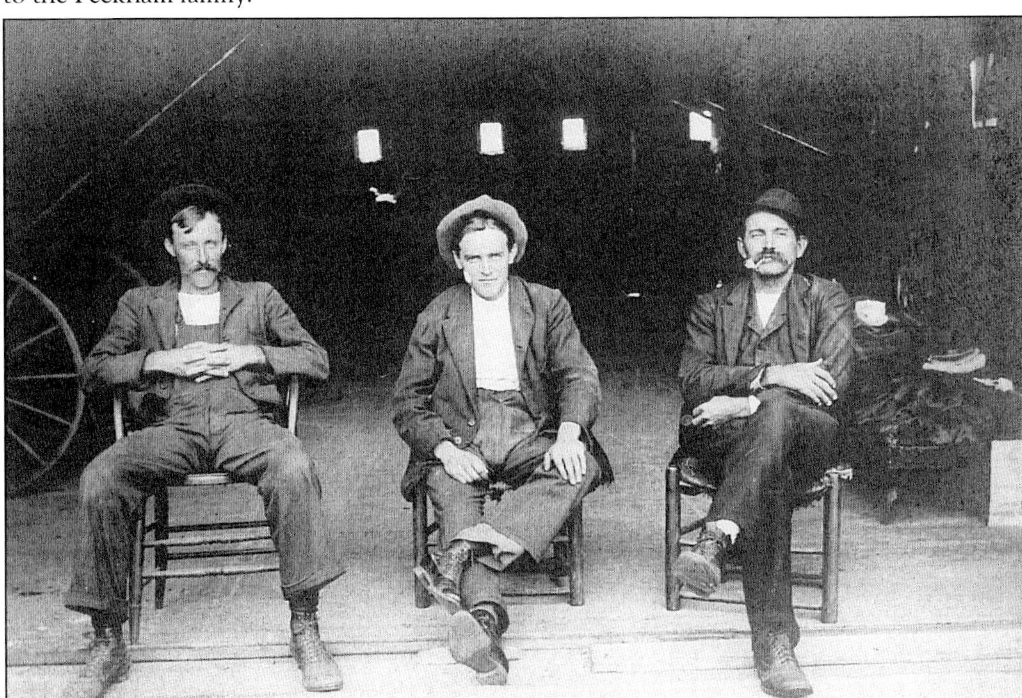

Charles Salisbury (center) is seen here with some unnamed visitors. This photo is believed to have been taken at Peckham's barn on Snake Hill Road about 1900.

Charles Peckham revisited the old Peckham Gristmill on November 10, 1957. With his hand on the grain hopper, he recalled the operation of the mill. The huge round grinding stones would be concealed within the wooden box below the hopper.

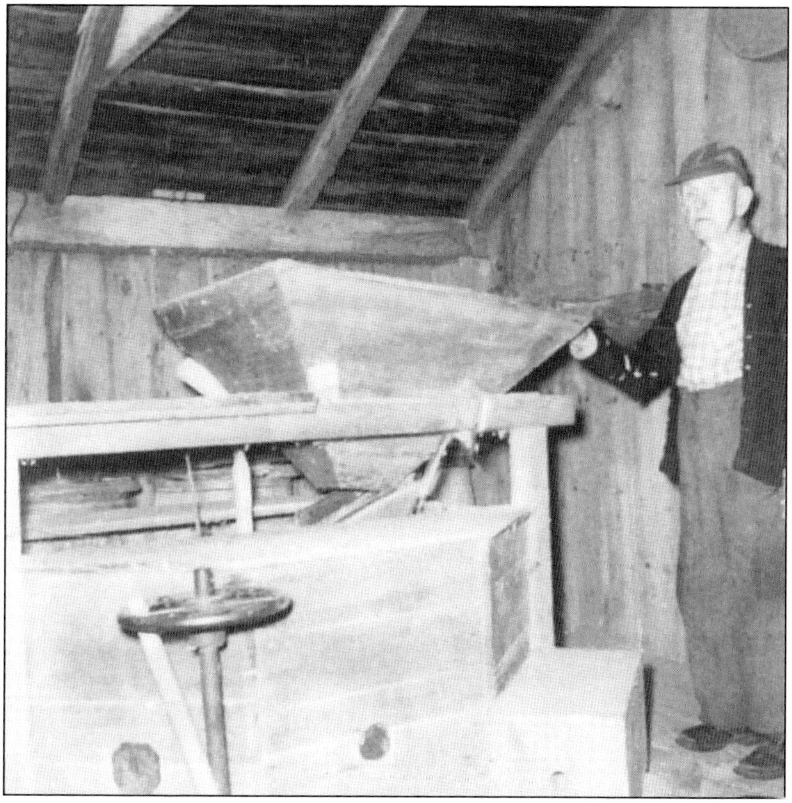

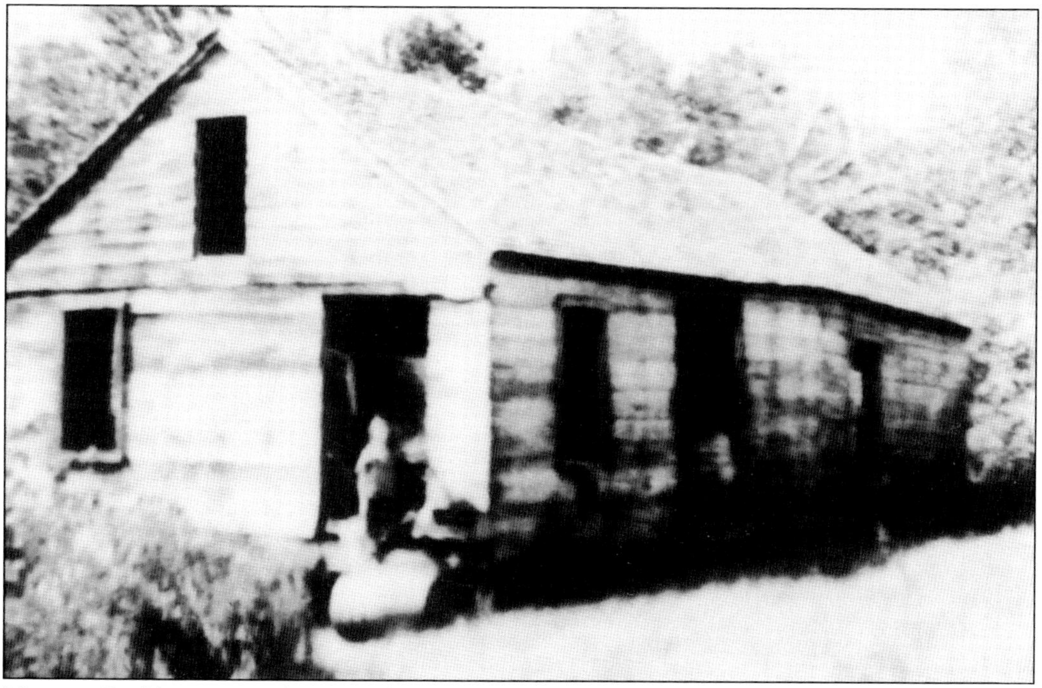

Marjorie Peckham is standing on a barrel at the door to Peckham's old cider mill on Snake Hill Road about 1940.

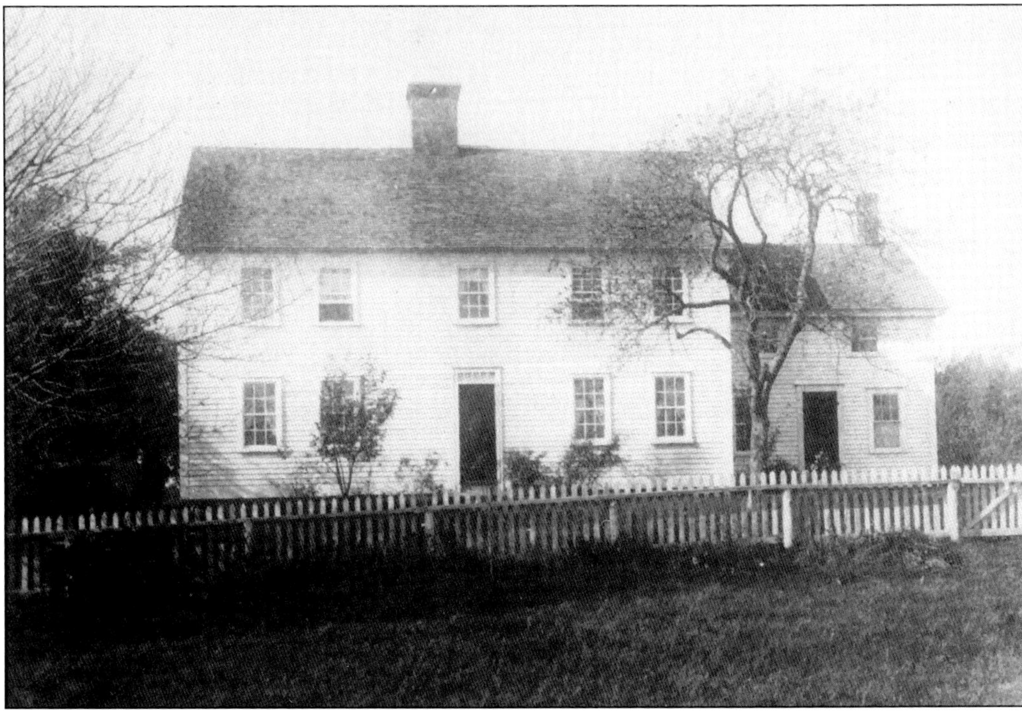

The old Parris Irons house is a fine example of an 18th-century, two-and-one-half-story country residence. The house faces south to take advantage of the sun for both heat and light. Parris Irons' Road runs north and south to the right of this early 1900s photo.

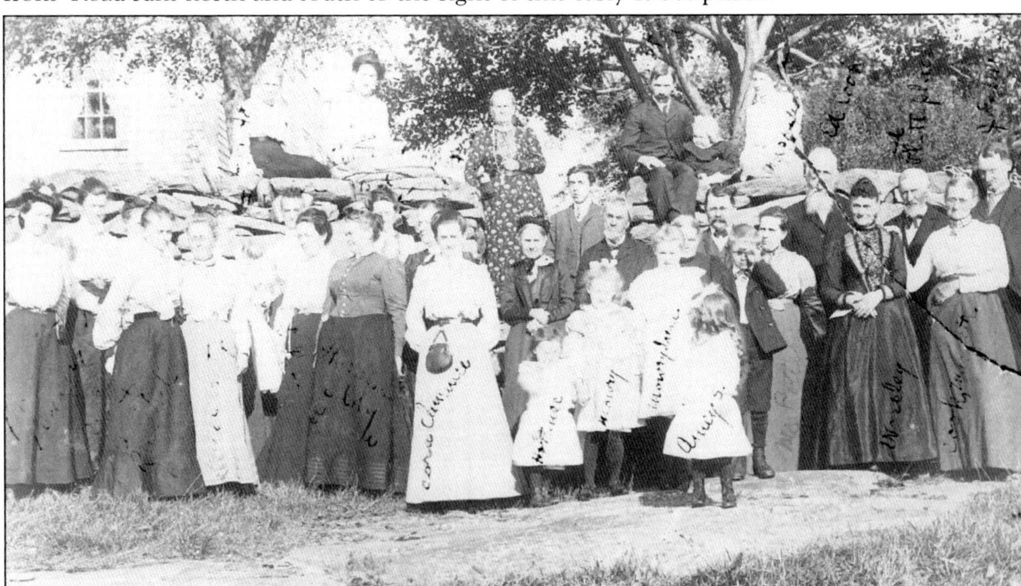

This gathering took place in September 1903 at Parris Irons Farm. Included are (front row) Florence Keach, Ella Steere, Rachael ?, Mrs. Swartz, Betty Potter, Hannah Eddy Penno, Cora Clemence, M. Potter, Mrs. Worsley, and Mrs. Cook; (the children) Hortense Steere, ? Mowry, Irene Mowry, Amey Steere, ?; (back row) Karen Steere, H. Paine, Belle Sweet, Ed Cook, Ed Phetteplace, and Jesse Mowry; (on the wall) Mrs. Spaulding, Marion Irons, and Annie Steere.

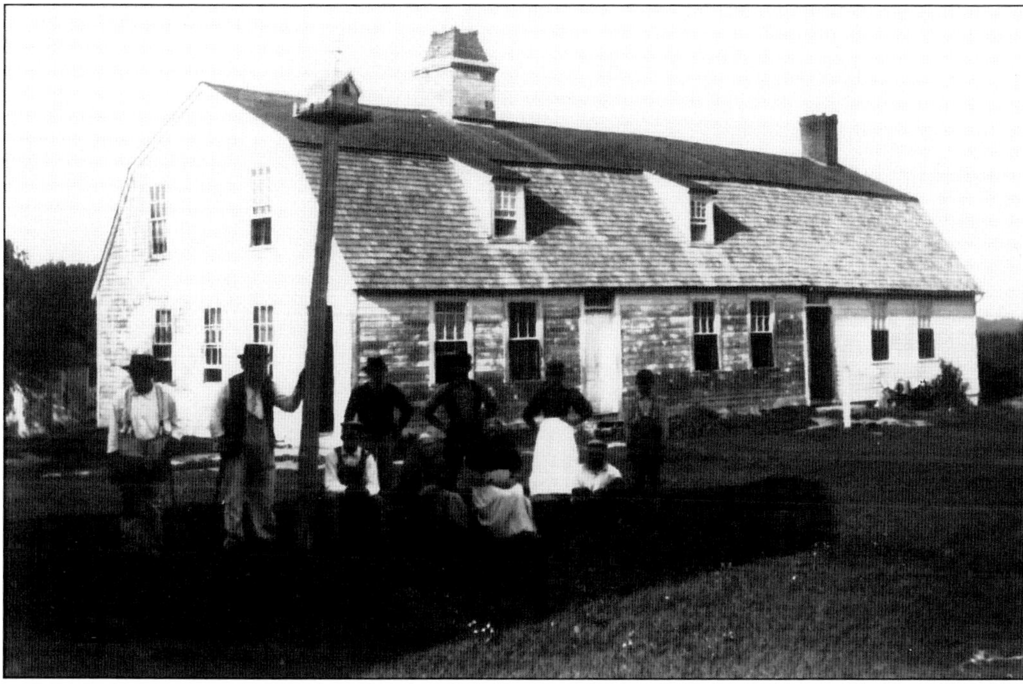

The Poor Farm residents on Tourtellot Hill Road posed for a cameraman in the 1880s. Stephen Paine's homestead farm since before 1732 became the Glocester Poor Farm when Jeremiah Mathewson sold it to the Town in 1851. In order to help with their upkeep, the residents at the Poor Farm cut wood, made fence posts and caskets, sold garden produce and eggs, and harvested apples.

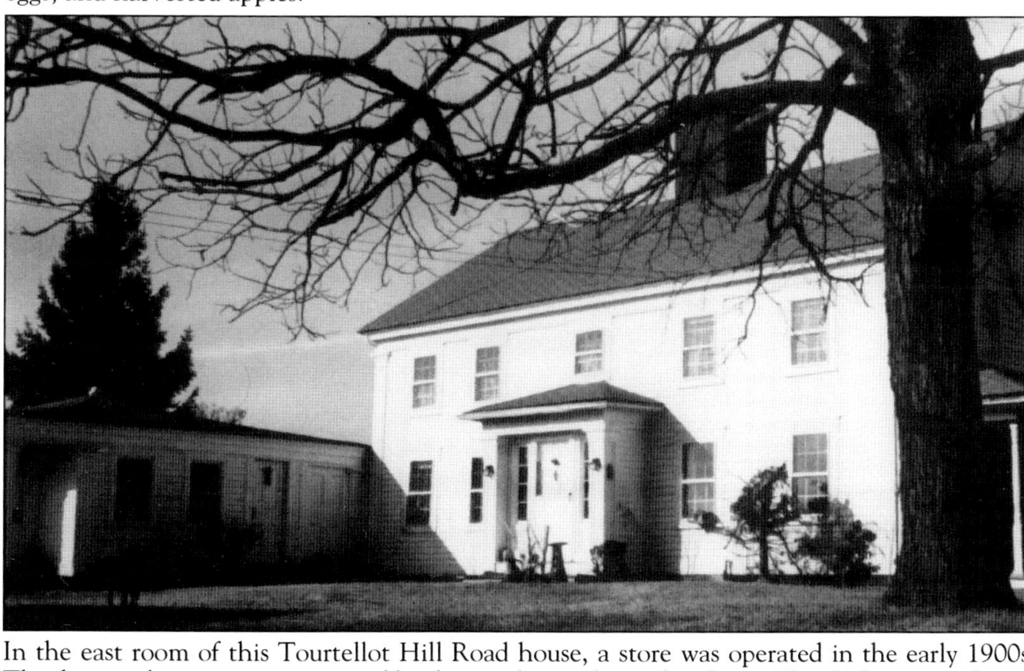

In the east room of this Tourtellot Hill Road house, a store was operated in the early 1900s. The door to that room was accessed by the porch at right in the photo. This 18th-century house belonged to Gideon Mowry before the Revolutionary War.

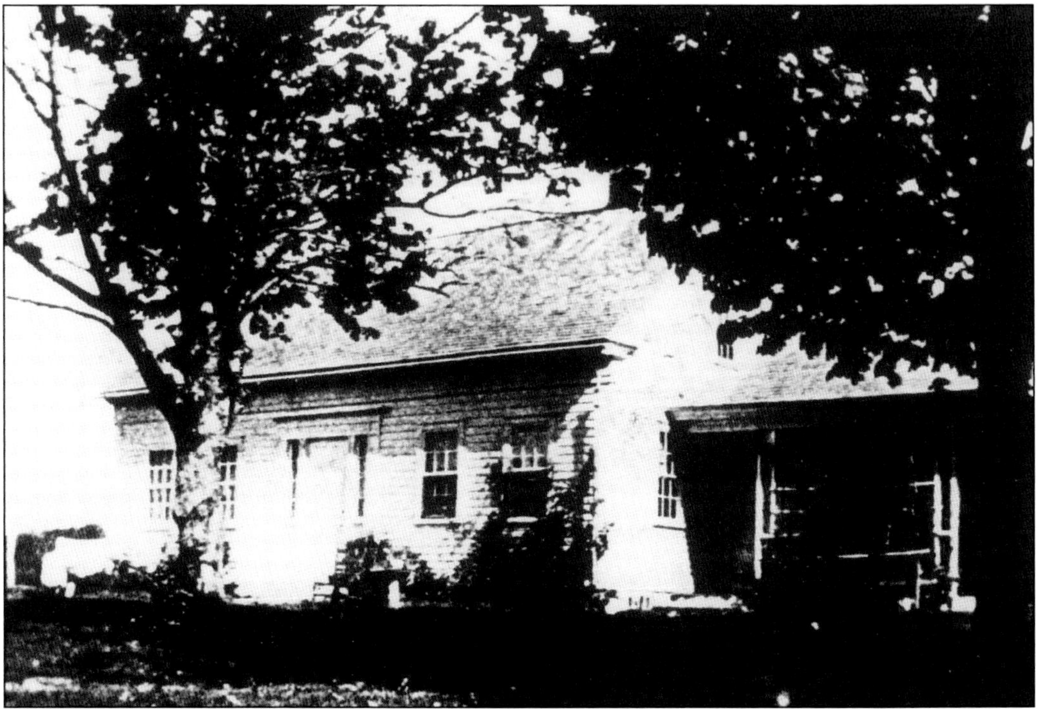

This Greek Revival house stood on Chestnut Hill Road around the corner from Elbow Rock Road. In the latter half of the 19th century, it was home to the G. Sprague family. It burned in the 1930s when John Lewin owned it.

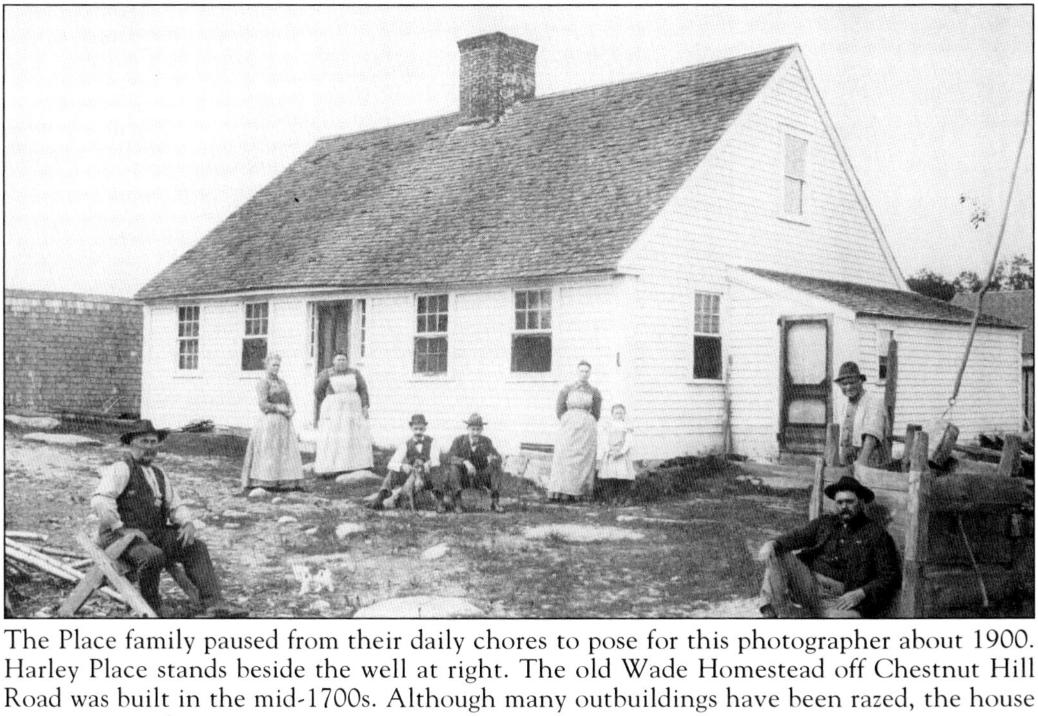

The Place family paused from their daily chores to pose for this photographer about 1900. Harley Place stands beside the well at right. The old Wade Homestead off Chestnut Hill Road was built in the mid-1700s. Although many outbuildings have been razed, the house is now restored.

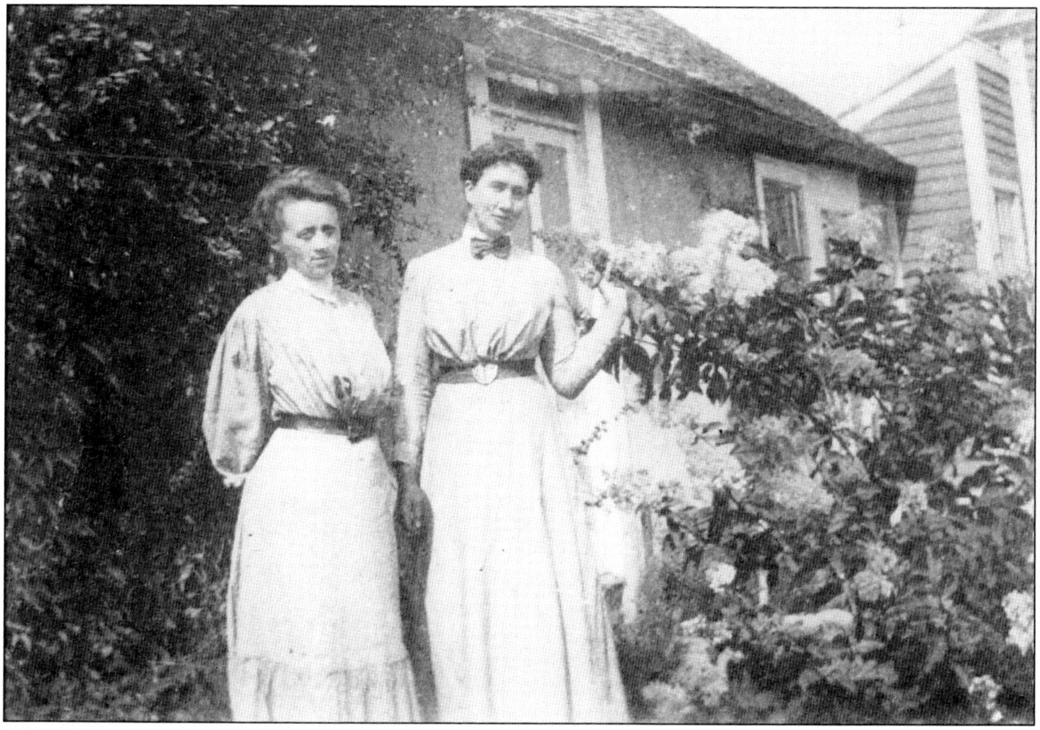

Clara Burgess and sister-in-law Effie stand beside the hydrangea bush at Burgess's house on Trap Schoolhouse Road about 1912. Effie Burgess was a midwife who tenderly administered to Cherry Valley's sick and injured, as well as delivering babies.

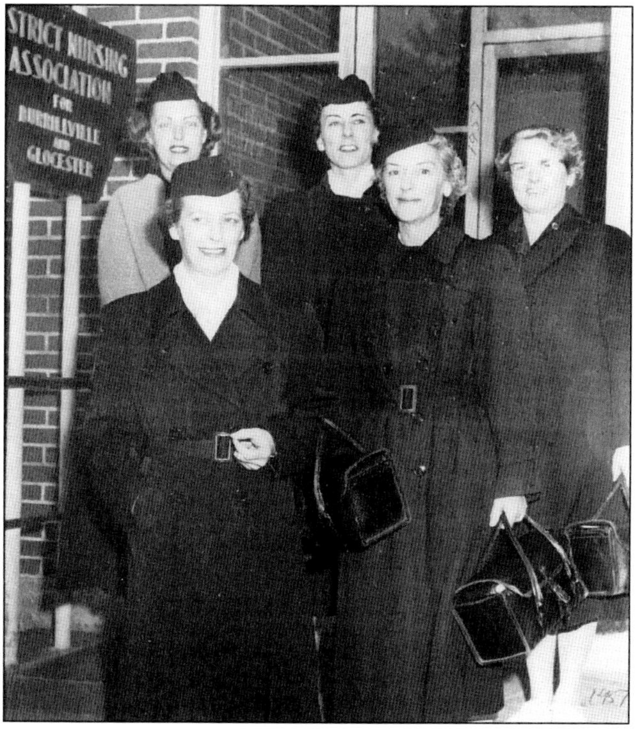

Ready for a day's work in 1957 are Marjorie Rhodes, Eileen Dwyer, Clarice Manly, and Betsy Pepper (behind Margaret Fogarty, who headed the District Nurses Association for the Burrillville/Glocester region). Through all kinds of weather these ladies logged hundreds of miles annually serving the health needs of the two towns. Their smiling faces and calm professionalism made the darkest day a little brighter.

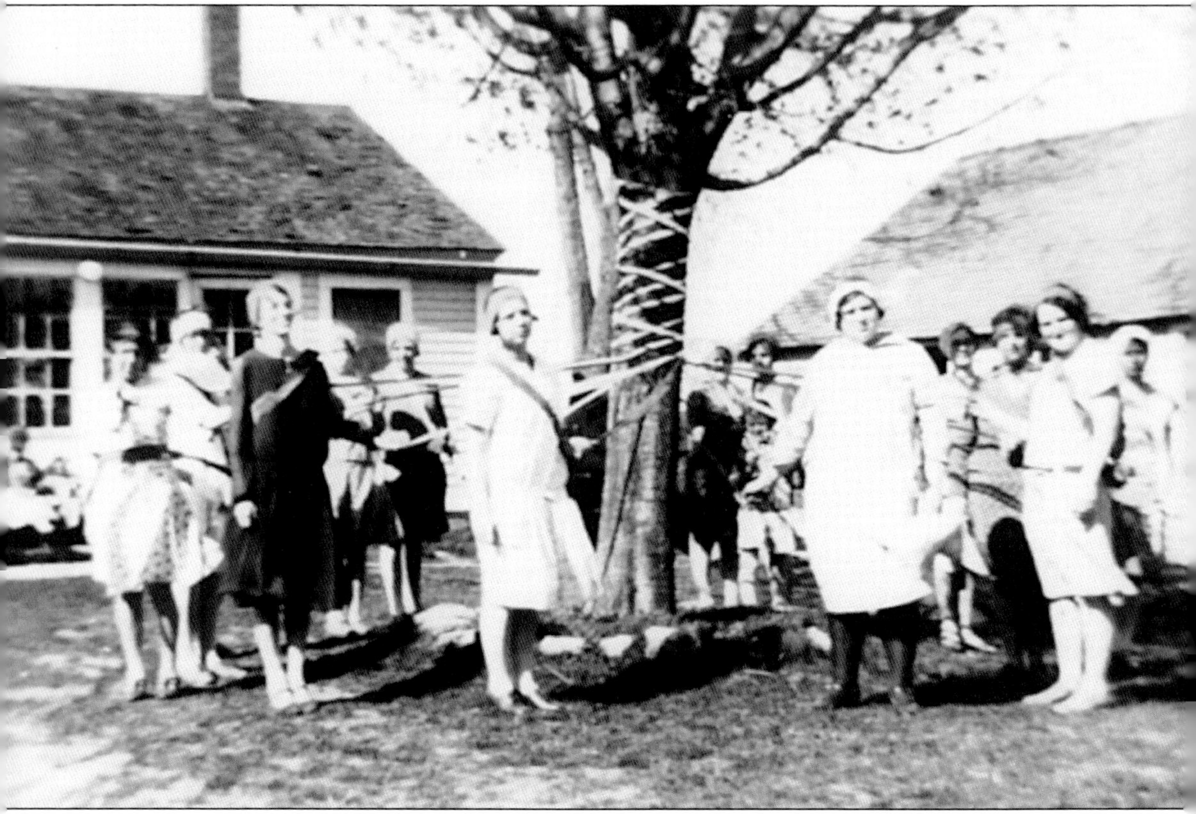

The ladies' group pictured here about 1937 were twining the Maypole on a tree at Marion Iron's home on Snake Hill Road. The older Irons house is in the background at right.

Eight

Parades, Entertainment, and Events

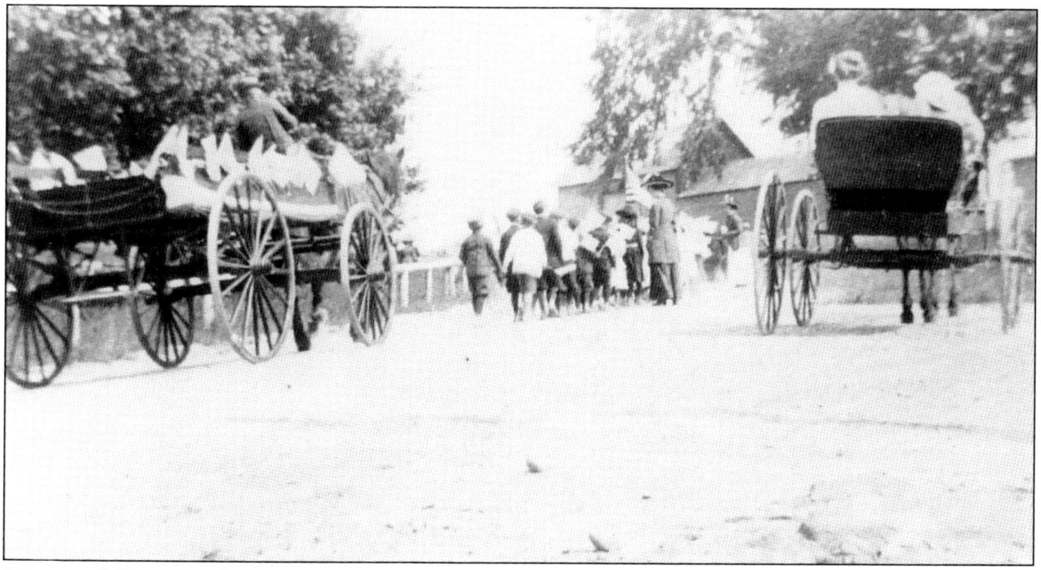

Memorial Day parade followers round the bend at Acote's Hill on the way to the cemetery in the 1890s. Ever since the Civil War, children have carried flowers and accompanied veterans to decorate the graves of those who died in battle. The photographer stood at the intersection of Putnam Pike and Chopmist Hill Road for this view.

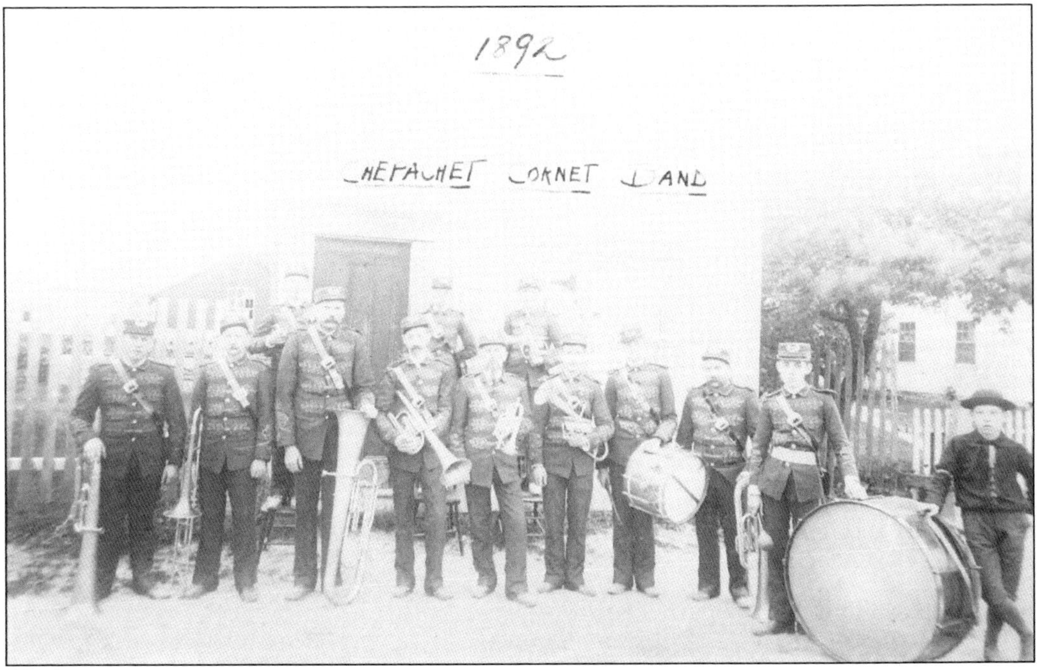

The Chepachet Cornet Band stands in front of the band house on Douglas Hook Road in 1892. J. Curtis Hopkins holds the cornet behind the tallest man, Eugene Eddy. James Greenhalgh is to the right, standing next to Eddy.

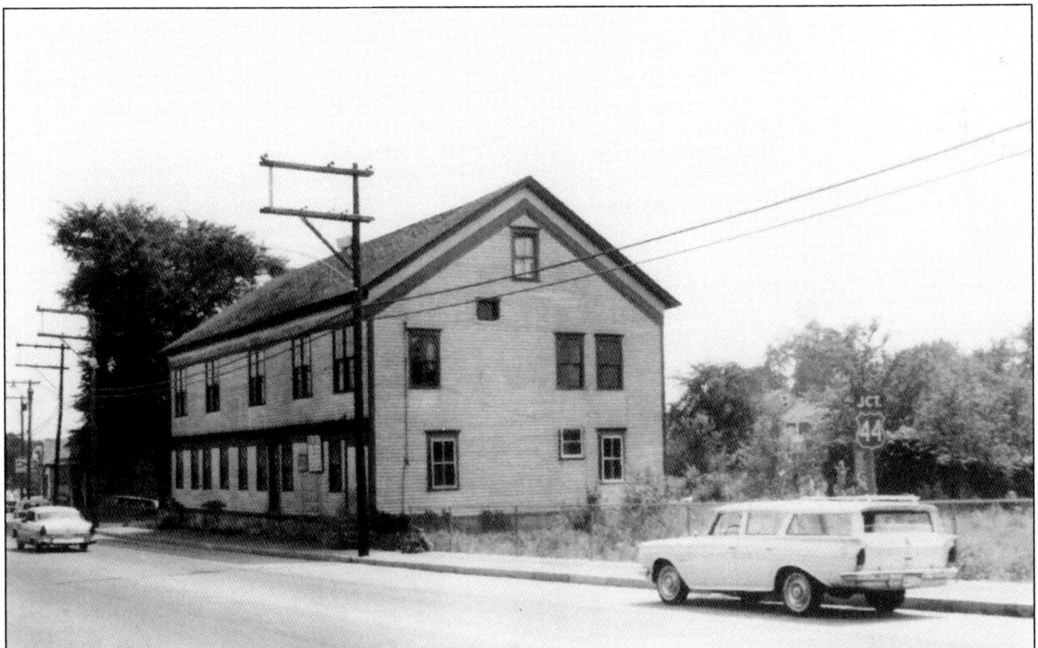

The AOUW Hall was last occupied by Clear River Mill. The "FOR SALE" sign eventually came down as did the building. It was originally built by Thomas Steere for the American Order of United Workers. On the second floor was a theater where plays, musicals, and, later, movies were presented. Today, Dairy Mart on Victory Highway occupies this lot.

Musical and Literary

ENTERTAINMENT

A. O. U. W. HALL,

Chepachet, R. I., ________

Saturday Evening, Jan. 25, 1896.

ADMISSION 10 AND 15 CENTS.

Doors open at 7 o'clock. Commences at 7.45 o'clock.

Programme

1 MUSIC—Instrumental . . . . . . Miss Maude Read
2 READING . . . . Edwin Dimock
3 TABLEAUX—Choice of State Flower.
4 MUSIC—Banjo Solo . . . . . . Mr. E. L. Leaf
5 DIALOGUE.
6 READING . . . . Edgar Potter
7 MUSIC—Solo . . . . Miss Flora Sweet
8 DIALOGUE—School Girls' Troubles.
9 TENNYSON'S DREAM OF FAIR WOMEN.

CHARACTERS:

Helen of Troy . . . . . . Miss Mary Wade
Iphigenia . . . . Miss Marian Angell
Cleopatra . . . . Miss Mary Towne
Jephtha's Daughter . . . . . Miss Maude Read
Rosamond . . . . Miss Flora Sweet

10 MUSIC—Duo . . . Messrs. E. L. Leaf and F. G. Widdoes
11 READING . . . . A. E. Legg

Burrillvile Star Print.

Home-grown entertainment such as this was enacted by townspeople occasionally with a guest professional or two who lodged in the village for several weeks. Some of the ladies may be recognized by their married names as follows: Maude Read Farnum, Mary Wade Marvin, and Flora Sweet Reynolds. Note young Edgar Potter listed here before he was a doctor.

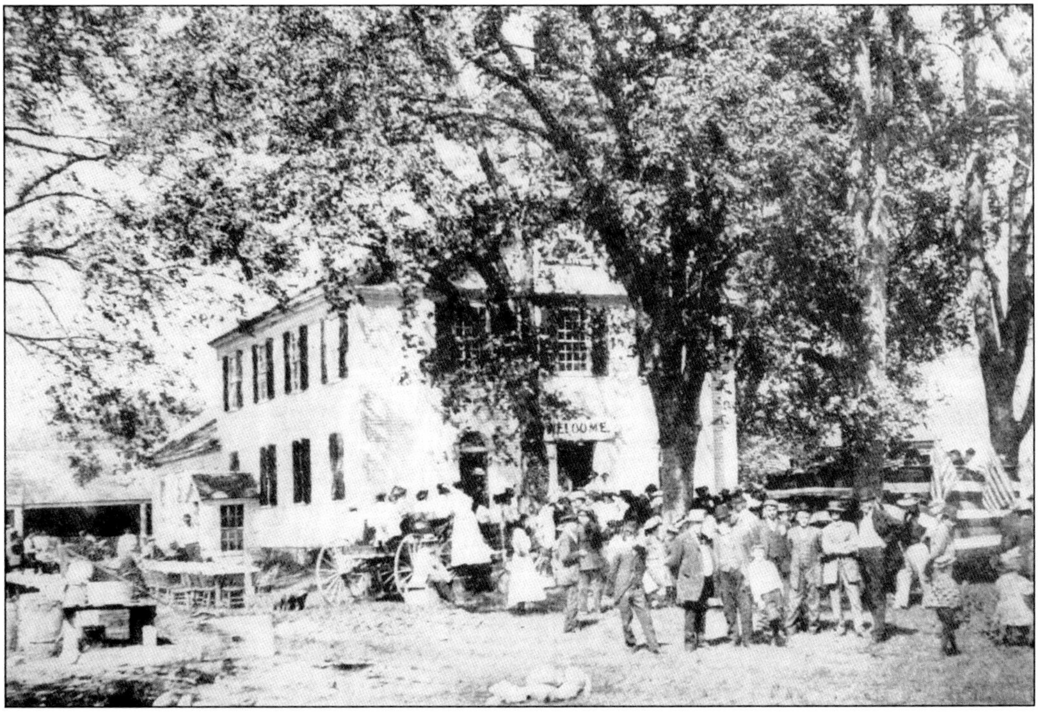

This is one of the first Old Home Days, which began in 1906, at Chepachet Freewill Baptist Church. A "WELCOME" sign over the door greeted old friends and family who had moved away and had returned for the annual reunion. The people may be waiting for the speaker or concert to begin. The long tables, at left, seated several hundred for a shore dinner.

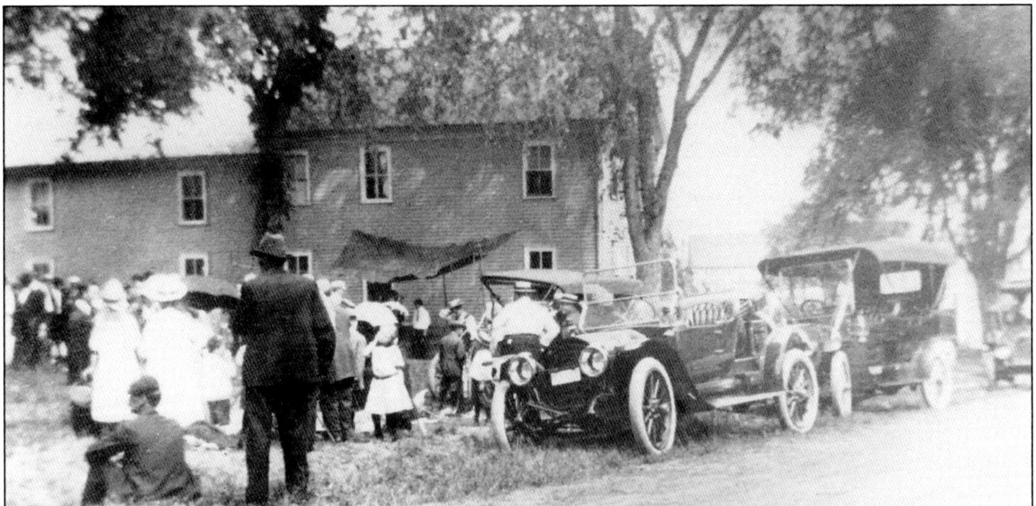

Old Home Day was a family reunion for the whole town, usually held in August. Each year the crowds grew larger. Cars lined the streets and flags and bunting decorated stores and homes. This photo was taken from Putnam Pike across the Baptist church lawn. The Benjamin White house is in the background.

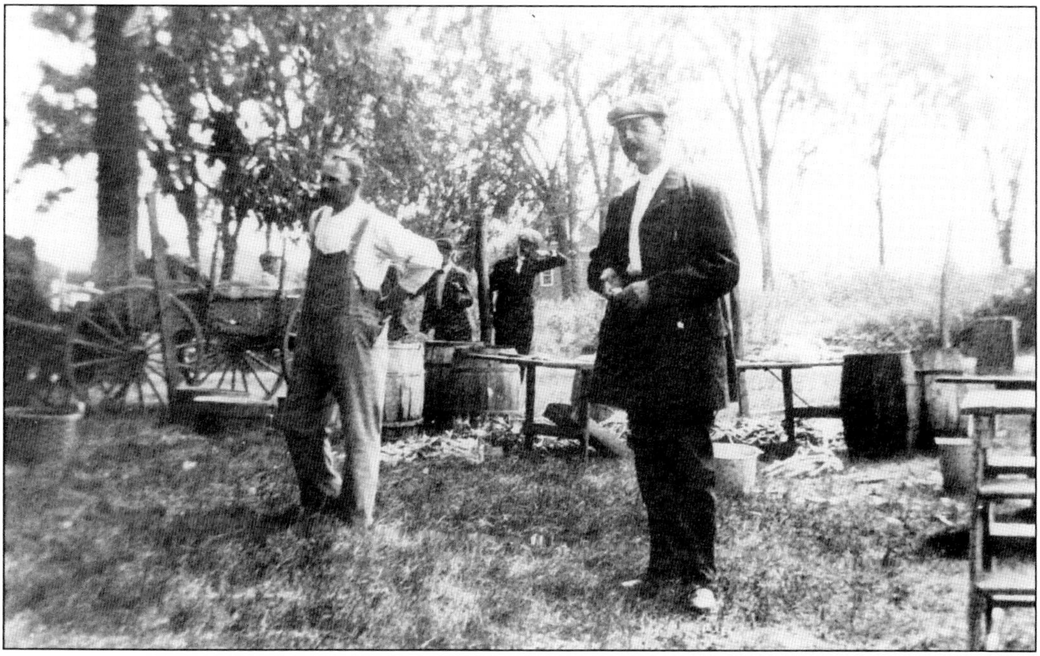

On the morning of Old Home Day, the barrels were lined with seaweed and then filled with clams. The watches are in hand and the men await the bakemaster's signal to begin. Everything was carefully timed so that all the food arrived steaming hot at the tables.

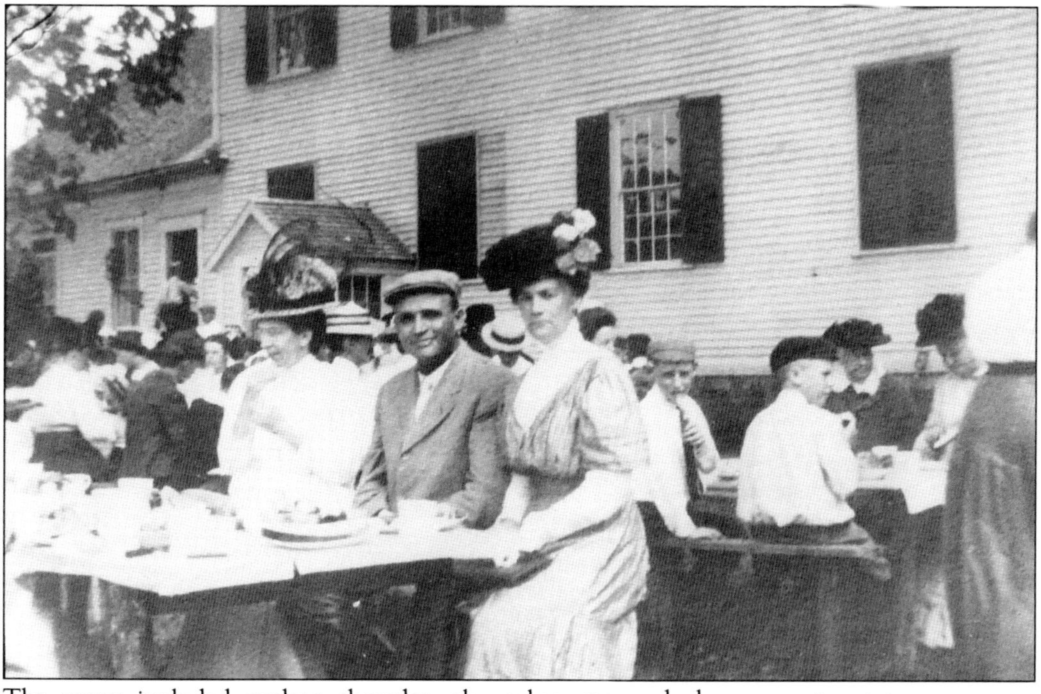

The menu included quahog chowder, clamcakes, steamed clams, sweet potatoes, corn on the cob, and watermelon. More and more seatings were necessary to accommodate the ever-increasing crowds that attended Old Home Day, which continued until World War II.

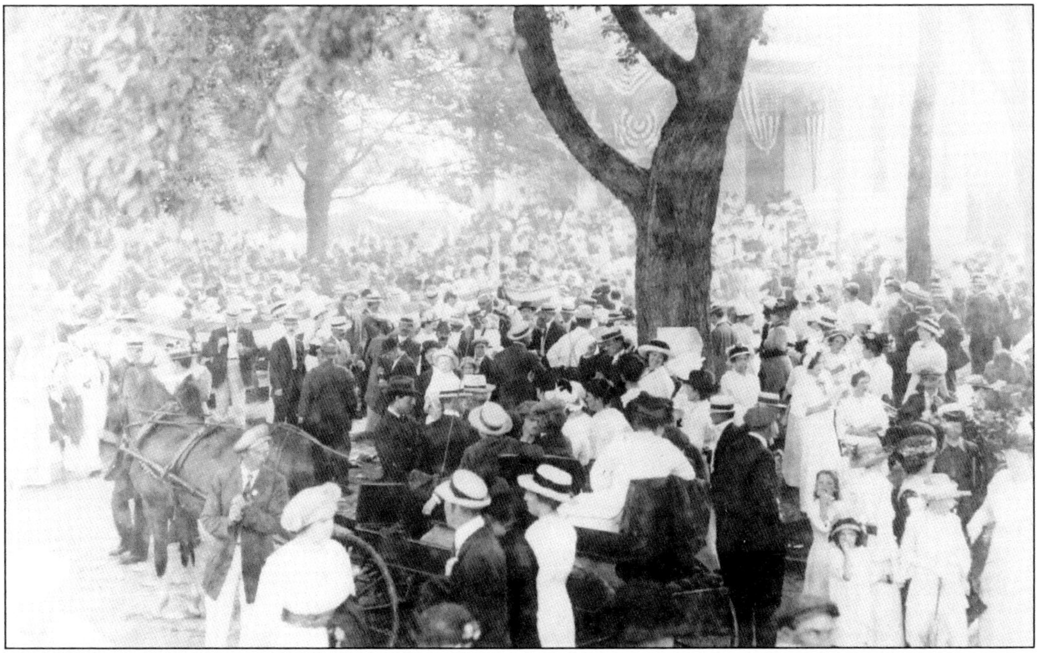

On July 25, 1914, the town put on the largest celebration Chepachet had ever seen. Bunting decorated most Glocester buildings along the trolley line on Putnam Pike. The shore dinner was prepared at the Chepachet Union Church with seating for five hundred. Those standing in this picture are most likely waiting for the next seating. Tom Shippee, in a cap, waits his turn beside the horse in the left foreground.

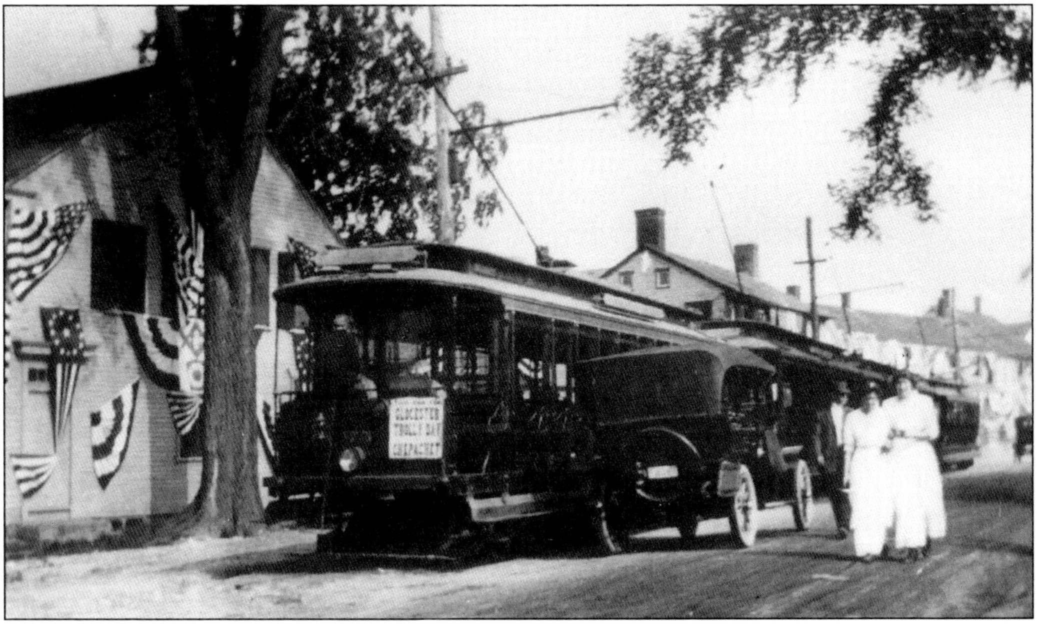

The trolley tracks ended in front of the Masonic Hall, so the trolleys that arrived on Trolley Day were backed up on that single track. There are five trolleys in this photo. These people appear to have come away early from the celebration at the church. Too many speakers, perhaps?

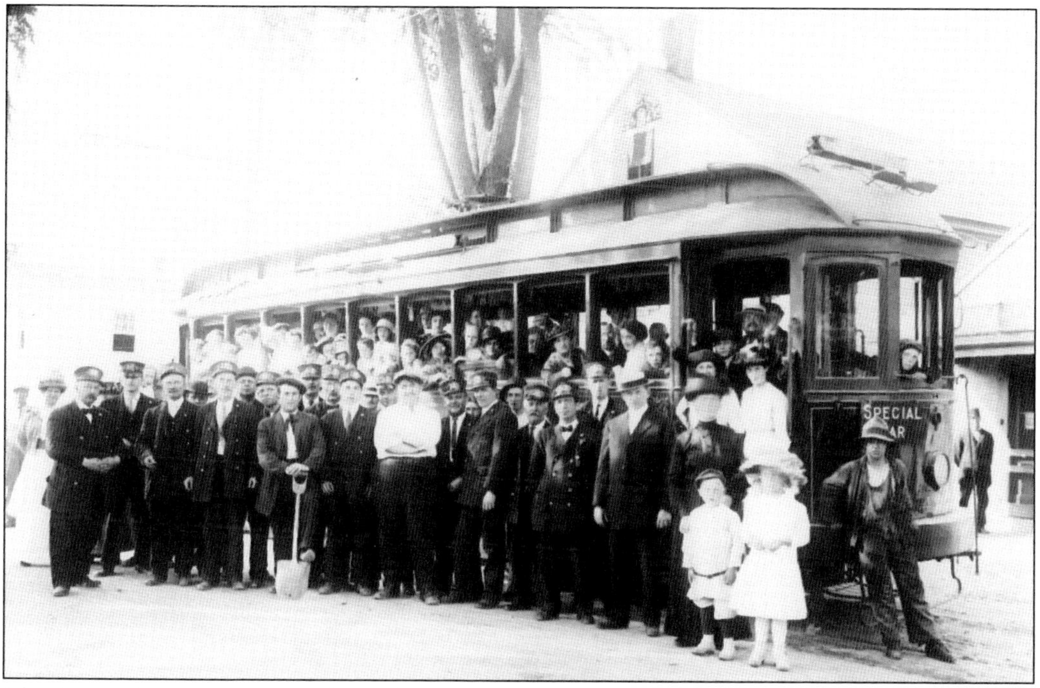

The first trolley to come to Chepachet arrived on June 30, 1914. Posing for the photographer are (in front) Frank Davis in a straw hat; the boy and girl are George and Dorothy Hopkins. Frank Potter, in a straw hat, stands behind Cora Shippee on the steps. Jennie and Cora Greenhalgh are seated inside with elbows out the windows. Deforest Richmond stands under the porch at the store.

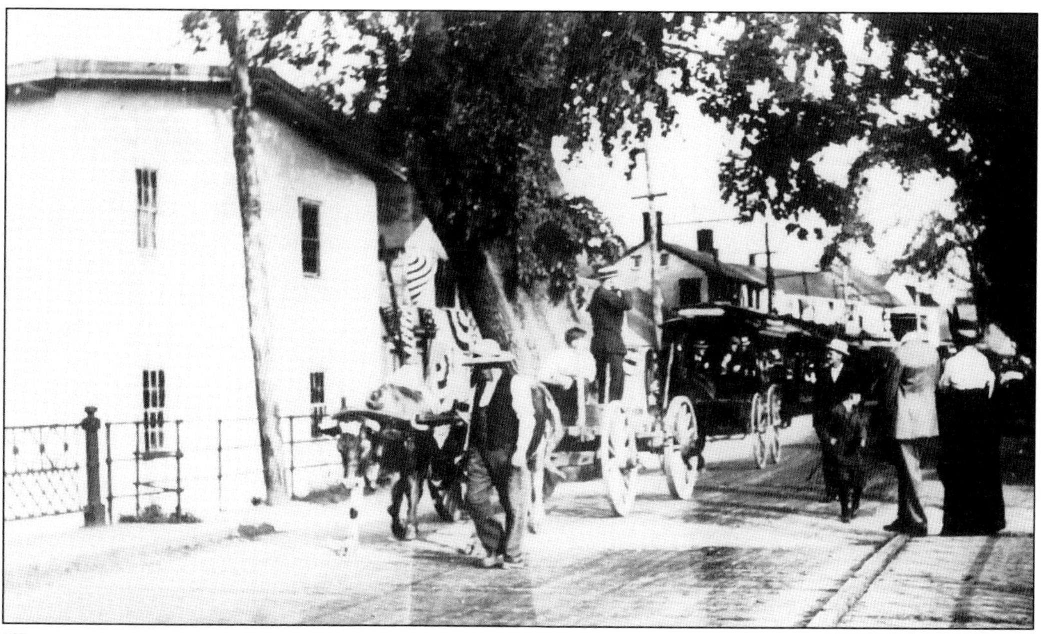

"Tot" Mars is leading his ox team across Chepachet Bridge after being in the parade. The trolleys can be seen in the distance. Everything from stagecoaches and autos to goat carts and bicycles, all decorated with bunting, joined in the Trolley Day parade.

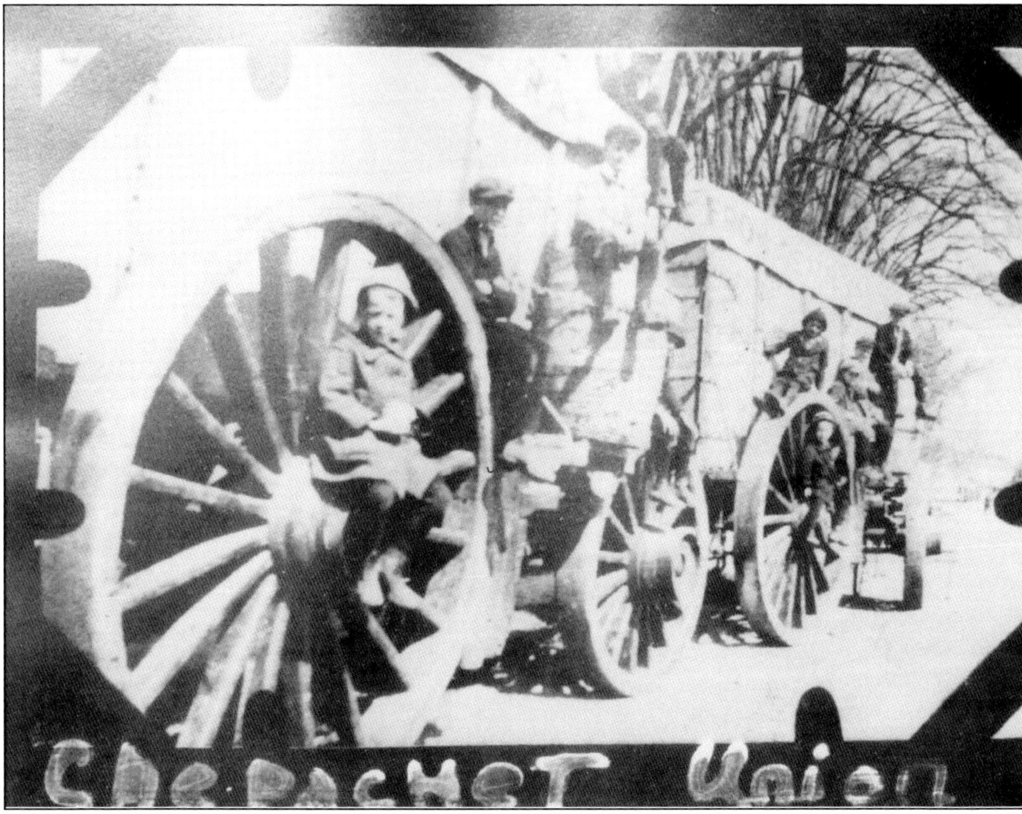

In 1917, the 20-Mule Team came through Chepachet hauling wagonloads of borax and stopped to rest their mules. They had traveled from Death Valley, California, and were headed to Portland, Maine. The boy on the closest wheel is Harvey Steere. The reason for the unusual frame around the photo is unknown.

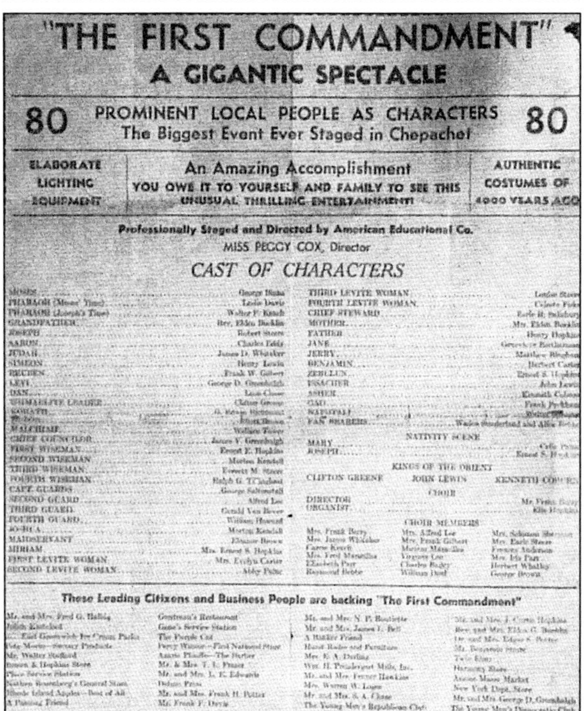

"THE FIRST COMMANDMENT"

A GIGANTIC SPECTACLE

80 PROMINENT LOCAL PEOPLE AS CHARACTERS 80

The Biggest Event Ever Staged in Chepachet

ELABORATE LIGHTING EQUIPMENT

An Amazing Accomplishment

YOU OWE IT TO YOURSELF AND FAMILY TO SEE THIS UNUSUAL THRILLING ENTERTAINMENT!

AUTHENTIC COSTUMES OF 4000 YEARS AGO

Professionally Staged and Directed by American Educational Co.

MISS PEGGY COX, Director

CAST OF CHARACTERS

These Leading Citizens and Business People are backing "The First Commandment"

Keeping up morale during the seemingly endless Depression of the 1930s was a challenge. Reverend Elden Bucklin rallied these 80 performers from church members and their neighbors and friends to act in *The First Commandment*. It was professionally staged by the American Educational Company.

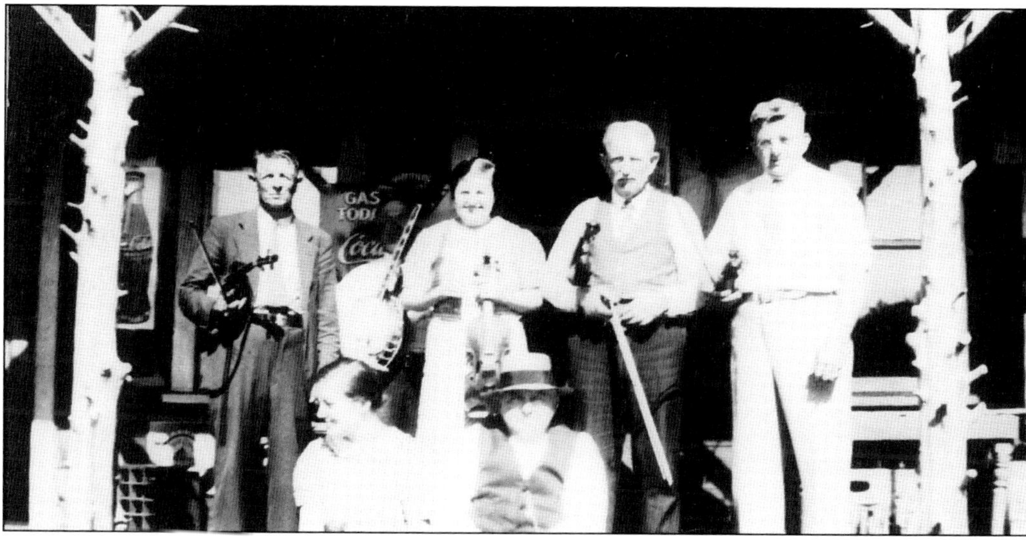

Here are some of the musicians who kept the dancers hopping at Ella Steere's dance barn in Cherry Valley at the corner of Snake Hill Road and Chopmist Hill Road. Popular local fiddler Bill Spink is holding his bow.

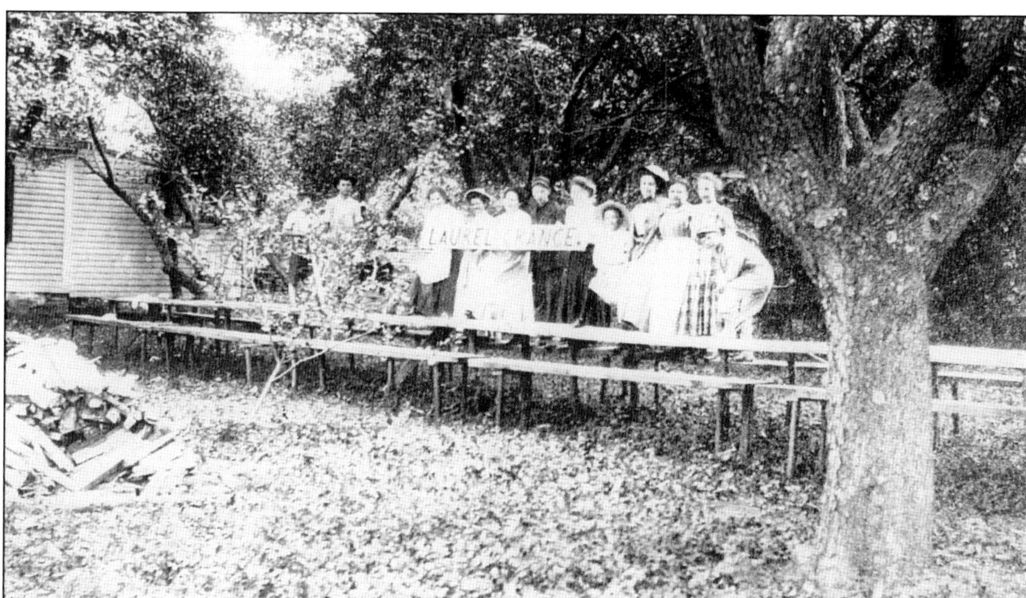

On Labor Day, September 7, 1908, these folks posed for the camera celebrating another successful fund-raiser to build Laurel Grange Hall. They are in Seth Steere's yard south of the house at Waldron's Corner.

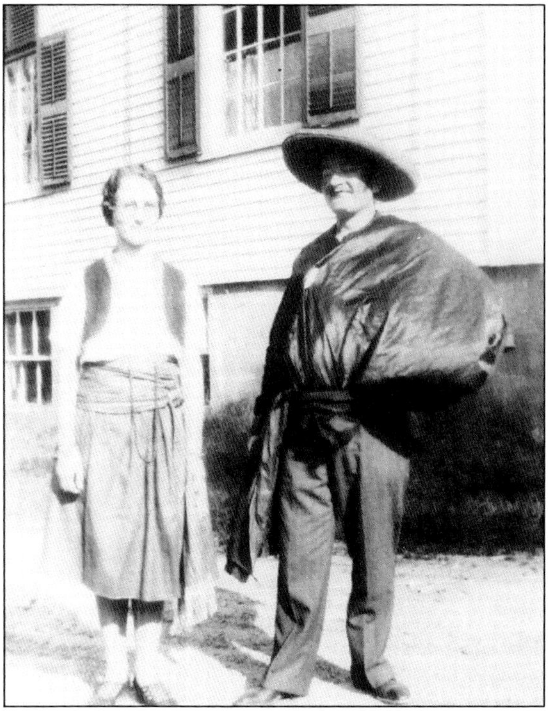

The Ancients and Horribles Fourth of July Parade began in 1927. In the first parade was this "Spanish lady" and "Mexican man"—Catharine Whitaker and James Whitaker. He was the chairman of the parade committee for nearly 20 years. They are standing beside the Chepachet Congregational Church, where the parade disbanded.

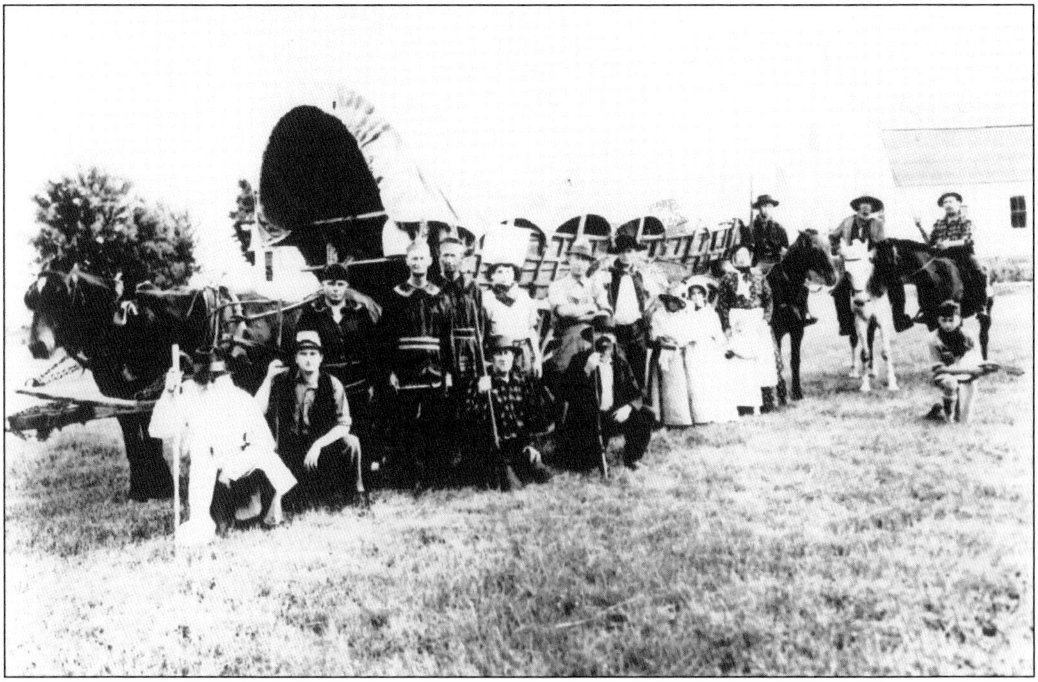

Whatever the parade entry, it was kept secret as long as possible. This Conestoga wagon came with its owners about 1936. Townspeople include, from left to right, Percy Townend, Lester Lee, Everett Steere, James and George Greenhalgh, Russell Blackinton (kneeling), ?, Harry Jacques, ? (kneeling), Art Slocum, Barbara Slocum, ?, Ira Townend, Andrew Townend (dressed as a little girl), three horsemen that came with the wagon, and ?.

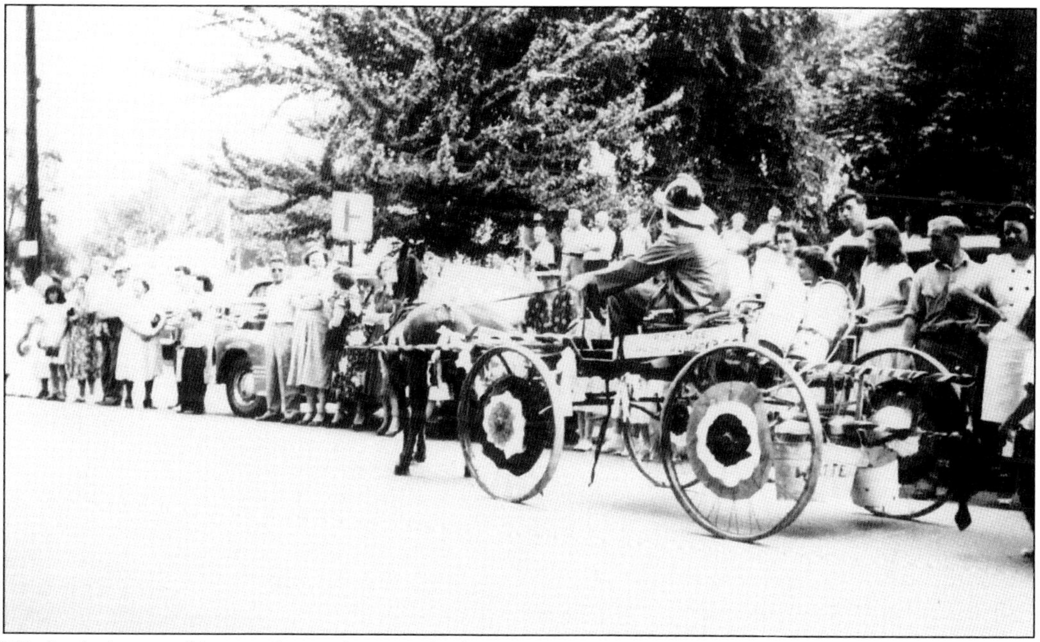

We had plenty of firetrucks in the parade, but never one like this. Everyone could participate—even "Hickville Hook and Ladder"—whoever that was! The cameraman caught some familiar faces in the background, too.

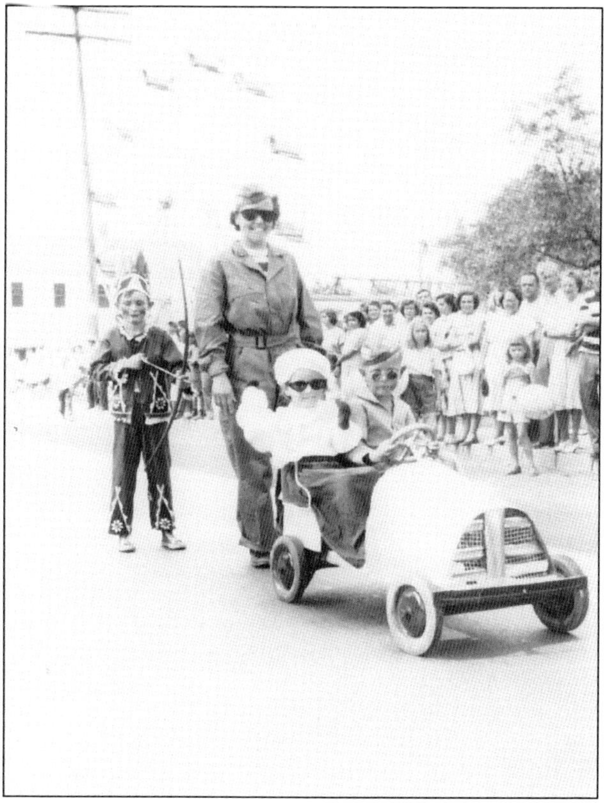

In the 1940s and 1950s, the firemen ran their carnival on the Chepachet Grammar School grounds. This photo was taken on the Fourth of July of parade participants; they are Neil Salisbury (the Native American), Carrie Tower, and Joyce and Bill Tower in the car. Behind them is the Ferris wheel that was set up at the corner of the schoolyard. In the background is the old town clerk's office.

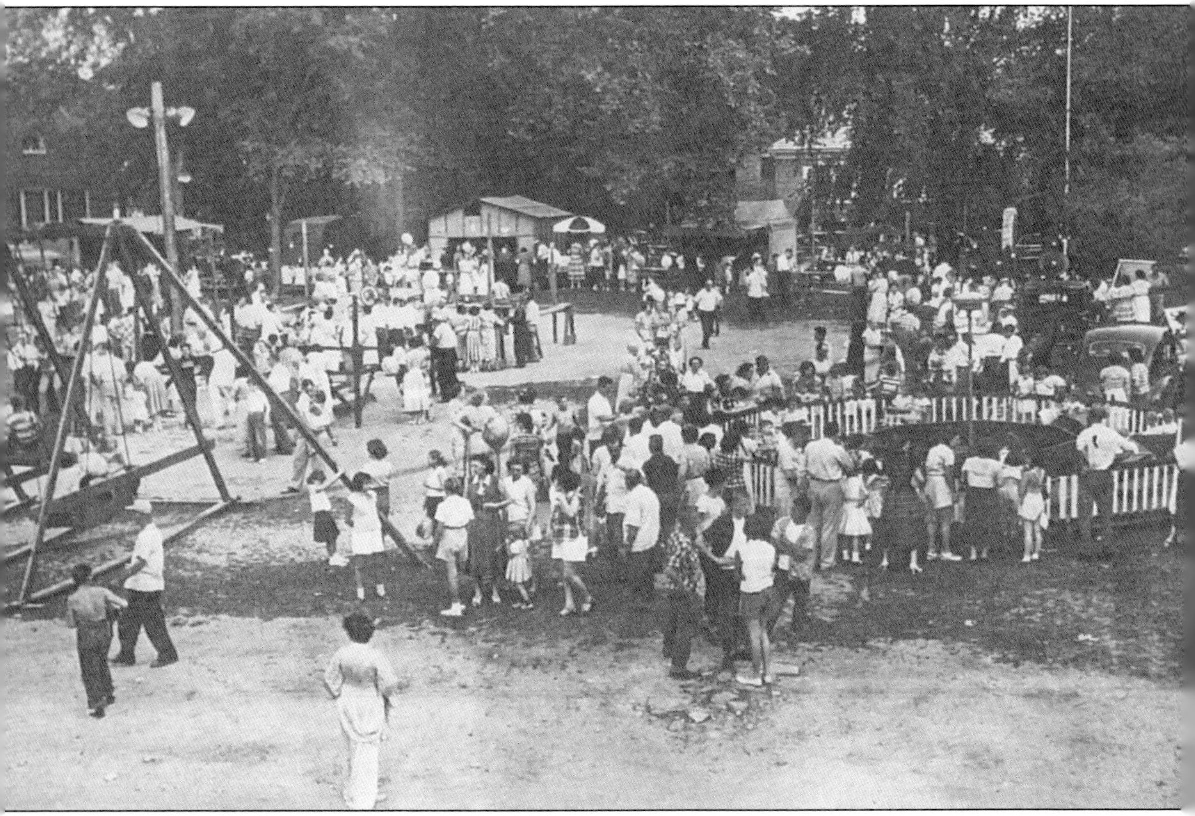

The photographer took this picture of the firemen's carnival from the second floor of the old town clerk's office in 1953. The Chepachet Grammar School is in the background (extreme left). The library and "new" town clerk's office are in the center background. A new car was raffled off every year (on the right). The Ferris wheel is just out of the picture to the right.

Laurel Grange Hall was still under construction when the camera caught the Hurdy-Gurdy man entertaining the workers at Waldron's Corner about 1914.

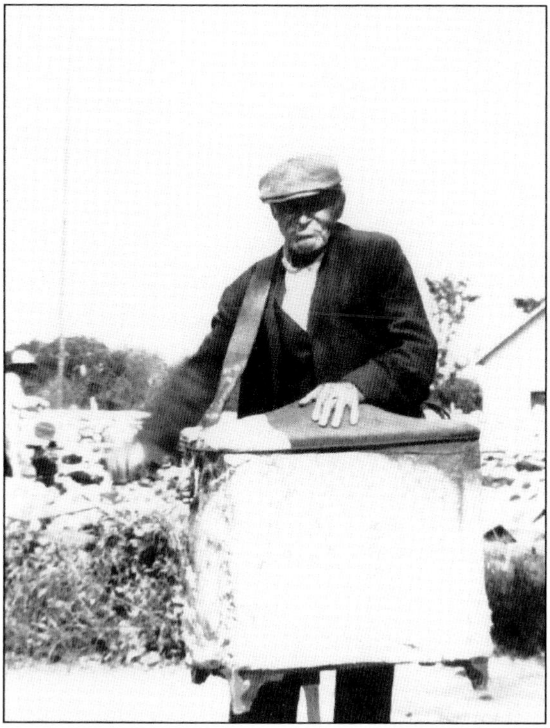

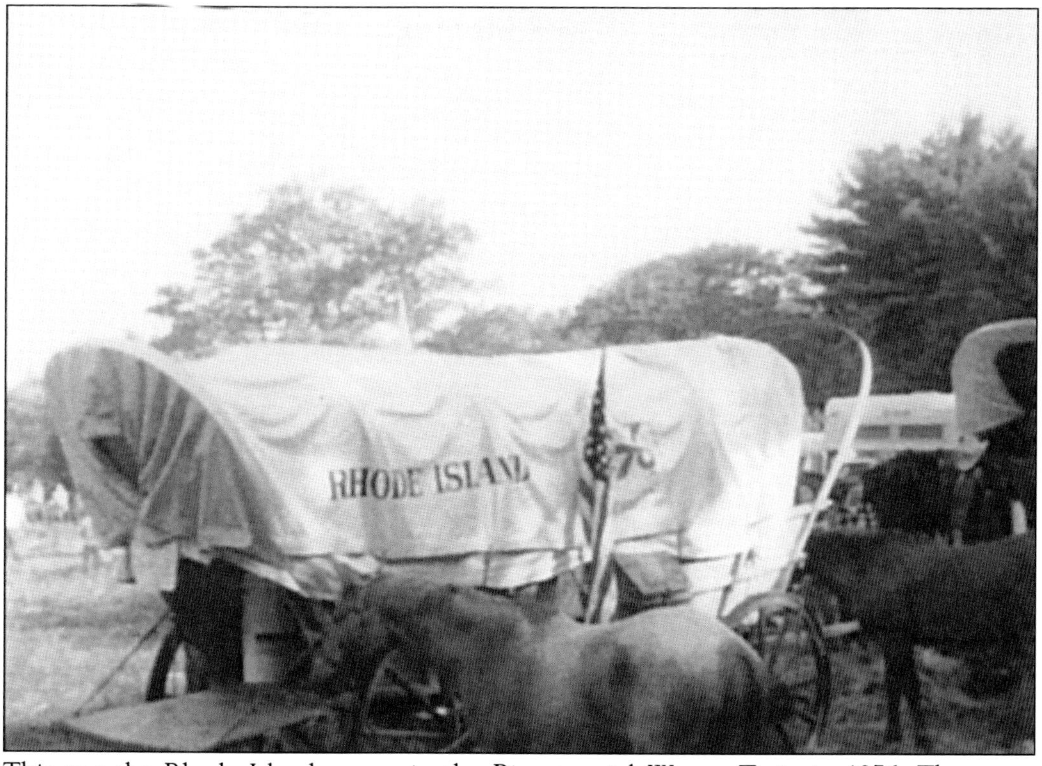

This was the Rhode Island wagon in the Bicentennial Wagon Train in 1976. They were encamped on Reynolds' Road in West Glocester.

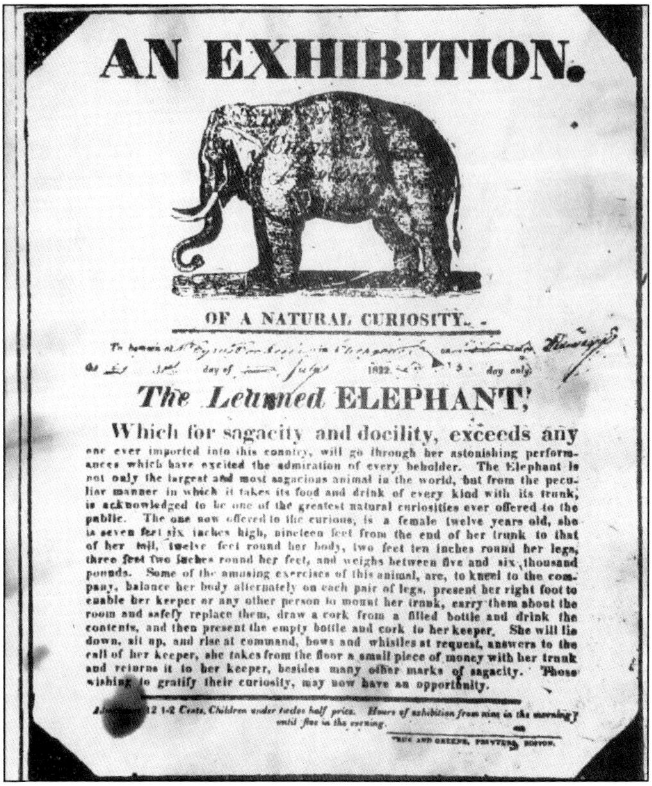

AN EXHIBITION.

OF A NATURAL CURIOSITY.

The Learned ELEPHANT,

Which for sagacity and docility, exceeds any one ever imported into this country, will go through her astonishing performances which have excited the admiration of every beholder. The Elephant is not only the largest and most sagacious animal in the world, but from the peculiar manner in which it takes its food and drink of every kind with its trunk, is acknowledged to be one of the greatest natural curiosities ever offered to the public. The one now offered to the curious, is a female twelve years old, she is seven feet six inches high, nineteen feet from the end of her trunk to that of her tail, twelve feet round her body, two feet ten inches round her legs, three feet two inches round her feet, and weighs between five and six thousand pounds. Some of the amusing exercises of this animal, are, to kneel to the company, balance her body alternately on each pair of legs, present her right foot to enable her keeper or any other person to mount her trunk, carry them about the room and safely replace them, draw a cork from a filled bottle and drink the contents, and then present the empty bottle and cork to her keeper. She will lie down, sit up, and rise at command, bows and whistles at request, answers to the call of her keeper, she takes from the floor a small piece of money with her trunk and returns it to her keeper, besides many other marks of sagacity. Those wishing to gratify their curiosity, may now have an opportunity.

[illegible] 12 1-2 Cents, Children under twelve half price. Hours of exhibition from nine in the morning until five in the evening.

TRUE AND GREENE, PRINTERS, BOSTON.

The celebrated Learned Elephant came to Chepachet on July 31, 1822. Broadsides on barns and fence posts announced the event for miles around. She was the second elephant ever to be seen in North America. Four years later she returned to Chepachet to be exhibited on the lot known to this day as the "Circus Lot" on Douglas Hook Road behind the Chepachet Hotel.

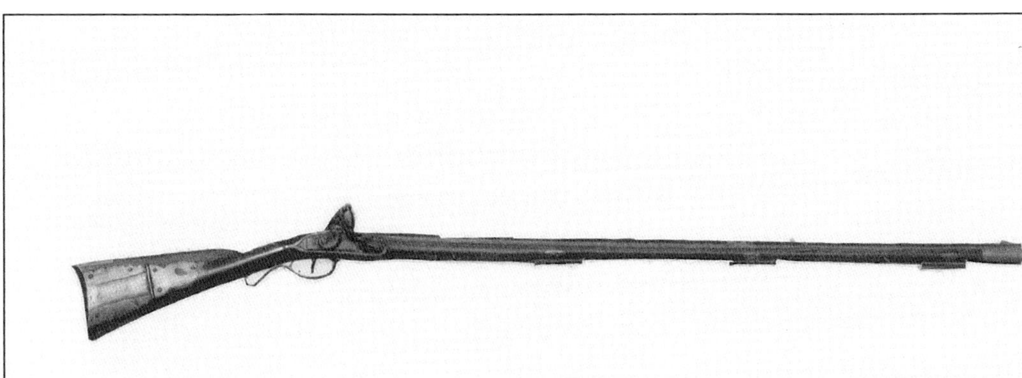

At the midnight hour on May 25, 1826, prompted by conspirators, the Learned Elephant was shot from a second floor window of Hawkins' Gristmill as she crossed Chepachet Bridge. The flintlock rifle that fired those fatal shots came back briefly to Chepachet to be photographed in 1997. The gun was made by gunsmith Welcome Mathewson of Burrillville.

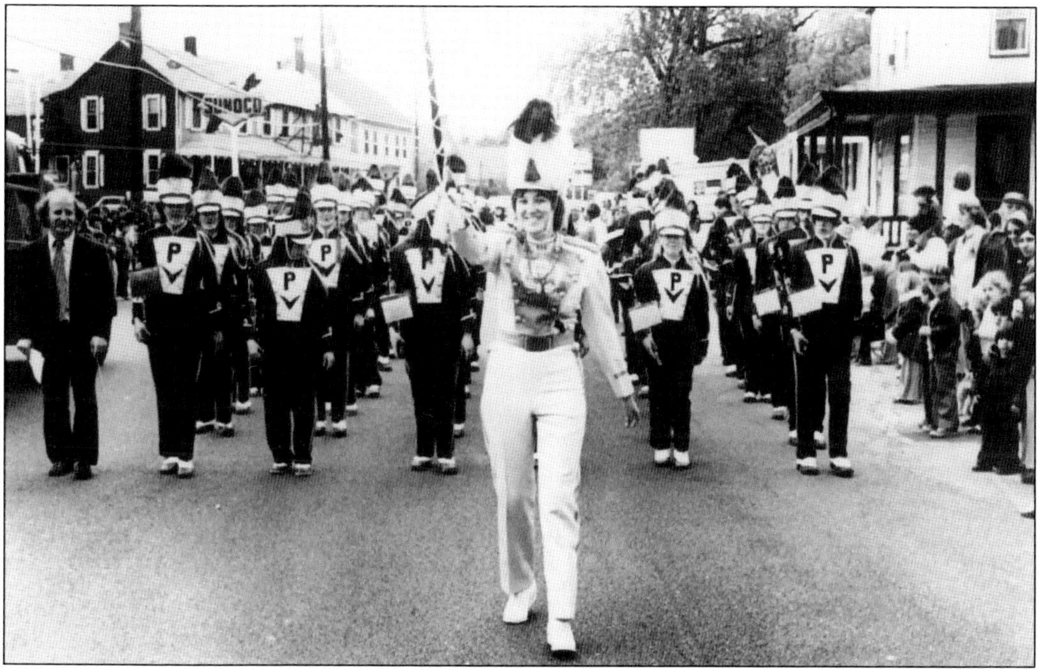

The Ponaganset High School Band directed by Nedo Pandolfi approaches Chepachet Bridge in the Elephant Day parade on May 25, 1976. Linda Steger is in the foreground. Elephant Day was a commemorative observation recalling the shooting of the elephant 150 years before.

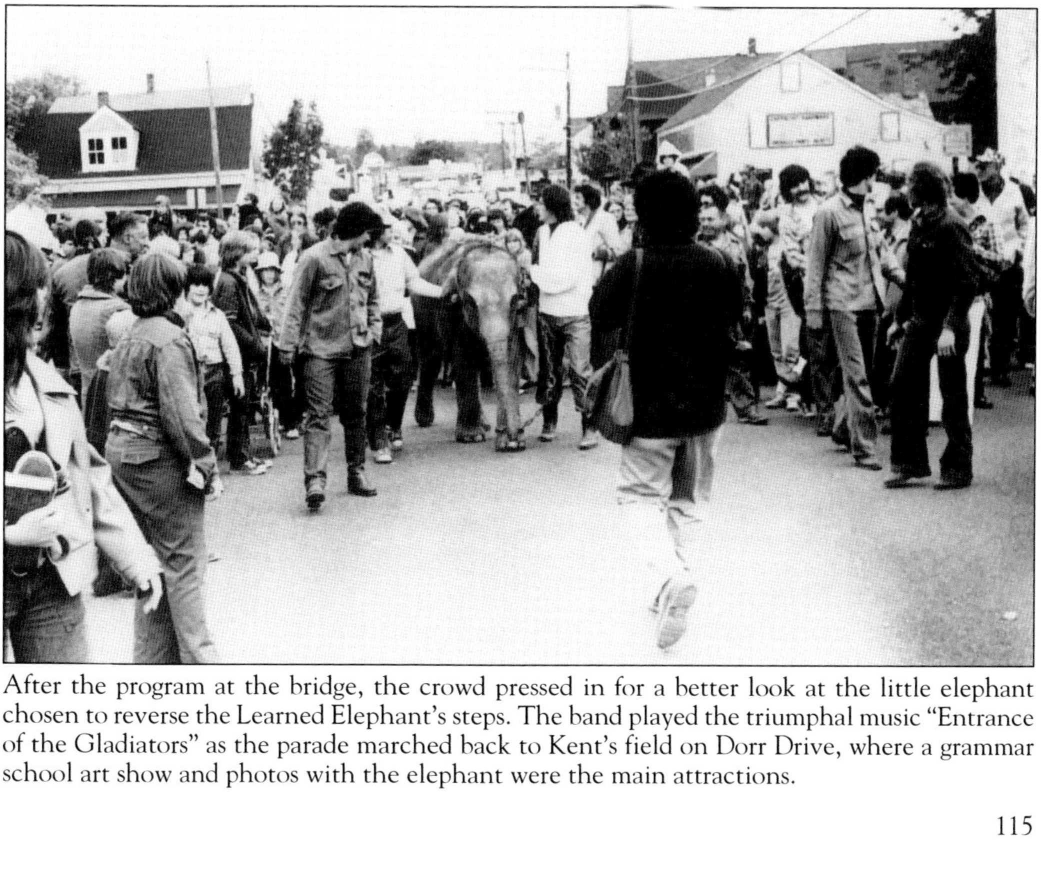

After the program at the bridge, the crowd pressed in for a better look at the little elephant chosen to reverse the Learned Elephant's steps. The band played the triumphal music "Entrance of the Gladiators" as the parade marched back to Kent's field on Dorr Drive, where a grammar school art show and photos with the elephant were the main attractions.

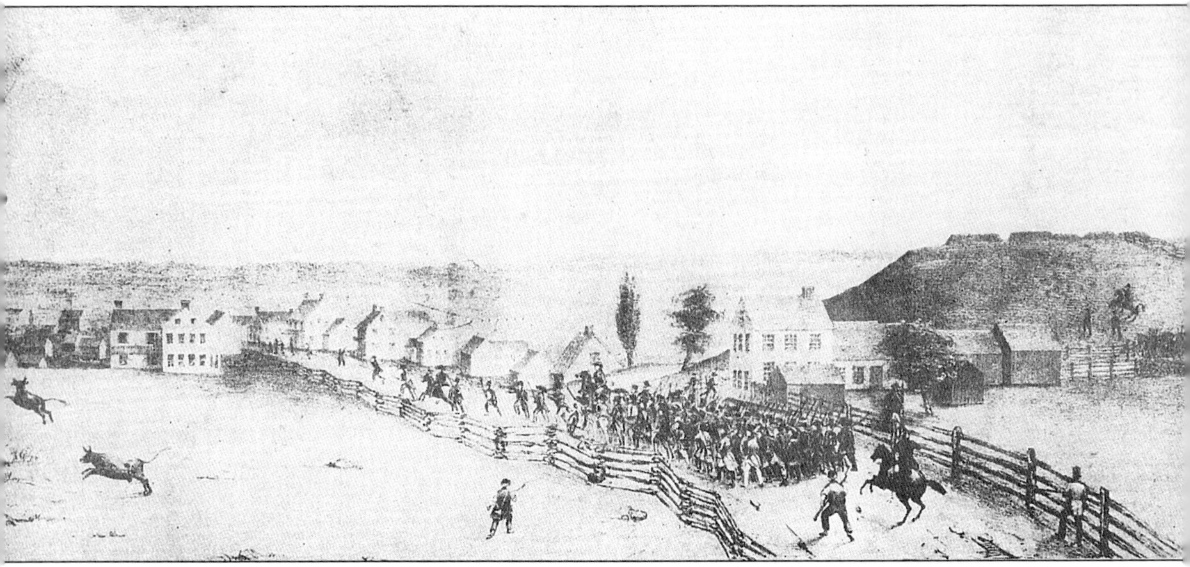

On June 18, 1842, state militias marched into Chepachet from Scituate (center) and Smithfield (right). Acote's Hill is at right with Dorrite entrenchments at the top. One hundred thirty innocent bystanders were taken prisoner at Chepachet during the Dorr Rebellion and were forced to march to a Providence jail. Henry Lord, who drew the picture, was incarcerated in a cell 7 by 10 feet with 13 others for 21 days.

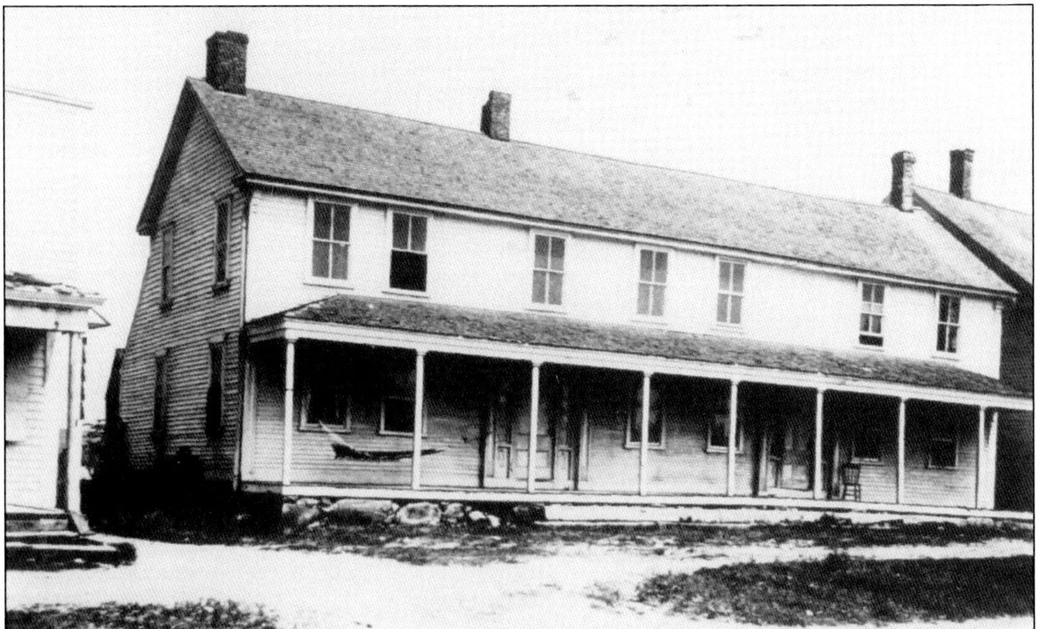

In the early 1900s, this building contained a barroom, billiard hall, and several apartments. In 1842, it was Jedediah Sprague's Tavern and Thomas Dorr's Headquarters during Dorr's Rebellion. Militiaman John Pitman fired through the keyhole of the door on the left wounding Horace Bardeen's thigh. Militia swarmed throughout the building, consuming extraordinary amounts of food and drink, for which the tavernkeeper was never paid. Today it is called the Stagecoach Tavern.

The Dorr Rebellion Reenactment was staged throughout the village of Chepachet on June 20, 1992, with nearly 200 in period dress. Several Rhode Island militias took their original roles. Pictured with a cannon atop Acote's Hill are Thomas Dorr (Dr. Patrick T. Conley) and his men. Lt. Col. Don Provost of the Gloucester Light Infantry leans on the cannon wheel.

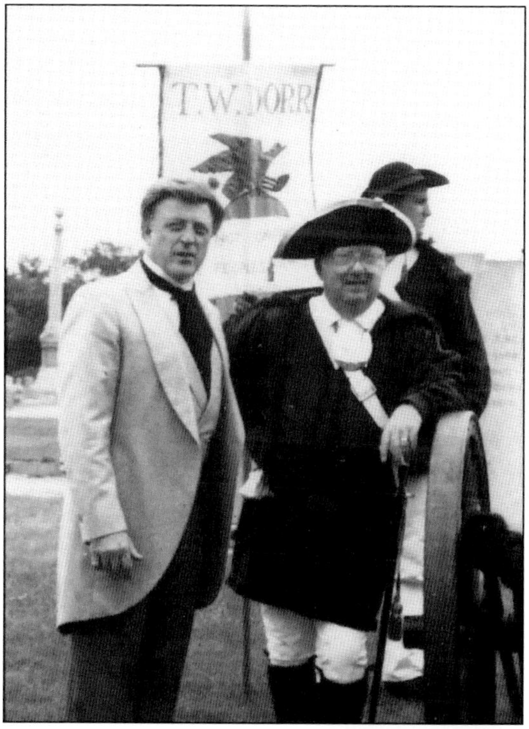

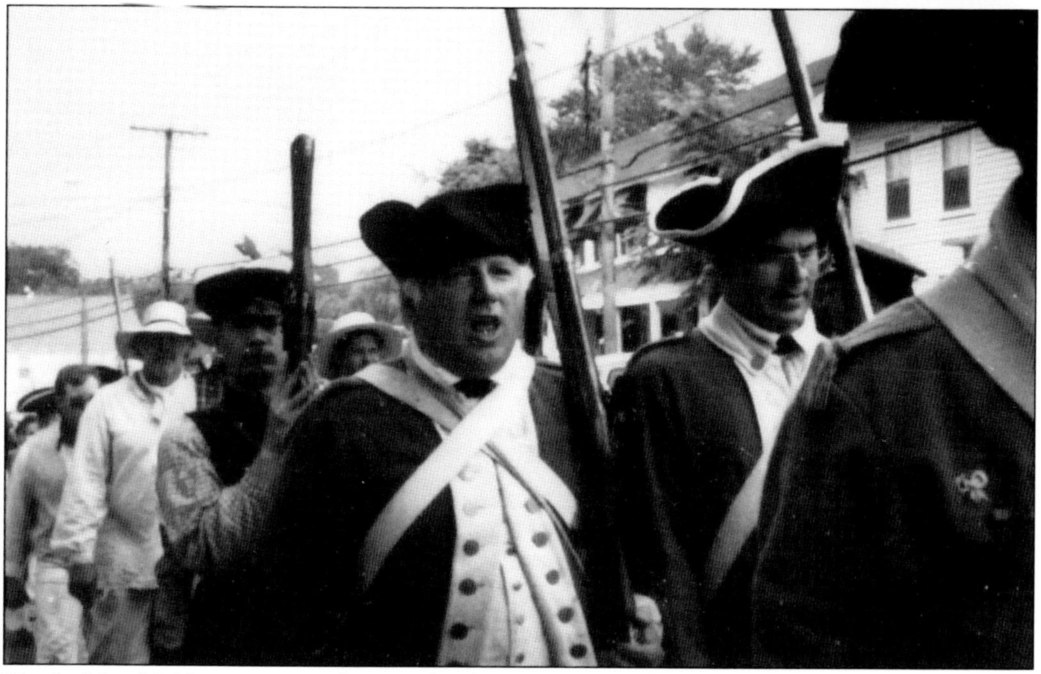

Rhode Island Militia reenact the march of prisoners to Providence jail. Stagecoach Tavern is in the background. There were speeches at "Dorr's Headquarters," a horseback charge up Acote's Hill, the flight from the hill, prisoners captured, a mock shooting at "Sprague's Tavern," period encampments, and a sacking of Chepachet. An official Dorr Rebellion Post Office sold commemorative cachets. Mock battles were held after the reenactment at Union Church field.

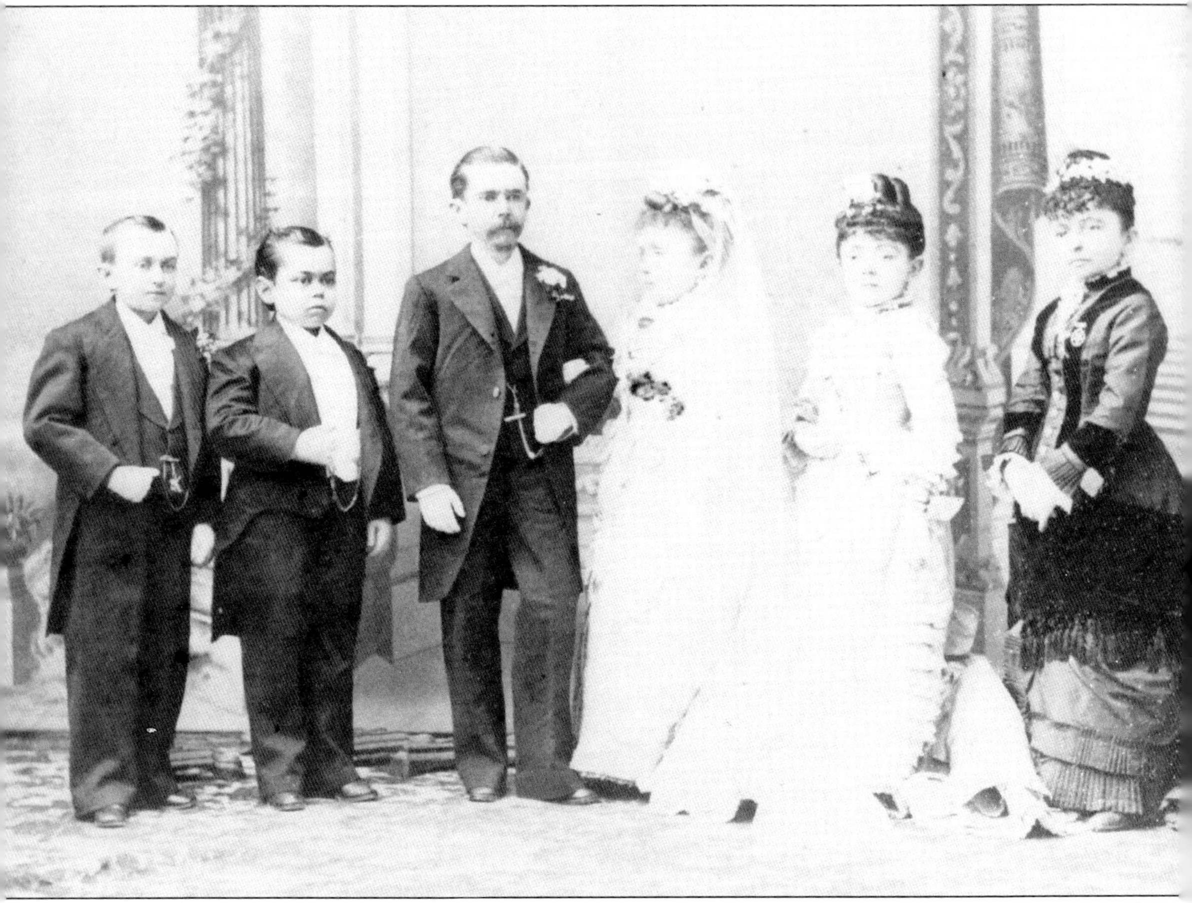

Chepachet native Col. Reuben Steere and Rebecca Ann Myers of Indiana married March 7, 1880, in Rochester, New York. Attendants were, from left to right, General Totman, Admiral Dot, Jennie Quigley, and Sadie Belton. The bride was 41 inches tall and weighed 39 pounds. The groom was 44 inches tall and weighed 43 pounds. They were members of the nationally renowned Lilliputian Opera Company. Reuben and "Annie" made their home in Chepachet in 1882. Reuben became Chepachet School's truant officer and "Annie" ran the restaurant and confectionery shop next to the Masonic Hall.

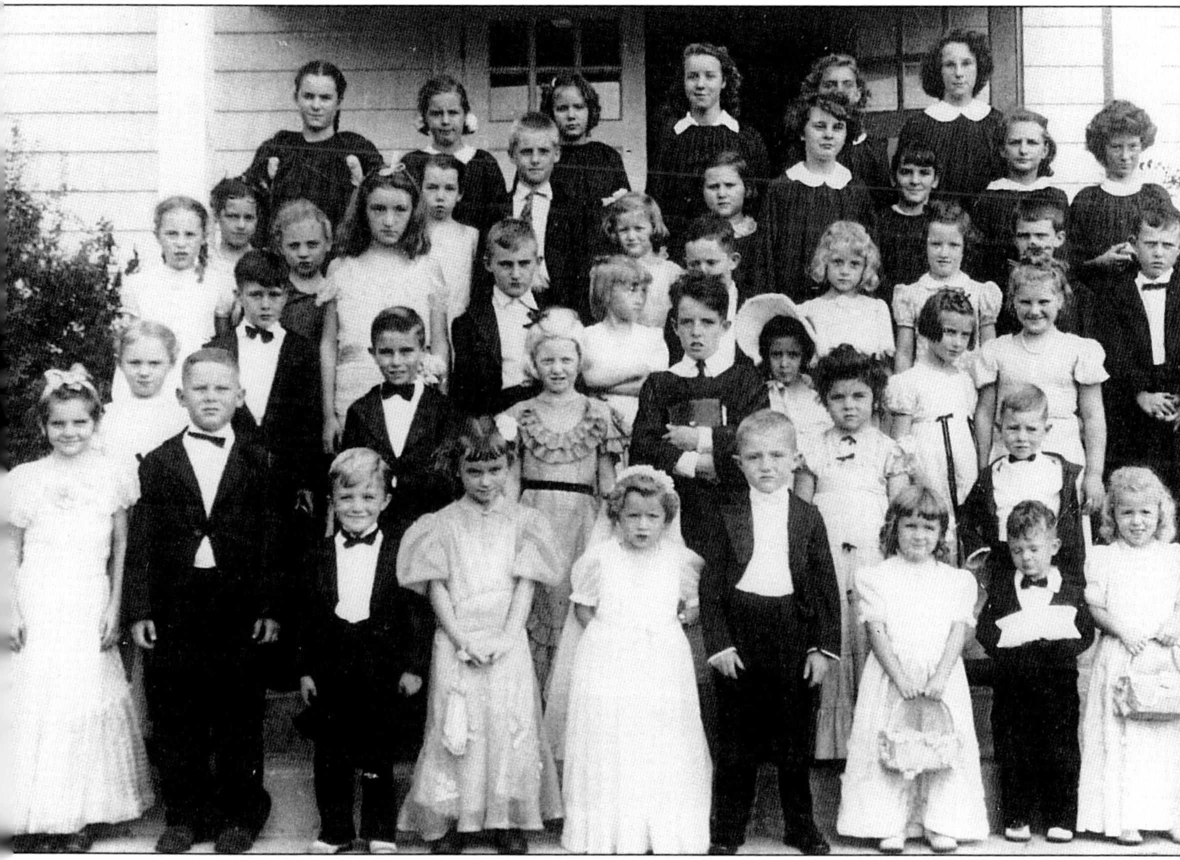

The "Tom Thumb Wedding" was staged at Chepachet Grange Hall in 1944. The participants were, from left to right, as follows: (front row) Clara Frazer, Robert Paine, ?, Edna Whitaker, Nancy Blackington, Bradley Steere, Blanche Davis, David Vickers, and Valerie Anderson; (second row) Barbara Hopkins, Phil Paine, William O'Donnell, Barbara Hodgson, Elden Bucklin Jr., Nancy Davis, Carole Morin, Beverly O'Donnell, Wayne Trinque, and Janice Leduc; (third row) Betty Hopkins, Lois Hopkins, Connie Chapman, Warren Olney, Roberta Hopkins, Bob Esty, Carol Anderson, Janet Brown, ?, and Frank Esty; (fourth row) Marcia Paine, Martha Steere, John Frazer, Ruth Goff, Mildred Vickers, ?, Sandra Place, and Shirley Peck; (back row) Audrey Clisdell, Harley Steere, Janet Champlin, Doris Greenhalgh, Betty Jean Levesque, and Ann Greenhalgh.

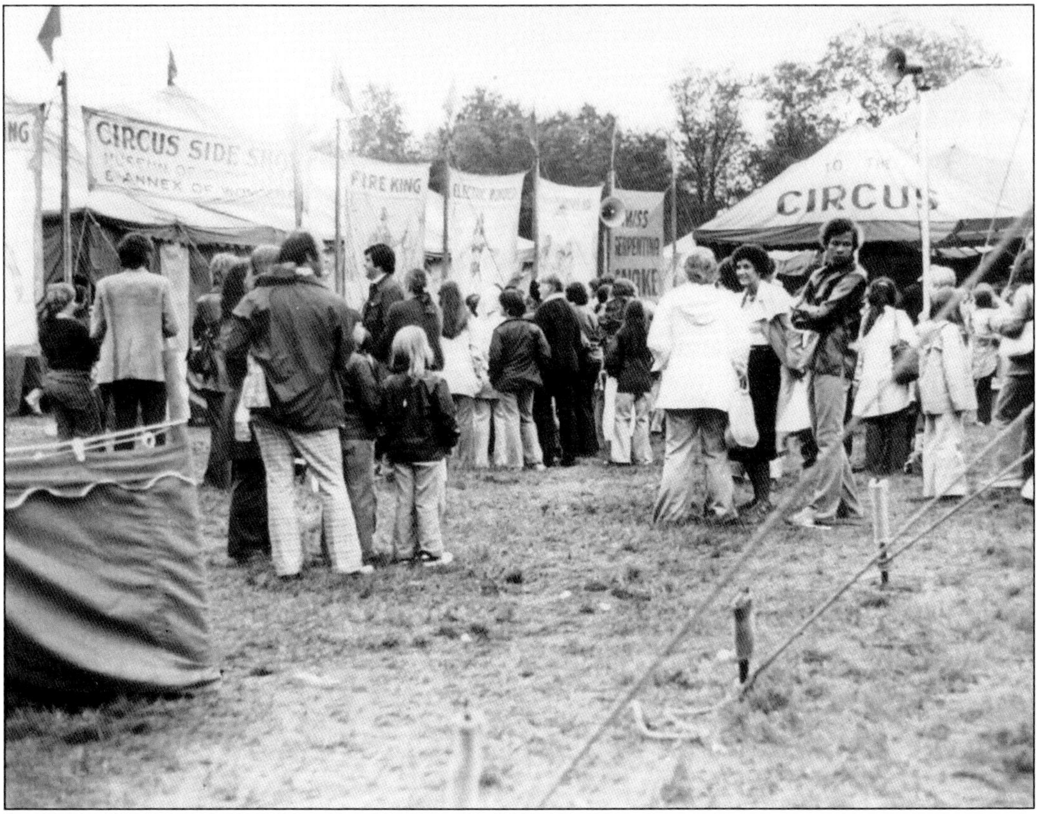

People view the sideshow while waiting for the circus to begin. The only all-student three-ring circus under a big top in the country came to Chepachet on July 31, 1976, and set up at Kent's field. Two performances played to capacity crowds. Circus Kirk brought their elephant to Chepachet Bridge to lay a memorial wreath from the Circus Fans of America in memory of the Learned Elephant.

Nine

Schools

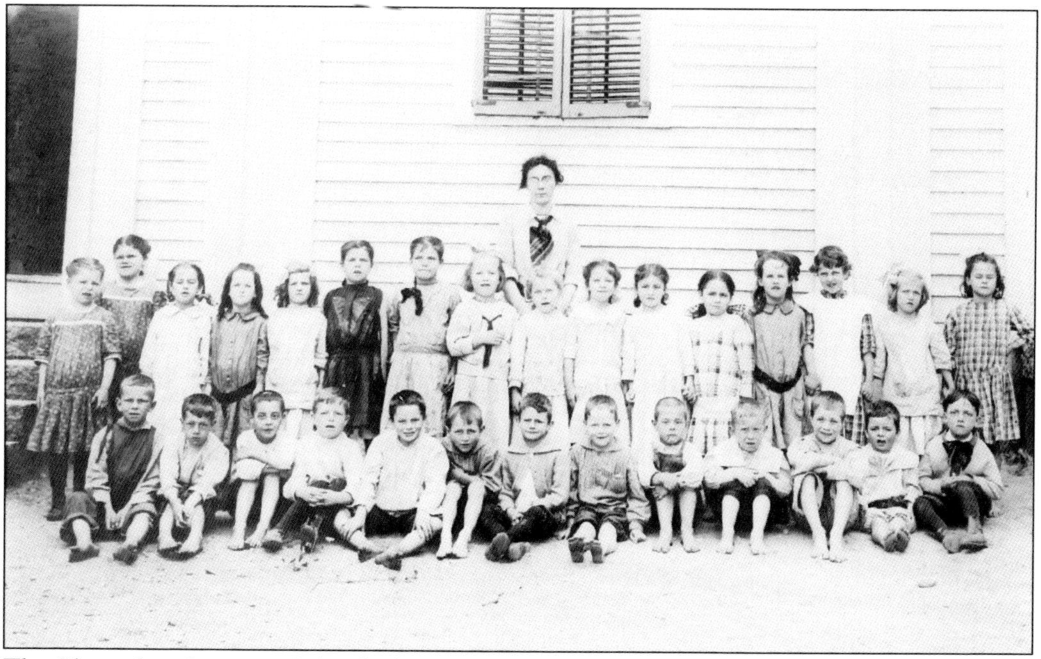

The Chepachet Grammar School Class of 1925 included the following, from left to right: (front row) Henry Paine, Arthur Paine, ? Ducharme, Phillips Steere, Walter Lange, Joseph Trinque, Henry Lange, Fred Trinque, ? Ducharme, Walter Paine, Earl Bates, Raymond Plante, and Arthur Steere; (back row) Ruth Irons, Esther Irons, Goldie Olney, Irene Keach, ?, Ethel Young, Viola Young, Violet Denoyelle, Mary Steere, Alice Clough, ? Bates, Yvonne Plante, Beatrice Keach, Anna Trinque, ?, and Pearl Lange. The teacher was Olivia Church.

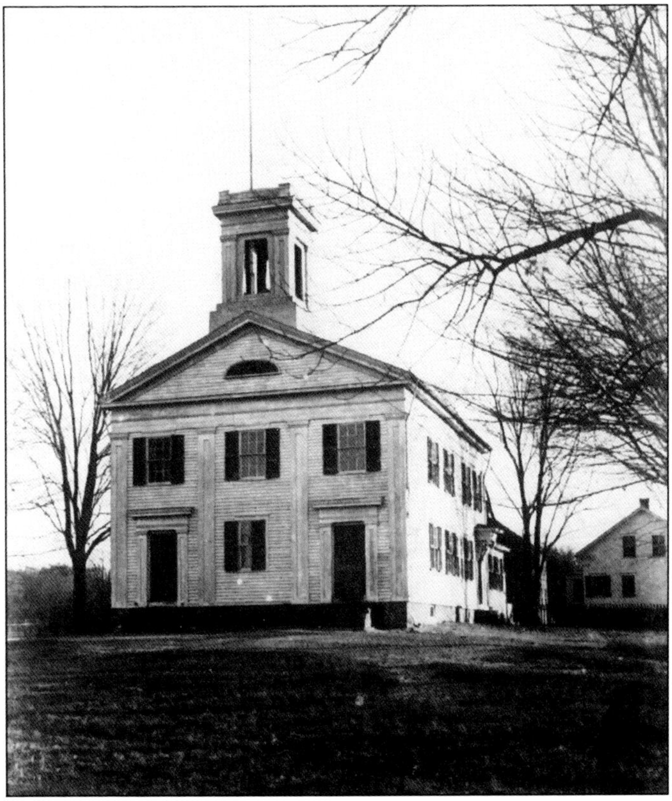

The Chepachet Grammar School was the largest district school in Glocester, taking students from three districts. It was located on Douglas Hook Road at the corner of School Street (Dorr Drive). It was built about 1835 by Eddy and Potter, who also built the Chepachet Union Church. The bell from this building was moved to the new grammar school in 1935. The Paine house is in the distance (now Hopkins).

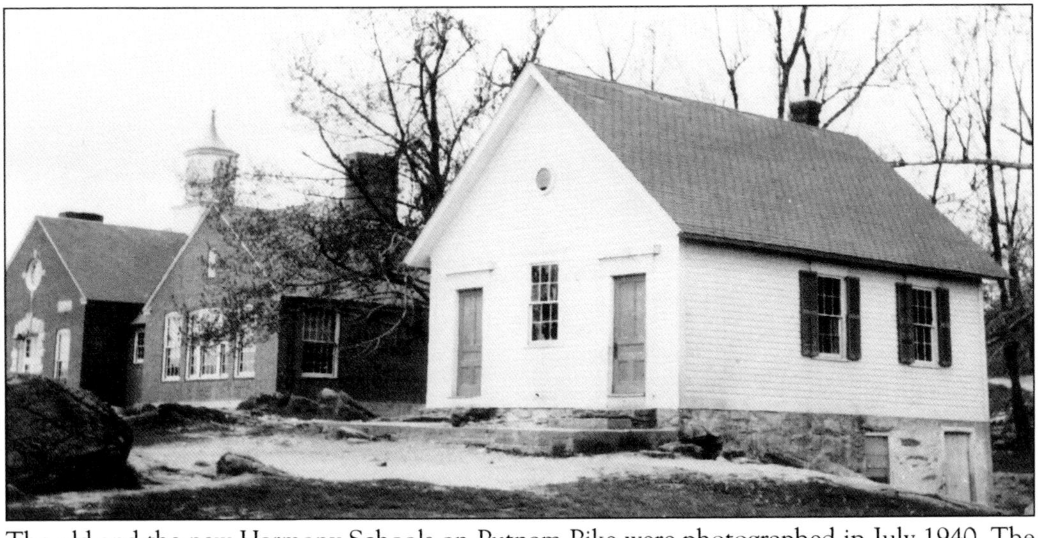

The old and the new Harmony Schools on Putnam Pike were photographed in July 1940. The old Harmony School was bought at auction for $52 and moved to Greenville to be the home of Phillip Galligan. It burned in the 1980s.

The teacher's name, Clemence, was misspelled "Clemens" on the front of the two-card graduate's souvenir booklet. Pupils listed on the second card are Ada Steere, Carrie Lapointe, Eleanor Wood, Eva Lapointe, Grace Winsor, Gladys Steere, Julia Winsor, Lois Newcomb, Albert Steere, Alan Wood, Earl Hall, Frank Berry, Merton Roder, Oscar Steere, Warren Jaques, Eva Barden, Florence Barden, Isabel Steere, Mabel Barden, Eber Jaques, Harold Barden, and Walter Steere.

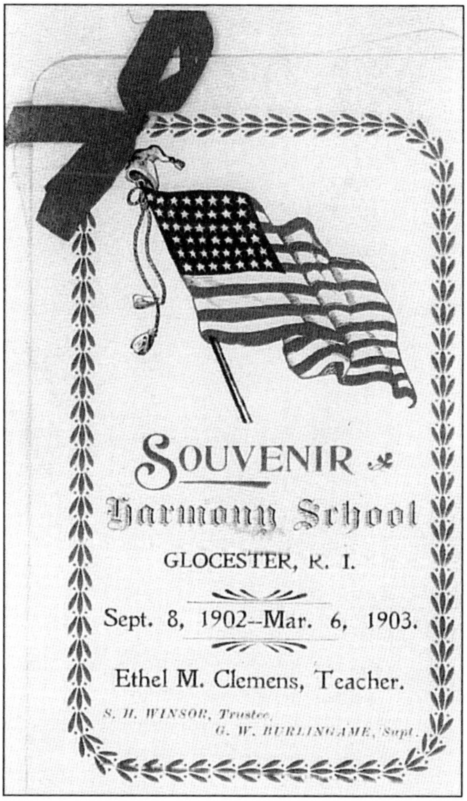

Even Rex, Marion Ottinger's dog, posed for the school photo about 1920. From left to right, the children are as follows: (front row) Harrison Ullman, Carlton Winsor, Grace Winsor, Harvey Staples, and Helen Coman; (middle row) Eliza Tucker, Billy Randall, John Ullman, Hazel Coman, Lizzie Tucker, Estelle Brown, and Beth Muncy; (back row) Raymond Lewis, May Willie (teacher), Marion Ottinger, and Ernest Winsor.

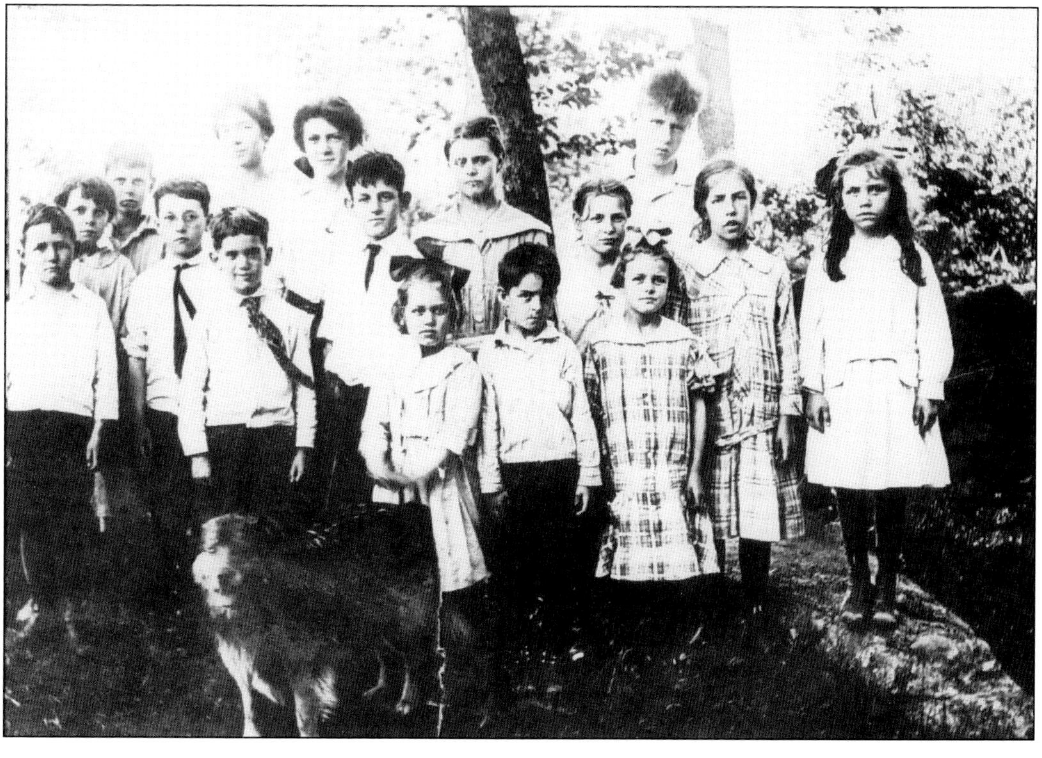

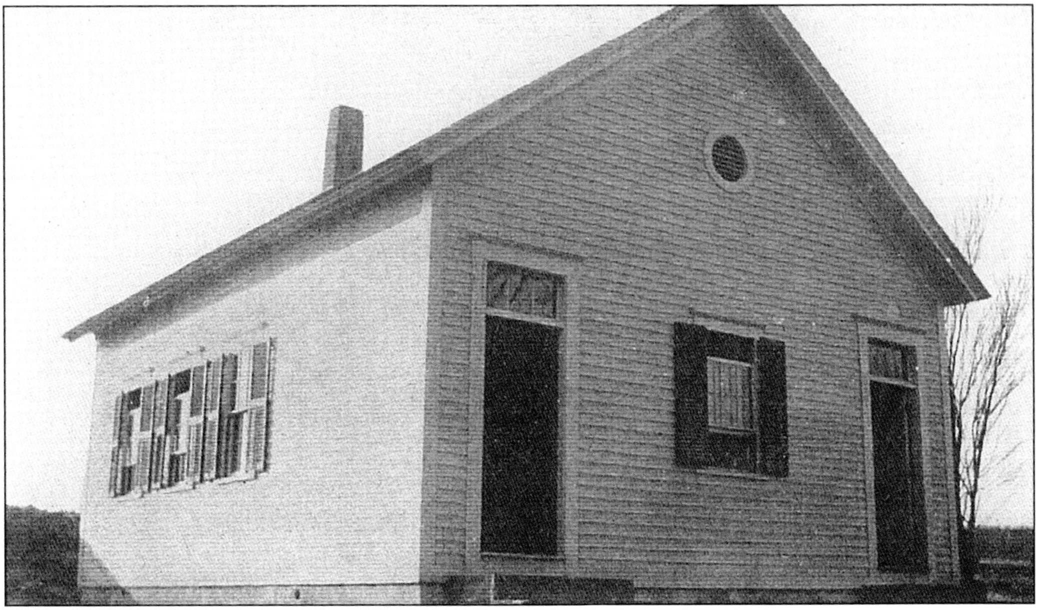

The second Clarkville School still stands on Putnam Pike in West Glocester. It was one of the last district schools to close, consolidating with Chepachet Grammar School in 1936, then reopening during World War II. Lucy Reynolds continued teaching there until it finally closed in 1944. The first district school at Clarkville was on a site now underwater at the Bowdish Reservoir near Putnam Pike.

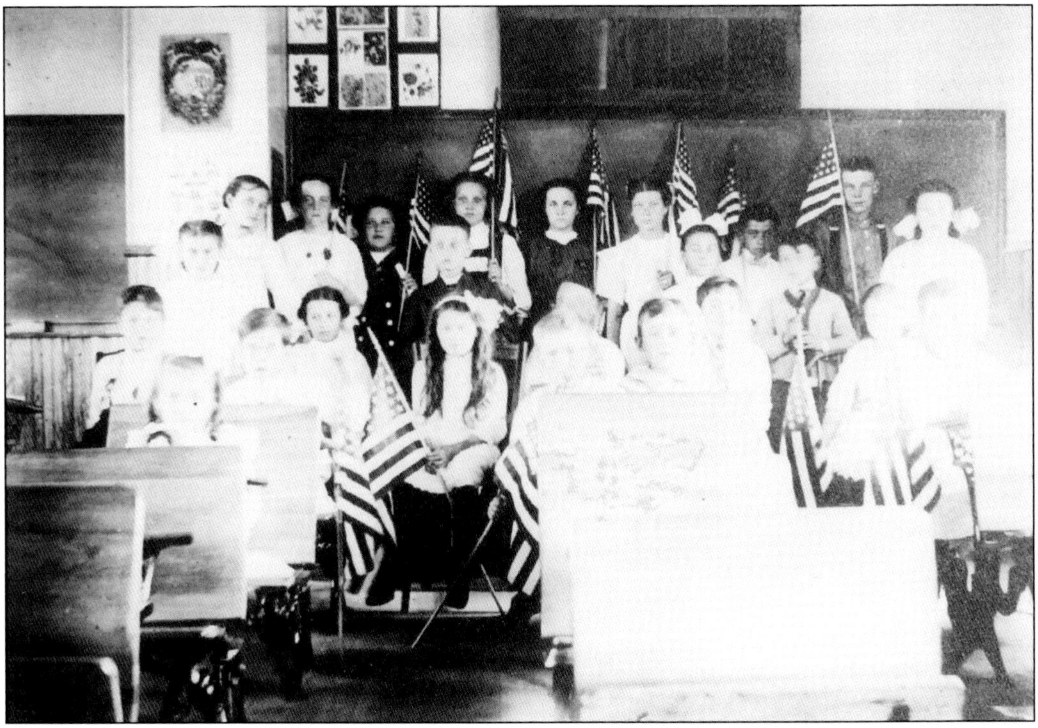

Students of Clarkville School District #7 pose for a photographer at the back of their classroom. The flags may indicate a Flag Day program in June.

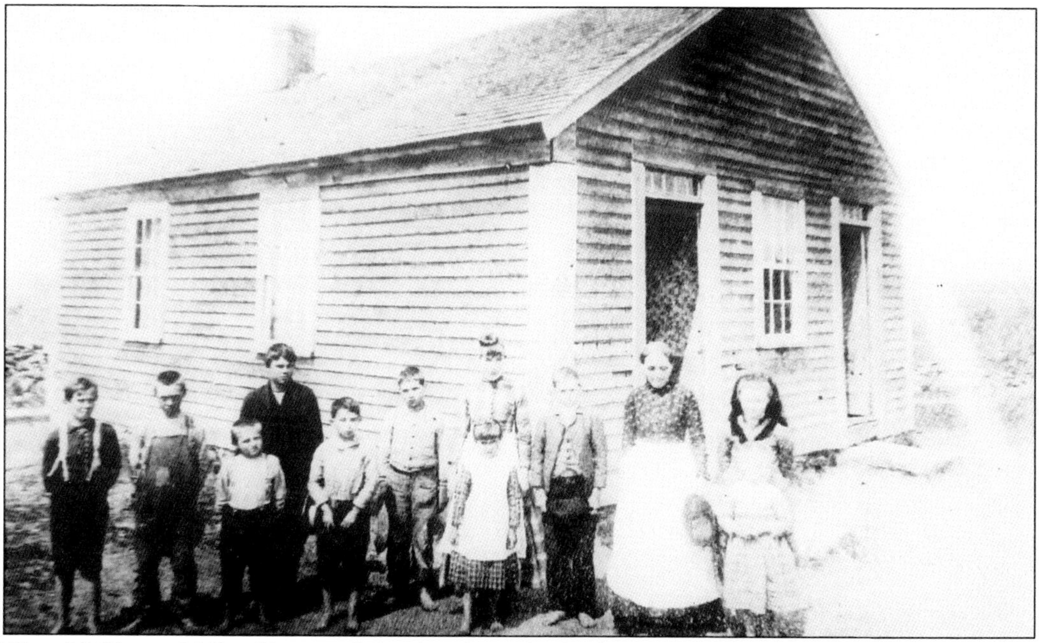

The old Cherry Valley District School #10 was built about 1849 on Snake Hill Road. Teacher Lydia Armstrong (in apron) stands with her pupils; they are, from left to right, Ella Steere, Una Aylesworth, Walter Sprague, Florrie Aylesworth, Mabel Sprague, Dexter Irons, Waldo Steere, Charles Young, Charles Salisbury, Clayton Bellows, and Roy Baxter.

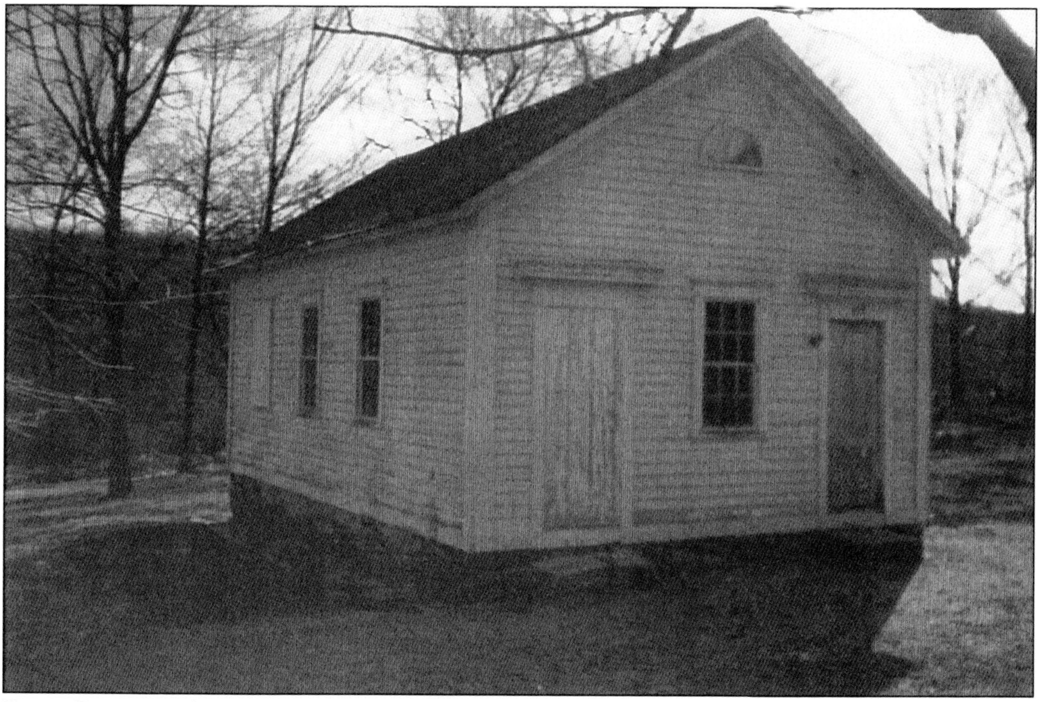

Evans District School #2, east of Mapleville Road in East Glocester, was built by Daniel Evans on his own property in 1867. He also hired a teacher and supplied lodging. This building was preserved for many years by the loving care of Emily Colwell.

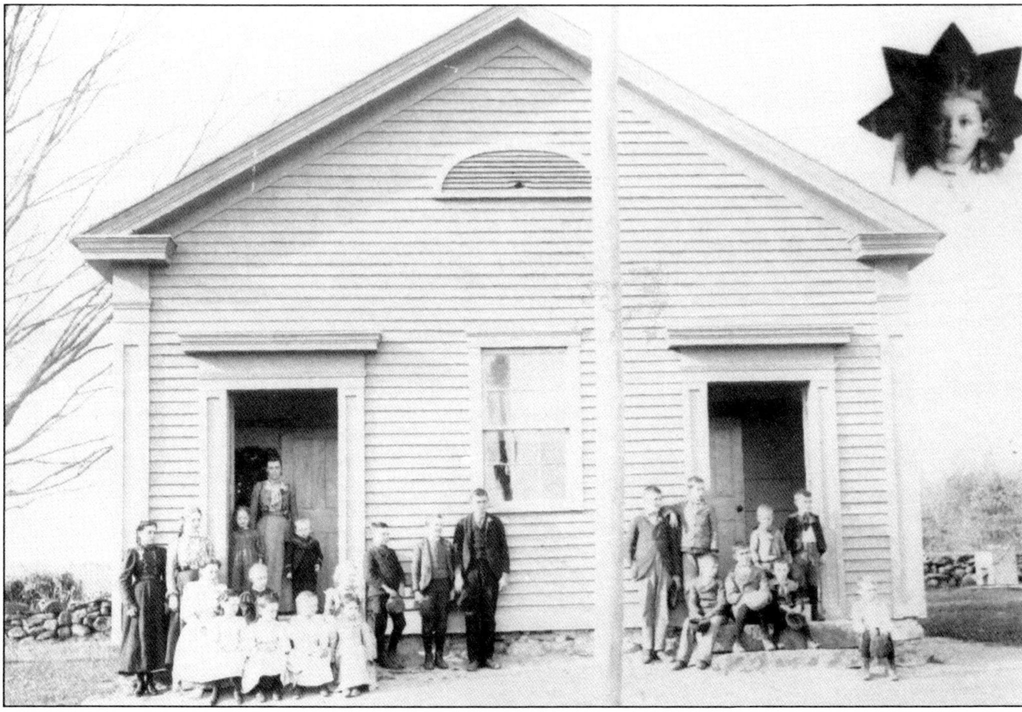

Central School District #12 was a large one-room school at the corner of Snake Hill Road and Tourtellot Hill Road. The land was purchased for $16 by Thomas Irons "for the benefit of a district school—and no other—except public meetings." In 1893, Ida Phillips was teaching 22 pupils. Stephen C. Irons instructed winter classes. No date or names accompanied the photo.

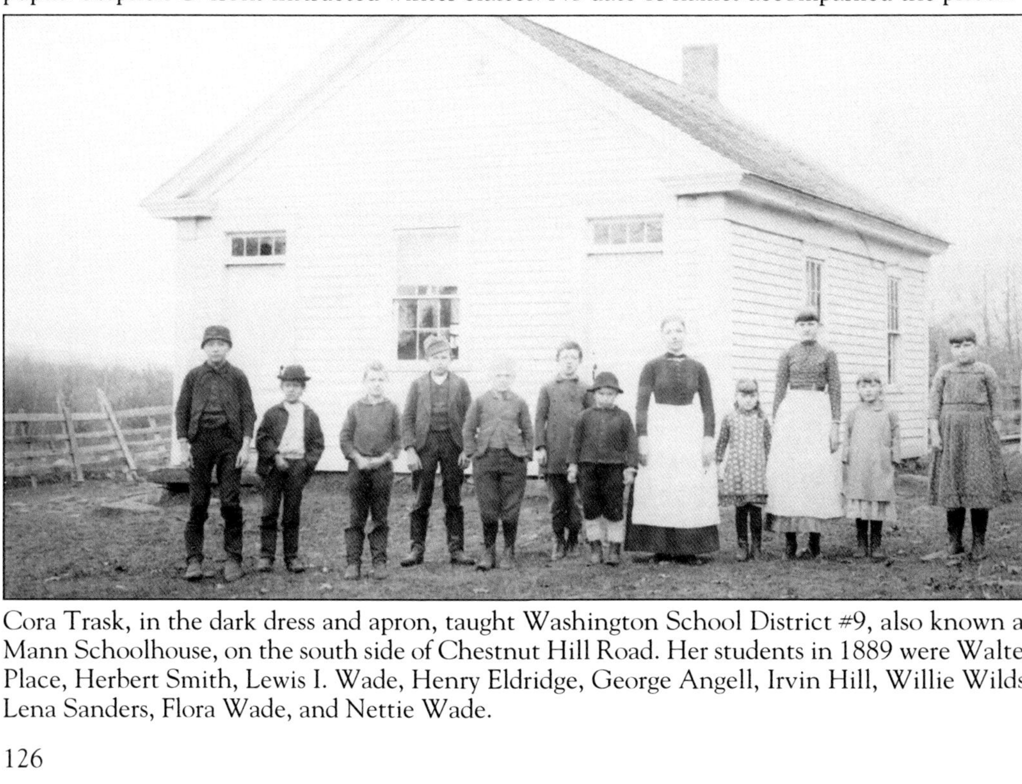

Cora Trask, in the dark dress and apron, taught Washington School District #9, also known as Mann Schoolhouse, on the south side of Chestnut Hill Road. Her students in 1889 were Walter Place, Herbert Smith, Lewis I. Wade, Henry Eldridge, George Angell, Irvin Hill, Willie Wilds, Lena Sanders, Flora Wade, and Nettie Wade.

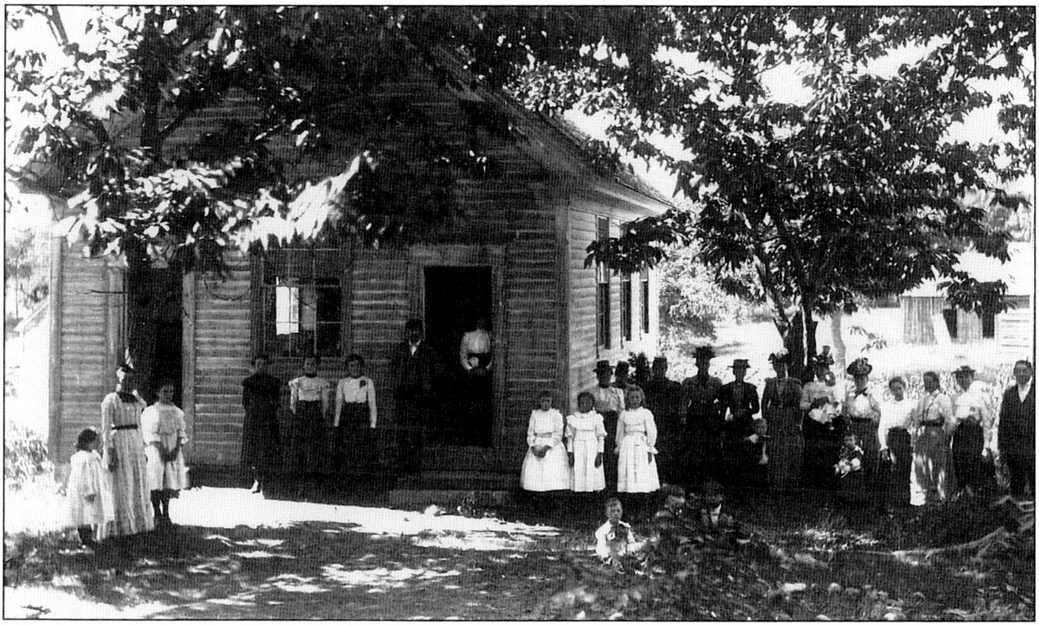

Parents and graduates are standing in front of Pine Orchard School District #6 at the corner of Pine Orchard Schoolhouse Road and Putnam Pike in 1898. Annie Steere is in the doorway. Built in 1857, it was the second school on that site. District #6 consolidated with Chepachet Grammar School after 1914. Today it is a residence.

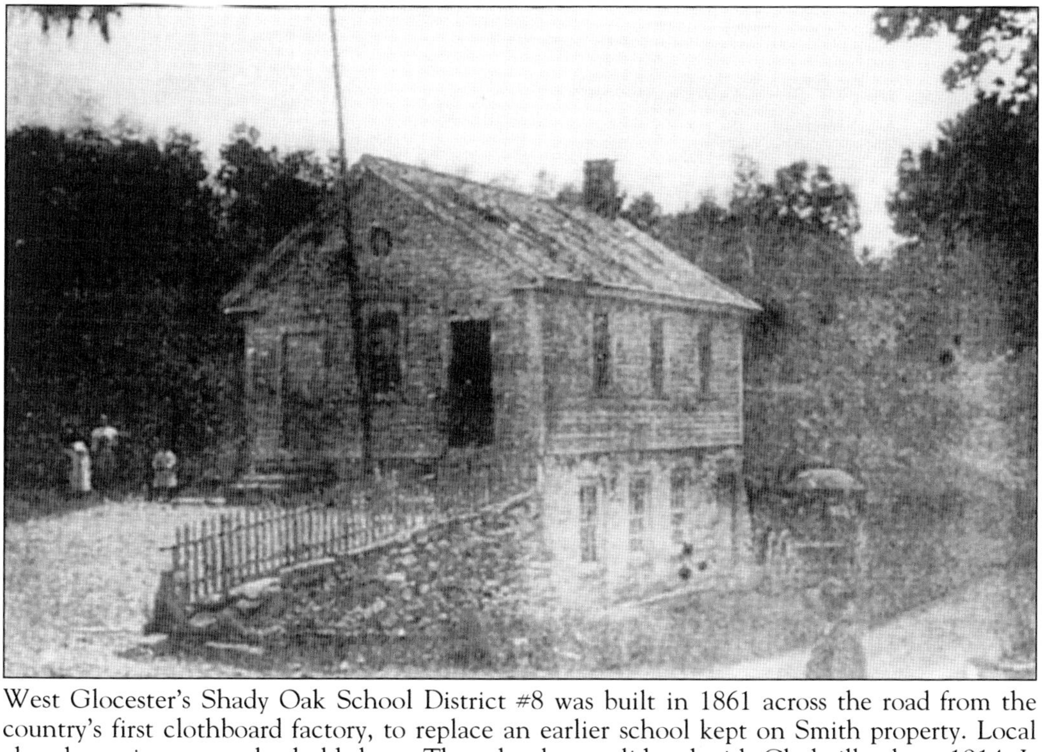

West Glocester's Shady Oak School District #8 was built in 1861 across the road from the country's first clothboard factory, to replace an earlier school kept on Smith property. Local church services were also held there. The school consolidated with Clarkville about 1914. It was demolished in 1955 when the new road (Reynolds' Road, Rt. 94) was built.

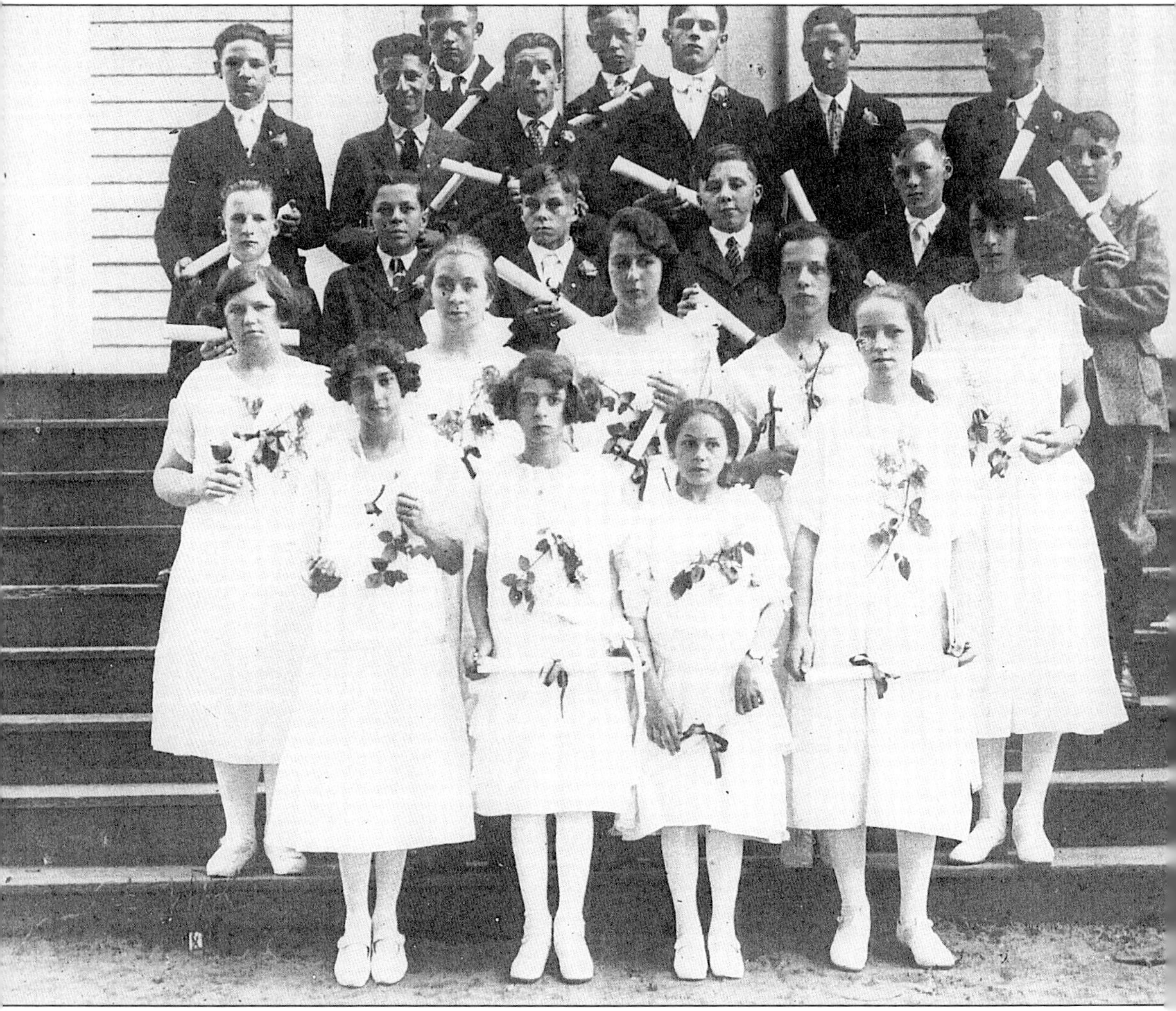

On June 19, 1924, the Central Cherry Valley, Chepachet, Evans, Harmony, and Washington district schools were represented in an eighth-grade graduation portrait on the steps of the Chepachet Union Church. The students are, from left to right, as follows: (front row) Beatrice A. Rivers, ? Flaim, Pearl L. Boyd, and Lydia M. Garrity; (second row) Ethel O. Colwell, Ethel L. Clough, Alice M. Allen, Bertha L. Weagle, and ? Flaim; (third row) Walter F. Keach Jr., George W. Gleason, Enoch T. Steere, Harvey B. Steere, Ernest S. Hopkins, and Harvey B. Staples; (fourth row) Edward A. Dutch, Anthony D. Shedyak, Sheldon D. Davis, Henry P. Salisbury, Earle F. Fuller, and Sumner C. Adams; (back row) Williard "Bill" Colwell and Frederick Arthur Eldridge.